CALM

Cloud Application Lifecycle Management

with Microsoft Windows Azure

Simon Munro

Copyright © Minttulip Limited.

ISBN 978-1-291-22688-1

Permission is granted to copy, distribute and/or modify this document under the terms of the GNU Free Documentation License, Version 1.3 or any later version published by the Free Software Foundation; with the Invariant Sections being "About this book", all text and images on Front-Cover Texts, and all the Back-Cover Texts.

A copy of the license is included in the section entitled "GNU Free Documentation License".

This document is provided "as-is." Information and views expressed in this document, including URL and other Internet website references, may change without notice. You bear the risk of using it. Some examples depicted herein are provided for illustration only and are fictitious. No real association or connection is intended or should be inferred.

Microsoft, Windows Azure, and Windows Azure SQL Database are trademarks of the Microsoft group of companies.

All other trademarks are the property of their respective owners.

Copy editor: Anna Greenwood

Diagrams and cover design: Damian Holland

Cover photo: Shard London by Vulture Labs. Licensed by Getty Images.

First released: September 2012

This release: v1.1 November 2012

Contents

Contents i
About this book 1
   Source 1
   Print and Kindle Versions 1
   Discussion Group 2
   About the contributors 2
Introducing CALM 5
   Who should read CALM? 8
Overview of the CALM Models 9
   Qualify 9
   Prove 9
   Workload Model 10
   Lifecycle Model 10
   Health Model 11
   Cost Model 12
   Security Model 13
   Availability Model 13
   Data Model 14
   Capacity Model 15
   Deployment Model 15
   Integration Model 16

- Operational Model 17
- Test Model 17
- Future Models 18

Qualify 19
- The Value Proposition 20
- Assessment 21
- Business Case 38
- Summary 38

Prove 39
- Why develop a proof of concept? 40
- What to prove 45
- How do you prove that it will work? 48
- When to do the POC 52
- Time and effort 53
- Failure to prove 54
- Summary 55

Workload Model 57
- The workload model, application architecture and architects 58
- Decomposing Workloads 59
- Indicators of differing workloads 62
- Implementing workloads as services 64
- Identified workloads 65
- Summary 65

Lifecycle Model 67
- Developing the lifecycle model 68
- Describing lifecycles 76
- Example 81
- Summary 85

Health Model 87

- Health monitoring 87
- Developing the health model 89
- Summary 102

Cost Model 103
- Costs differences in the cloud 103
- Opportunities presented by cloud cost models 106
- Problems with cloud cost models 107
- Developing the cost model 112
- Summary 123

Security Model 125
- Developing the Security Model 126
- Summary 132

Availability Model 133
- The cloud computing availability myth 134
- Availability empowerment of cloud platforms 135
- What is availability? 138
- Developing the SLAs 143
- Cost of availability 149
- Availability business rationale 153
- Development approaches for availability 164
- Organisational behaviour 191
- Availability as an engineering discipline 193
- Summary 194

Data Model 197
- How the data model has changed 197
- The influence of cloud computing on data models 199
- Risks of inadequate data modelling 199
- Data is widely dispersed 201
- The need for multiple data stores 204

The emergence of NoSQL 205
  The case for SQL 214
  What data to model 218
  Determine data schemas 219
  Model each schema 221
  Assess data storage options 246
  Problematic Data 251
  Big data 251
  Summary 253
Capacity Model 255
  Capacity planning on the cloud 255
  Influence of capacity planning on application development 257
  Developing the capacity model 258
  When to develop the capacity model 267
  Summary 267
Deployment Model 269
  Differences with cloud deployments 269
  Principles of the deployment model 273
  Developing the deployment model 274
  Summary 288
Integration Model 289
  Challenges of integration in the cloud 291
  Opportunities of cloud-based integration 296
  Developing the integration model 299
  Summary 315
Operational Model 319
  Principles for cloud enabled operations 320
  Developing the operational model 322
  Summary 334

Test Model 337
    Testing Opportunities 338
    Testing problems 340
    Test plan content 348
    Summary 358
License 359
    GNU Free Documentation License 359

About this book

CALM has been developed by Minttulip Limited and released to the Windows Azure community under a GNU Free Documentation License. This license similar to the GNU General Public License, giving readers the rights to copy, redistribute, and modify a work and requires all copies and derivatives to be available under the same license. Copies may also be sold commercially.

This means that the works are free to use and modify provided that the previous authors are attributed, changes are logged, derivate works are under the same license, the full text of the license and invariant sections, disclaimers and copyrights are included, and DRM may not be may not be used to control or obstruct distribution or editing of the works.

Source

The repository for the book is located at github.com/projectcalm/Azure-EN. The repository contains the markdown source, images, and downloads in various readable formats.

Updates to CALM will be made form time to time and pushed to the Git repository.

Print and Kindle Versions

CALM is available for purchase as a printed book from Lulu, Amazon and other online booksellers. It is also available for purchase on Amazon Kindle. These versions are priced to cover distribution costs.

Discussion Group

People interested in CALM can join the Project CALM group at https://groups.live.com/projectcalm.

About the contributors

Minttulip Limited

minttulip.com

Microsoft's announcement in 2010 that they were betting their future on the cloud was the catalyst for the formation of Minttulip. Minttulip specialises in the consultancy, delivery and platform benefit realisation for all Microsoft Online Services, including Office 365, Azure and Windows Intune.

Minttulip is on an uncompromising mission to become the UK's leading Microsoft Cloud Power Technology Partner of choice. We've scoured the marketplace for the best talent in the business. Collectively they have transitioned over 65,000 users to Microsoft Cloud services for the UKs largest FTSE organisations.

The Minttulip Application Development practice has specialist people that focus on building applications on Windows Azure. The services range from brief consultation services, using CALM as a framework, to large-scale bespoke application development.

Together, our primary goal is to deliver exciting, tangible benefits to customers through a single cloud only, Microsoft only vision, and to do it better than anyone else.

Simon Munro

Principal Cloud Application Architect at Minttulip Limited

simonmunro.com

Simon Munro is leading the formation of application architectures, processes and frameworks for the delivery of applications on Windows Azure within Minttulip. He has more than fifteen years of experience in building applications across a wide variety of technologies in many industries and over the last few years has developed an in depth understanding and hands on experience with building applications on cloud platforms.

This is based on his interest in highly available and scalable applications that can support the growing demand that is fed by ubiquitous broadband, millions of users and the amount of data that is generated. He believes that it is only by having a fundamental understanding of the architectures and the related mindset shift of development teams that we can take advantage of the opportunities that this presents to business, individuals and broader society.

Introducing CALM

Cloud computing promises that an application can be hosted in the cloud and immediately take advantage of infinite scalability, high availability, low maintenance and no upfront cost. Like any good marketing message there is enough truth to that promise to deem it correct, but things are a little more complicated than that. The benefits of cloud computing can only be realised by an application that is engineered specifically for, or adapted to, a cloud computing environment. However, the skills to achieve this are scarce and knowledge unclear. So if cloud computing is the future (at least for some applications), how do we go about building 'cloud engineered' applications without the seemingly necessary and obviously unavailable skills?

Of course existing non-cloud development teams are not incapable, but they do need to be made aware of what needs to be done differently, will need additional skills or training, and will need to follow a process that encourages thinking about the application in a way that implements engineering that is better aligned to the cloud.

The challenge is that existing material tends to be too focussed on lower level technical tasks, such as working with the SDKs or infrastructure, and seldom covers topics that are shared by other domains, such as scalability patterns or data consistency. It can be argued that cloud computing offers a new paradigm for business, in which case such technical depth is of little use.

The constant focus on developer technologies means that individuals may have high confidence in their ability to deliver, due to familiarity with base technologies, but are not aware of risks until it is too late. Simply put, development teams embarking on their first cloud development, regardless of their technical abilities, will struggle to ship as expected; because they don't have a process to follow which ensures they ask the right questions of the business or which focuses their attention on unfamiliar aspects.

However when it comes to training these development teams to deliver cloud applications, they are usually ahead of the skill curve and, in most cases, have done a fair amount of tinkering and research before recommending that an application be developed in the cloud. So we are talking to mature and capable individuals with a vast array of technical capabilities.

Our solution was to make assumptions about what they would know, taking Application Lifecycle Management (ALM) as a familiar set of practices, in order to highlight the differences in cloud computing application. This allows experienced teams to identify unfamiliar areas and ensure they are covered. The decision to address the entire application lifecycle is deliberate, because while the application code (say ASP.NET) is familiar to most developers, it is the operational environment and the designs that have the greatest influence on the application's architecture and implementation.

CALM (Cloud Application Lifecycle Management) applies specifically to Windows Azure and is the result of this demand to highlight what needs to be done across the entire application lifecycle. The format is easy to read, immediately useful and not prescriptive to a specific framework (other than Windows Azure) or methodology. This allows development teams to make use of CALM within their existing development processes by adding to, rather than replacing, current practices.

Most cloud guidance is either a statement about the market (players, maturity, technology etc.), a set of solutions to particular problems (the cookbook guide), or a walkthrough of a fictitious case study. Whilst these are useful training aids, neither format is directly applicable to the project at hand and doesn't play a part in actively reducing risk. CALM has been developed as a guide that can be used throughout the project and outlines the specific steps and deliverables that are required. This is achieved by working with specific models that can be built quickly, but which can also be evolved in more detail as the project progresses. The primary models addressed are the Workload Model, Lifecycle Model, Capacity Model, Availability Model, Health Model, Operational Model, Deployment Model, Security Model, Cost Model, Integration Model, Test Model and the Tenancy Model, with supportive processes around qualification, proof of concepts and development approaches.

CALM describes the differences, opportunities and problems in cloud computing applications and the specific output required for each model. The output cannot be produced at once, or during a specific stage of the project, and the models describe what needs to be produced at what stage. For example, in the deployment model, having 'an idea' of how an application is deployed is critical early on in the project, but the model needs to evolve to depict exactly how an application is deployed by the time it is handed over to operations.

Whilst developed specifically for Windows Azure, CALM deliberately spends little time discussing the underlying technology. Firstly, the principles being communicated are not technology specific and the solutions to them are architectural practices rather than technical implementations. Secondly, too much technical detail would be overbearing for a broad audience who need to understand the problems and solutions (a tester has no need for much detail on Windows Azure). Finally, there is plenty of material and reference for the technical detail, so the communication of low level technical detail is largely a solved problem.

Whilst not filled with detailed code samples, CALM is not theoretical and does not shy away from practical use. It contains definitive references to deliverables and is scattered with examples that apply to the given topic. The approach and examples have been jointly developed by Microsoft and Minttulip, bringing together years of 'from the field' consulting experience by senior practitioners. Whatever use is made of CALM, from a single reading to a reference companion, we are confident that by highlighting differences and areas of focus we can reduce the risk of costly mistakes. After all, we know that the cloud can deliver; we know that technical solutions exist, and we know that our teams have the ability. We just need to make sure that it all works together in a way that delivers the best product.

Who should read CALM?

- Software Architects, Senior Developers and Developers should read through CALM to understand how the content applies to their particular project. They are the people making the day to day decisions that have far reaching impacts on architecture and the ability of the application to live up to its delivery promise.
- CTOs and Development Managers should at least read through the 'problems' and 'opportunities' presented in each model. This will help them contextualise the cloud hype and how it maps to their own organisation's capabilities and initiatives.
- Business representatives should read the introductory sections of each model in order to understand how they can contribute to the project.
- Project Managers should understand the deliverables of the models in detail so that they can be discussed with the implementation team and worked into the overall project plan.
- Cloud computing concepts will be new to Testers who have a critical role to play in making sure that everything works, and cloud computing concepts will be new to them. CALM will help them to understand both their responsibility and the architectural decisions they will need to validate.
- Operations staff are responsible for maintaining availability on a platform that has high expectations and is assembled in a completely new way. CALM will ensure that the ability to operate the application remains a fundamental requirement.

Overview of the CALM Models

Qualify

Not all applications fit well in the cloud, and some applications are better positioned to take advantage of the cloud to seize business opportunities or resolve existing challenges.

The qualify process is the first step on embarking on a cloud project, and the model helps ensure that the best candidate application is selected to run on the cloud. It considers the business value, risk, and cost factors across a number of projects in order to select those that are viable. Together with some indicators of what types of applications to avoid, and what types of applications to look for, working through the qualify process should result in a strong business case for an application that is to be developed on the cloud.

Prove

One of the primary reasons for following the CALM guidance is to reduce the project risks as early as possible. Early in the project lifecyle, the most important method to remove risk is to prove that both business and technical assumptions made about the application and its architecture are valid and that the application is still a good candidate for the cloud.

The prove process pays particular attention to the technical proof of concept (POC). Running code on a production Windows Azure platform developed to prove the specific design decisions made in the application, is the only way to sufficiently prove that the application will work.

Workload Model

Cloud implementations favour the development of loosely coupled services that perform specific functions. The removal of infrastructure influences on the cloud allows the services to run in the most appropriate fashion. Determining what is appropriate is achieved by first of all defining workloads that are either logically separate or separated by differing attributes and behaviours across other models.

The workload model requires that fundamental architectural decisions as to how functionality is decomposed into workloads is made by a capable architect early on in the project lifecycle. The influence of the output of the workload model on other models is profound as they form the basis for the architectural separation and physical isolation of implemented services.

Lifecycle Model

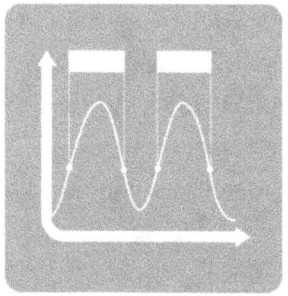

Cloud applications are undertaken on the promise that they are able to handle spiky traffic. The ability to scale-out based on demand is, as cloud vendors highlight, based on the capacity available in the platform, but it is also something that needs to be engineered into the application. An application that has been built without any idea of what load it is going to be subject to, will either fail to perform to expectations or be over-engineered to handle traffic that never arrives.

Creating a common understanding within the team as to what is meant by 'load' or 'traffic' is critical to architecting and implementing the application correctly. Getting business to think hard about the load, and the cycles over which it is expected, is the first step in building a scalable cloud architecture that is fit for purpose. The lifecycle model is about documenting the relevant workloads through various lifecycles, be that hourly, daily, weekly, monthly or any other relevant interval.

One of the most valuable aspects of the cloud is the ability to handle irregular workloads, thus optimising the consumption of resources in order to keep costs under control. Making sure that this irregularity is modelled and understood is critical to building applications that unlock the value of utility computing. The lifecycle model describes and communicates that understanding so that everyone on the team is clear on what they are trying to build.

Health Model

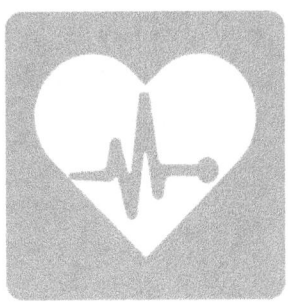

Cloud applications need to be able to respond rapidly to changes in load, and they need to do this on a platform that is built on commodity infrastructure with variable performance and reliability. The application has to run in an environment where the heartbeat can continuously be monitored, so that responses to diminished health can be fast and efficient. This requires that the business is clear on what constitutes good or diminished health, that developers implement mechanisms to collect health data, and that operators are able to see, at a glance, what needs to be done.

The health model provides a framework for defining the healthy states of the application in SLAs, the methods for collecting health and viewing monitoring data, and the processes needed to restore the application to a healthy state.

Cost Model

The costs of cloud computing are frequently used as the justification for moving applications to the cloud. There is definite value in consuming compute resources as needed and paying for them monthly, instead of large infrastructure investments. Unfortunately for many projects, the costs are quickly calculated when the business case is being drawn up, and promptly forgotten about once the project gets the go-ahead. In order to deliver on the cost saving promises of the cloud, costs need to be understood, planned, and kept under control.

The cost model creates a better understanding of the operating costs of the target application, and requires that a custom model be developed with sufficient detail and is constantly maintained. The cost model encourages the understanding and sharing of cost considerations amongst all members of the team, so that they can understand their individual influence on the running costs of what they are building.

Security Model

Security is one of the major concerns about the public cloud. Whilst this concern may be unwarranted, in comparison with any other infrastructure, security still requires careful consideration. Whilst there are specific security, compliance, and regulatory aspects to understand about Windows Azure, applications that run on the cloud do not need to be treated differently to any other application. Full attention should be given to security across all levels of the application and its operation. CALM is not prescriptive about security model specifics and, in a highly specialised and fast-changing industry, encourages the adoption of a recognised security assurance process or methodology.

The security model sets the groundwork for understanding some of the cloud security concerns, and points the implementation team in the direction of credible security processes to be adopted.

Availability Model

Modern applications have high availability expectations. The adoption of the cloud, where a small application can have massive adoption without the need to build expensive and reliable datacentres, puts pressure on applications to be highly available. Cloud computing patterns reflect modern application architectures by building applications that are designed for failure. This is implemented through various technical approaches, such as redundancy, resiliency, scalability, fault isolation, and many others.

The availability model starts by establishing a common understanding of availability, which is then used to encourage the business to describe their requirements in terms of availability expressions that are contained within the SLAs. Before delving into implementation, the costs of availability and the business rationale that supports those costs, is considered within the availability model. Finally, the model helps the team to select and describe the approaches to availability that will be implemented within the application.

Data Model

Modern applications have drastically changed the data model. No longer are applications built on monolithic SQL databases, but make use of multiple data stores with specific strengths for specific purposes. Cloud applications are architected to run as isolated services that store their data in the best data store for the particular service; from SQL, to key-value stores, to persistent messaging. Applications can choose from a vast array of available technologies including services offered by cloud providers, such as Windows Azure Storage.

The data model describes the need for multiple data stores in terms of specific functionality and the needs of cloud applications. The data model then outlines an approach to resolving the data model across all workloads and their data schemas, including all of the aspects to be documented. The choice of databases and approaches to data is one of the most important aspects of cloud computing. A cloud application that has a data model that does not scale cannot take advantage of the scalability benefits of the cloud platform, and may fail to satisfy its availability requirements.

Capacity Model

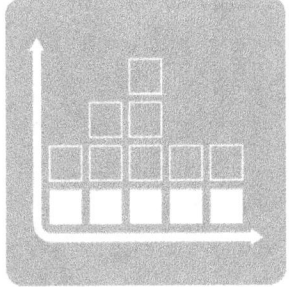

Due to the 'infinite capacity' offered by cloud platforms, it would seem that capacity planning for the cloud is unnecessary. Capacity planning for the cloud is completely different from on-premise capacity planning; there is no need to estimate future resource requirements in order to procure the necessary hardware. Capacity planning on the cloud is about making optimal use of capacity, and making sure that the application can take advantage of the available capacity.

The capacity model is workload-based and introduces scale units for individual workloads. Scale units allow the capacity needs of workloads to be determined and rationalised. Once scale units have been determined, and the application engineered to work with any number of scale units, the provisioning (and de-provisioning) of capacity to handle load is as simple as an operator spinning up additional units.

Deployment Model

Cloud applications are not deployed as single applications during downtime, but as changes are made and within a production environment that is serving live requests. This is made possible by an architecture that is loosely coupled, designed for failure, isolated, and other patterns. It is assisted by the cloud platform itself, which provides the available capacity and the cloud 'operating system' to enable services to be easily swapped in and out of production. This type of deployment may be unfamiliar to most members of the team including developers who are not used to developing for such principles and operators who are used to deploying to a fairly static infrastructure.

The deployment model ensures that deployment is considered early during the development process and that any requirements positively influence the application architecture. The deployment model requires that the specifics of what needs to be deployed are described in the layout view. It also requires that the process view is described, so that this is considered within the application and the operating environment.

Integration Model

Application integration is difficult and complex regardless of the platform that it runs on. Whilst cloud applications have the advantage of being accessible and having sufficient bandwidth, they are more difficult to integrate with on-premise applications. On-premise applications implement integration interfaces using outdated protocols, and hide behind robust firewalls that refuse to let in anything without a static IP address. But applications do not exist in a vacuum and cloud applications will require some integration work to be done.

The integration model describes some of the differences with cloud integration, and highlights potential problem areas. The integration model requires that integration points be worked through in detail, early in the project to minimise risks, and describes the detail that may be required. It also discusses some of the technical options that are available, specifically on Windows Azure, which can be used to assist with integration.

Operational Model

Operations in cloud environments will be unfamiliar to operators. The ability of an application to respond to load and meet its availability targets requires that the application is designed for operations and used by operators with the correct skills and knowledge.

The operational model takes into consideration the CALM models, deployment, health monitoring and release management processes. These are used to determine the required proactive and reactive operational activities. In an environment that needs to operate at scale, with multiple services running, and which needs to respond quickly to load variations and failures, the degree of automated response must be high. The operational model provides a context for increasing the operational maturity of the application and operations team in order to meet these complex operational demands.

Test Model

Cloud computing platforms offer production capacity and configuration for testers from the day that the project starts. This is a massive opportunity for testers, and allows them to run tests with production simulations as soon as the first build is checked in. Testers have other considerations when testing for the cloud, such as the new technology, the operating environment, the complexity of testing loosely coupled services, and the need to simulate tests of scalable applications.

The test model highlights the opportunities and problems associated with cloud testing and the important role that testing plays versus traditional environments. The test model then describes the types of tests to be included in the test plan, and flags those which may be new to testers, such as the scale test and operational test.

Future Models

Cloud computing is an emerging market and application architectures are bound to evolve, as are the platforms on which they run. This first release of CALM is focused more on the design aspects of application lifecycle management. The authors are aware that not all aspects of ALM have been covered, such as developer centric tools and processes. We feel that this release is in line with the current maturity of most cloud development teams and covers the parts that are important in ALM at present. Over time the models will be adjusted, and others added, based on our experiences in the field, feedback and demand.

Future releases of CALM are planned to contain the following models:

- Tenancy Model — This model deals specifically with the needs of developers building multi-tenant and SaaS applications.
- Development Model — This model deals with different development approaches for the cloud. It includes both technical approaches as well as processes that are specifically relevant for developers.
- Migration Model — This model deals with the need to migrate applications from on-premise to the cloud, and considers hybrid applications and IaaS-based applications on their way to becoming well architected PaaS-based solutions.
- Scalability Model — In this release, CALM scalability is part of the availability model. The scalability model deals with specific detail on scalability concerns and patterns as a solution to availability.

Qualify

Businesses embark on software development programmes to achieve their business goals, not (to the surprise of many developers) simply to play with the latest technology.

Any new technology or process can be considered if there are business **opportunities** that can be seized by adopting the technology or existing **challenges** that can be overcome. The new technology may offer something more cost effective, quicker to bring to market, lower risk or simply beyond the capabilities of existing technologies. Cloud computing is such a new technology. Embarking on a cloud computing project for little business benefit is not worth undertaking and should be qualified out. One possible exception is delivering a 'simple' application for the purposes of learning the technology, which lowers risk for the 'real' project. Even then, the most significant project to be undertaken at a later date will still need to be identified.

The process of qualification is cyclical and composed of two primary tasks. Firstly, candidate projects need to be selected based on business need. Secondly, these projects need to be assessed in terms of their cost, risk and benefit. This assessment can be fed back into the selection process to narrow down the candidates, which in turn can then be assessed further.

At the end of the qualification process, the primary output is the business case for the cloud computing project as well as documents that facilitate the process.

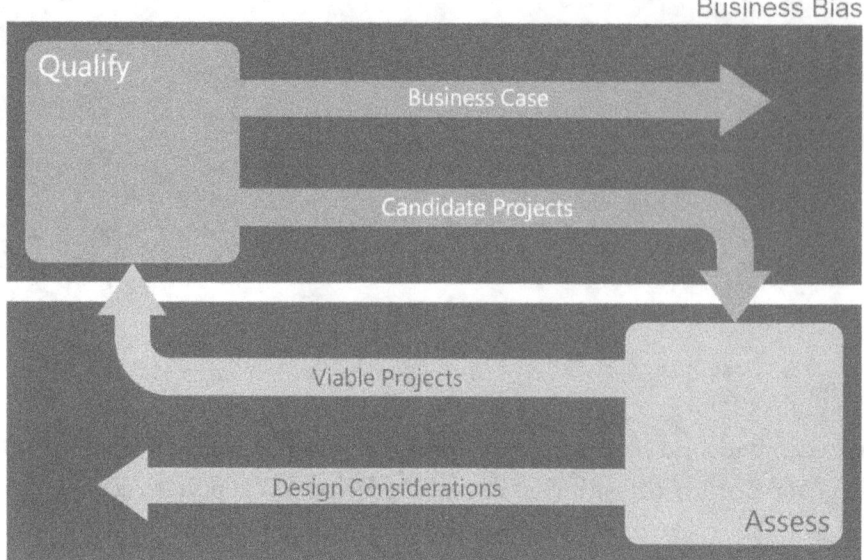

The Value Proposition

Business needs to understand the value of running an application on Windows Azure, rather than the benefits of the technology. Most of the information provided to, and understood by, technical people is about the platform and technology that make little sense to the business.

The difficulty is creating an environment where existing mental models which may be based on traditional IT are cast aside. This enables business to see opportunities that are candidates for cloud projects. Perhaps the business is used to the long lead times of their existing IT and would not even consider an opportunity that needs to be brought to market quickly? Perhaps they are used to large, up-front IT costs and therefore cannot adopt fail-fast business tactics?

Ideas to get the discussion going include:

- Rapid provisioning — this may get the business thinking about bringing new products to market faster than they thought possible
- Ability to handle and afford brief high loads — this may get the business thinking about social campaigns, pop-up virtual shops of similar activities that run for short periods.

- Fail-fast tactics — if up-front infrastructure investment is minimal, perhaps business will be prepared to take a chance, and if the opportunity doesn't pan out, be able to shut the application down.
- Applications that need to pivot. Because the infrastructure is provisioned as needed, the application may be able to adapt to change based on customer input.

Prioritisation and focus

Once opportunities have been identified, they need to be whittled down to a selection of candidate projects that require a more detailed assessment. The most likely candidate projects can be prioritised for assessment, where they can be focussed on individually.

Mutual Benefit

The application developers, whether in the form of an external organisation or an external provider, also need to see the value in undertaking the project. This is often overlooked in the enthusiasm for solving the business need and can result in failure if not done correctly. Apart from the obvious benefit of margin, the candidate projects also have to be possible from a resource availability perspective, allow for reasonable development time and do not promise what cannot be delivered.

Assessment

Assessment is a primary task driven by the technical team, as it is the technical team that can get a handle on the costs and risks. These costs can include development effort, processes for operations, migration and platform costs. The technical team also needs to provide input to assess the risks of the development. This can include technical complexity, integration risks, timescales and available skills. Business may also contribute by adding their business risks and costs to the assessment.

Note: The assessment has to be done by people that are familiar with cloud computing and have at least some experience in building applications on

Windows Azure. If such experience does not exist internally, it is strongly suggested that an external supplier is approached for consultation.

The costs, risks, and benefits need to be discussed and described. They can also be weighted, summed and plotted in order to create a view on viable projects. Factors to consider are listed below.

Business Value Assessment

This assessment attempts to identify those projects that are of highest value to the business. An application that increases revenue by 20%, for example, would be of higher value than one that makes sure that stationary drawers are fully stocked. Specifically look at factors that make particular projects better suited to running on the cloud.

Increase

- Support of business agility — being able to bring products or campaigns to market quickly. Most revenue increasing projects fall into this category, but it is not limited to revenue. Depending on the business, this agility could include improved customer service, improved logistics processes, debtor management, and so on.
- Spiky usage patterns — high, unpredictable growth, regular traffic spikes and planned campaigns.
- Operational efficiency — reduction in the number (or cost) of full-time IT staff to feed and water infrastructure.
- Fail-fast business tactics — ability to try out an idea without significant sunk infrastructure costs.

Decrease

- High complexity — an overly complex solution to the business need may decrease the value to the business. This decrease in value may manifest itself as increased time to market over an on-premise solution due to the higher risk of complex solutions.
- Existing legacy application — an application that is currently running and cannot take advantage of the benefits of the cloud may waste resources if moved to Windows Azure.

Cost Factors

The influence of the cloud on cost, over on-premise solutions, is well-covered ground, so it should be fairly easy to run through the cost factors. Despite marketing to the contrary, not everything on the cloud is cheaper than a traditional on-premise application, so make sure that you include any factors that increase the cost.

Increase

- New developer skills required — developers need to learn a new API and new approaches to processing data.
- New deployment and operational processes — existing processes used for deployment and operations need to be adapted for Windows Azure.

Decrease

- No upfront purchase of infrastructure.
- No need for overestimating of required capacity.

Risk Factors

New cloud computing projects that are started within organisations that are new to developing for the cloud will have higher risks than their traditional on-premise alternatives. Since the objective of the assessment is to choose one cloud project over another, look for particular warning signs (such as compliance) that would make building the application for the cloud significantly risky.

Increase

- Compliance and security — it is possible that there is a regulation that makes it difficult to store data in, or process on, Windows Azure.
- Low tolerance for latency — some applications need low latency, which is difficult to achieve on Windows Azure.
- Legacy Applications — trying to run applications on Windows Azure that are not designed for it is possible but can cause problems.

- Legacy Integration — some integration points may require private protocols that cannot be easily accessed from a publicly hosted client.
- Fear, uncertainty and doubt — there may be influencers in the organisation that are anti-cloud and will voice concerns over data storage, security, compliance and other problems highlighted to them by incumbent IT suppliers and operators.

Decrease

- Early testing — architectural assumptions can be tested very early on in the development cycle because a 'production' platform is always available.
- Non-fixed infrastructure — as the application matures and changes, the underlying Windows Azure platform configuration can accommodate the changes.
- IaaS — an architectural bias towards an infrastructure-based (IaaS) solution as opposed to a platform-based (PaaS) solution can decrease the short-term risks. Although it is not recommended, in some cases it may be practical if re-engineering for PaaS is considered too risky.

Assessment Output

After assessing the costs, risks, and business value across the candidate projects it should be possible to identify the projects that have the highest value for the lowest possible risk and cost. This knowledge can be fed back to business to qualify the final project and write the business case.

The assessment also provides some early warning for the implementation team regarding possible problems as well as highlighting the expected benefits to the business. This will influence the design, reducing risk during development and ensuring that the objectives are met.

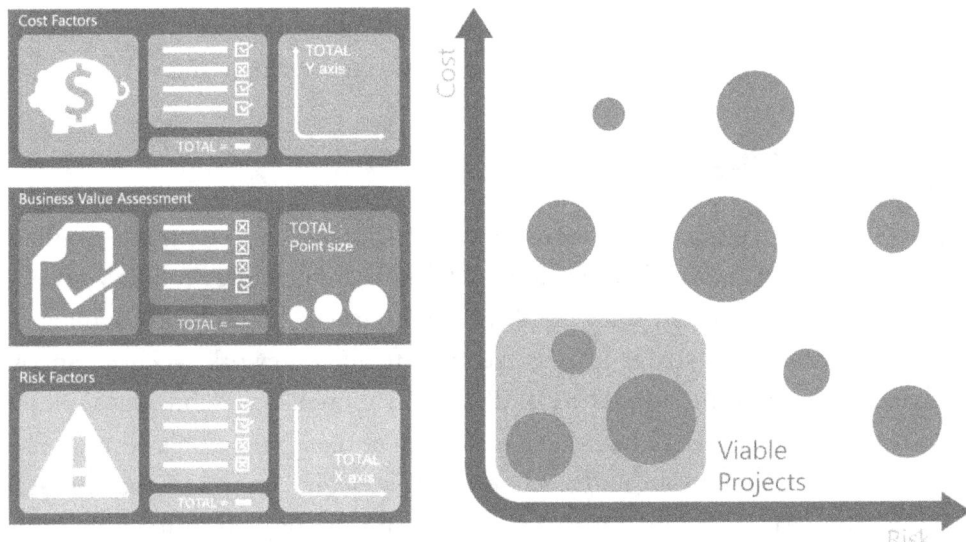

The assessment also provides some early warning for the implementation team on problems that may be encountered as well as highlighting the expected benefits to the business. This will influence the design, reducing risk during development and ensuring that the objectives are met.

Assessing the suitability of the application for Windows Azure

The assessment process of formally weighing up value, costs and risks of various projects should provide a clear indication of the best candidate projects. A double-check of this process is to look at some of the things to seek or avoid when choosing whether or not an application should run on Windows Azure. These are described below for reference but because each application is different, and may not fall directly into one category or another, the diligent weighing up of value, costs and risks should still be applied.

Things to Avoid

Many Windows Azure applications are undertaken where a target project is intended as a 'Proof of Concept' and the effectiveness of the application will be assessed before others are undertaken (the assessment may be conducted formally, informally, by business or IT). In this scenario, there are some applications that should be avoided if at all possible, otherwise the project may fail and remaining Windows Azure endeavours will be scuppered.

Too much legacy

The Windows Azure style means that applications are assembled somewhat differently. That means that existing application architectures follow a style that either clashes completely with the Windows Azure style (such as assuming fault tolerant architecture) or at least make it difficult to rework (such as an over-reliance on a high throughput RDBMS). Even though the Windows Azure style is relatively new, it would be ridiculous to expect that there won't be any existing approaches, code, tools and technologies brought into a Windows Azure application. At the very least we need to bring existing skills to bear, such as .NET development capability. Windows Azure provides compelling support of established and credible technologies, such as Windows Azure SQL Database (as a variation on the well respected SQL Server). However, there are some legacy indicators to look for that may rule out an application for Windows Azure.

Dependence on Premium Products

The Windows Azure style is to avoid commercial, high-end technologies as much as possible because many commercial products have a high dependency on the underlying infrastructure. A customised ERP system may be complex to run on Windows Azure because it has not been developed specifically for the PaaS model of Windows Azure and because it has a high dependency on high-throughput SQL Server, complex manual configuration and load on individual servers. Additionally, premium products have licensing options that are immature for running on Windows Azure, and besides, running all the various pieces of legacy applications only in virtual machines, doesn't make much architectural sense. Applications that have a high dependency on these products should be passed over until their vendors mature the products and make them more Windows Azure friendly.

Data on ACID

If, after an extensive analysis of database requirements, you discover that the bulk of the application has a high write:read ratio and that most operations require consistent transactional operations, then you should avoid building the application on Windows Azure. Although possible, there are applications, such as high read web applications, that will realise much better benefits than an ACID oriented application. The question as to whether ACID is required is explored in detail in the data model.

Single Instance Components

Because we need to design for failure, we need to put redundancy into our application layer. Some components that are commonly used are single instance, non-distributed components. This can become a problem if the functions that they perform are long running. Consider, for example, an ETL (Extract Transform Load) operation executed by SSIS (SQL Server Integration Services). The SSIS task may need to be scheduled, and run on a single machine for a long time (importing thousands of rows). If SSIS falls over, or the instance it is running on falls over, it may be difficult to detect, rollback and restart. This may not just be a limitation of SSIS but also the design of the ETL operation, and illustrates a single instance operation that should be avoided.

Organic Installations

Many third party applications, particularly those from small vendors, have a long, custom installation process. This may involve installing software, making configuration changes in many files and applying a number of patches before the application can be used. The Windows Azure style leans on components that have fairly simple installation and configuration that can be scripted. In Windows Azure, backups should be used for data and not configuration. Applications or entire instances, and the dynamic naming and IP addresses of instances, means that applications with complex configurations done by hand should be avoided. If the application cannot be baked into a package and easily deployed using the Windows Azure SDK and tools, then it should also be avoided.

Persisted virtual machines, virtual networks and other IaaS features of Windows Azure do allow some organic installations. It should be seen as an exception for components where there is little choice, rather than an architectural principle. An application that is mostly IaaS is not a primary candidate for running on Windows Azure.

Complex Regulatory Compliance

Windows has certifications and compliance for ISO 27001, SSAE 16/ISAE 3402, EU Model Clauses, and HIPAA BAA, but crucially, no support at the time of writing for PCI-DSS. This compliance should take care of many of the general requirements that applications may require and in some cases (PCI DSS) requires integration with a compliant third party payment provider or a certified on premise system. However, regulations vary across industries and countries and are the domain of regulatory specialists to untangle them and advise what needs to be done in order to comply. Because public cloud computing is still in its infancy, many regulations seem to work against cloud computing principles. How, for example, is data expected to be stored in a single country if it makes sense to distribute it around the world to take care of availability or latency?

Indeed many regulations are expensive to implement and favour large multinationals that have extensive in-house infrastructures and hordes of legal advisors and auditors on hand. This doesn't fit with the Windows Azure model of enabling SMEs, who may not be aware of regulations that affect their business or their customers.

This will undoubtedly change in time. Most of the concerns about regulatory compliance come from a lack of concrete legally backed (and tested) knowledge and are often based on myths of misunderstood regulations. For example, the UK Data Protection Act is widely understood to prevent the storage of data outside of the UK. Closer inspection of the act reveals that it is just 'personally identifiable' information that needs to be dealt with and it may be overcome by simply encrypting the postal code.

While attention should be given to necessary regulations any application that needs to operate in a highly regulated industry or region should be avoided. If your application must comply with regulations, get started early and involve the right stakeholders (legal, audit etc.). It is far better to encounter regulations, so that they can be considered within the implementation, than to fail just before go-live when legal has to give the application the once-over.

Low Latency Tolerance

Certain types of applications have requirements that are closely tied to extremely low and controllable latency. The obvious example is in financial trading, but others exist in manufacturing (monitoring equipment) and other areas. Because the underlying commodity infrastructure is beyond our control, there is no way to tweak the infrastructure to gain a few milliseconds by adding extra fast disk, networking or other infrastructure. Applications that have a low tolerance for latency should be avoided, as the architectural solutions for achieving low latency in Windows Azure are labour intensive. Bear in mind, those applications that need to be performant may have a tolerance of high latency; the low latency requirement is very specific and is unrelated to general performance and responsiveness.

Big Bang Implementations

Any organisation's first Windows Azure implementation is likely to face a few difficulties, take longer and cost more than was initially expected (or hoped). The platform is different, the tools are different, new skills are required, and the approach to development may be quite different too. If things are going to be late or cost more, it is better if they are small things. The fallout from a small project with a developer or two that overruns by a few days is going to be easier to deal with than a large project with a large team that overruns by months. So 'big bang' architectural implementations that bet the entire business or entire departments (however the politics in a particular enterprise may work) on a wildly successful implementation should be avoided. The first implementation should be one of the following:

Small tactical project

Chose a fairly simple project; perhaps a microsite to test social media, such as an application that integrates with Facebook. The idea is to take something small, low cost and tactical that can probably be thrown away once the campaign has run its course. This way any error margins in estimation have a low time or cost impact and usable business functionality can be developed and deemed a success. The throwaway nature means that the next project can then be reworked based on the inevitable lessons, and the long-term commitment is low. Internal IT will kick up little fuss at a 'crapplication' and business will not be frozen by risk aversion.

Extension to an existing solution

Assuming existing systems exist, there is always a need for added functionality to support the business. This is not necessarily an embedded piece of functionality that is part of the core processes, but is often related to the transfer of data used for other purposes. It could be the frequent (daily/weekly/monthly) importing of data that is used for further analysis, reporting or some other operational function. Assuming that the data in question is not subject to complex regulations (or internal control), the application can satisfy a long standing business need that IT has never been able to get around to. Again, the ability to have something low risk, low cost and successful, where lessons can be learned and taken forward, makes a fairly simple application a good candidate for a first project. This type of application also opens the door on hybrid public/private cloud applications, which is both architecturally relevant and an important discussion subject within any enterprise.

Greenfields iterative development

If no suitable tactical projects can be found, and the decision is made to start from scratch, it is imperative that valuable interim functionality is delivered incrementally and as soon as possible. This is part of the agile approach, and the reasons for this are discussed at length in the agile community. The important aspect is not the agile processes part (e.g. scrum), but the iterative deliverable of working software. For a Windows Azure project, you have to be deploying to production and serving up production traffic (even if it is pre-launch) in order to address the issues of availability, scalability, monitoring and so on. This can become a problem when re-platforming or replacing an existing system, where the application cannot be swapped out until all features are complete. In such a case, it would be better to develop new functionality first as extensions to the existing solution, before starting the big rewrite.

Things to Look For

When selecting a candidate project for Windows Azure you need to select one that plays to its strengths. When you have finished you want people to say,

"Wow, we could never have pulled that off using our normal stuff!" You don't want a "Meh..." response where the application is not that much cheaper, easier or deployed faster than any other application that comes out of existing IT practices. While most of the success of a project is down to the team, technologies and architecture, choosing a business need that ticks all the right boxes for a Windows Azure solution is key to creating a successful base from which to launch other AWS initiatives. Look for the following attributes for good candidates.

A need for agility

While cost (or operational expenditure rather than capital expenditure) is often taken for granted as the biggest advantage of Windows Azure, when the numbers are run this is not so obvious. By far the biggest advantage of Windows Azure over traditional IT, is the ability of IT infrastructure to respond immediately to the agile needs of the business. Not the needs of IT or developers wanting to play with a shiny new toy, but the needs of the business. If the business that you are serving is lethargic, happy with revenue streams and set in its ways, whether because it is an old dinosaur or constrained by industry, then no amount of agility from developers is going to be taken seriously.

Spiky usage patterns

One of the biggest advantages and equally one of the biggest technical challenges with Windows Azure is the ability to scale up and scale down capacity depending on demand. The advantage is in the rapid provisioning and decommissioning of capacity and its associated financial benefits. Obviously an application that has flat usage and a finite number of users (which translates into predictable traffic) cannot take advantage of the benefits of scalability, because there is no need.

The Scale of Spikes — one man's spike is another's little blip and it is important that all stakeholders including developers, operations, business and finance, share the same metric when describing spikes. A web application may not break a sweat with a few thousand extra requests an hour, but business may think that it is enormous. After all, a small increase in web traffic may translate into huge sales that may be difficult to fulfil.

Wishful Thinking

Everybody wants to build the next Facebook or Twitter, and the likelihood of this occurring is close to zero. So building a scalable application just because someone hopes that it will become the next big thing, sets everyone up for disappointment. An application that has a hundred thousand users is still significant, but not if the plan had one million in the first month. The same goes for a campaign launched in the hope that it will go viral. These days viral traffic is seldom accidental but the result of clever marketing. So check that the traffic spikes expected are reasonable and match them with the business plan before assuming that the application usage will be spiky in nature.

High, Unpredictable Growth

The business plan may expect high growth, but cannot plan accurately for the growth. The growth may be related to marketing campaigns, product development, operational readiness, manufacturing capability, competitor response or any number of business related issues that might affect, either positively or negatively, the growth in regular traffic. The key with unpredictable growth is that there is a clearly defined market of a large enough size that can be tapped with the right marketing spend, partnerships or other reasonable investment as per the business plan. Windows Azure offers an advantage in this scenario as there is no need to plan for the provisioning of infrastructure at all. Assuming that there is a direct correlation between traffic and revenue (or market penetration, if that is the business objective), as the traffic increases more Windows Azure resources can be brought online in order to serve the load.

Not all high growth is unpredictable. In some cases, such as the migration of a fairly static set of customers from one system to another, the growth can be predicted. In these instances, the ability to plan, source, fund, and provision infrastructure within a traditional datacentre may work out best. So look for an application that has high growth that cannot be predicted and your Windows Azure application will really shine as it easily responds to the demands.

Regular Traffic Spikes

When building an application on Windows Azure, you have to build it so that services can be started and stopped without affecting the overall behaviour. The side effect of this is that the ability to increase, and importantly decrease, available resources is built into the application. This means that an application with regular spikes in traffic is perfectly suited to Windows Azure because it is easy to respond to the extra, or reduced, load. The frequency of spikes needs to be carefully understood. Are the spikes during the day, week, month or year? This will determine your approach to handling them. Pre-paid, six month plans can be bought for baseline traffic, and pay-as-you-go can handle short-term unpredictable load. Existing roles may even be able to cope with intra-day spikes if there is enough capacity, or the service is degraded. There are so many options open on the Windows platform, that the optimal and low hassle handling of regular spikes shows off the best of a Windows Azure application.

Planned Campaigns

While we often think about unexpected demand, in most cases it is part of a particular business campaign. Perhaps it is an end of season sale, the announcement of a new product or a new advertising campaign. Traditionally applications and their infrastructure would be sized according to the expected demand during planned campaigns, such as having enough capacity for the holiday season sales. In most cases business wouldn't even bother to tell IT that a campaign was planned or underway.

With Windows Azure, the applications can be engineered for the demand of planned campaigns and only provisioned once the campaign is underway. While it may be possible to autoscale the application, it would be preferable if IT had a close relationship with the business in order to be prepared for additional demand. This could include running a few tests, just to make sure that the system can handle the demand, or spinning up additional roles manually, pre-populating caches, and so on, to ensure that the application is immediately responsive.

Operational Efficiency

While we mostly concern ourselves with scalability of infrastructure and applications, it is the operational processes that support those applications that need to be scaled. Consider for a moment providing scalability in a non-virtualised environment, where an increase in traffic requires the purchasing and provisioning of new physical hardware. You can picture the stress and panic within an operational team to power, network, plug in and configure the new servers; if they have enough time to do it at all.

Windows Azure allows operators to easily (and even automatically) provision and maintain required infrastructure. Not just roles but also queues, databases and other infrastructure. This tends to suit applications that require a high degree of operational efficiency. Striving for operational efficiency may sound like something that everyone would want to do, but Windows Azure encourages the practise by reworking the approach and architecture. Most enterprise environments endeavour to gain efficiency within existing processes that, by comparison to Windows Azure, exist within a broader inefficient environment.

Much of the inefficiencies in enterprises are arguably valid and necessary. For example, operating a highly specialised Oracle platform supporting core ERP systems may be inefficient but necessary, because of vendor support of the platform, existing investment in infrastructure, regulation and risk. In this case, speciality of the underlying physical assets may make sense and should not necessarily be argued.

On the other hand, some business cases exist where running an application on the incumbent infrastructure does not stack up, and the costs blow the business case out of the water. For example, the marketing department wanting to run a promotional campaign for a specific product such as a Facebook campaign, may not be able to absorb the cost of three additional support staff working in shifts, DBAs on call or even the installation and configuration of a server or two. After all, any money spent operating the application could be utilised to attract people to the application in the first place.

There are many plans for applications where the cost of operating infrastructure has not been considered or simply has to be lower. These applications should be sought out and built on Windows Azure. Building an application that needs to be operationally efficient, and building it properly, is a great way to take advantage of what Windows Azure oriented applications will offer.

Fail-fast Business Tactics

Start-up businesses are primarily looking for plans that they can get up and running quickly, with little investment and, if it works, continue evolving. If it fails, it can be terminated quickly without too much investment. These plans are based on the principal that something is worth trying if the costs and other risks are low. In established businesses, similar applications could be the offering of a new product on top of an existing platform. For example, creating an application to sell a new short-term insurance product on top of the existing systems by packaging it in a unique way. While fail-fast tactics support business models that require more than just IT, they generally have a large IT component. Windows Azure oriented applications suit these business plans; not only because the applications can be rapidly provisioned with minimal hardware and licensing investment, but also because the applications can be architected from the beginning with scalability in mind. So if the application becomes successful, it can continue operating without having to pay for a rework in order to make it more mainstream.

Applications that need to Pivot

Within entrepreneur and start-up circles, the term 'pivot' refers to changing the product that was initially planned to something else because customer take-up was too slow or customers asked for radically difference features. Translated into application requirements, rather than business strategy, this means that the application requirements may need to change quite radically and quickly.

The ability of an application to support this pivot in the evolving business plan requires certain architectural elements that match the practices encouraged within Windows Azure oriented architectures, such as loosely coupled services. Some components in a well-architected application, such as user login and registration, can be reused in the new application without a significant rework.

Beyond the software architecture, the infrastructure in a Windows Azure oriented application can change as the application changes.

While not necessarily that common within an enterprise environment, the concept of pivoting is echoed in applications that are highly responsive to changing user demands. This is not an excuse for lazy business analysis or failure to manage scope creep, but a genuine evolution of requirements as the application starts being used.

Considering Hybrid Applications

To software engineers, it may make sense to run the entire application on Windows Azure, and they seldom consider that applications can span Windows Azure and a traditional datacentre. Many of the options listed in 'Things to Avoid' may be perfect candidates to run part of the application on-premise.

It would generally be architecturally irresponsible to create an application where a single synchronous process has to span completely different systems; but in some cases, it is unavoidable. Perhaps an existing authentication mechanism exists that can and should be used? In which case it should be wrapped up in a service and called from the Windows Azure application. Maybe there is a requirement for integration with an existing order viewing and fulfilment system that supports processes far beyond the application front-end?

This opens a can of worms (and associated pain) of application integration which can only be avoided in a perfect or isolated world. The integration with existing (or even new) applications in and around the enterprise has to be considered when building applications for Windows Azure. Integration and integration patterns are discussed in further detail in the integration model, but in the context of this discussion about what to look for and what to avoid, the following should be considered:

- Avoid synchronous integration where possible — you can build a highly scalable and available system, but if a web request is dependent on, and has to call, another service before rendering a result, it needs to be up to the same standard. For example, if you need to pass orders to another system for fulfilment, it may be preferable to add them to a queue and send them in a separate process, just in case you get a traffic spike that you can handle, but the recipient system cannot.
- Keep contracts simple and concise — when sending data to other systems, try and keep the interface down to a clear method call (REST or RPC style) with a simple document (such as JSON) and only the bare minimum of fields. Interfaces with large schema compliant XML documents are unwieldy and prone to errors and breaking schema changes.

- Keep as much data to yourself as possible — the ability to store data in the optimal data store (say a NoSQL database), and on the application cache are fundamental scalability techniques and this needs to be in your application's control. Having to re-query an external (service based) data store every time you need to fetch a crucial bit of data, will create a scalability bottleneck that may never be overcome.

When building a large and complex system on Windows Azure it is better to focus on what the platform is good at; public facing scalable web applications (in terms of our reference architecture). Some aspects of the application may be suitable for your Windows Azure application, but you can leave them out when it isn't a requirement. You could plan to re-architect them in the future, but for now, it could be easier to use existing infrastructure, licenses and people to do the work external to Windows Azure on the incumbent platform and architecture. If your application has a requirement for data to be sourced from the central corporate database, you might as well use the existing ETL tools and services running in the on-premise datacentre to run the data into your database; rather than trying to do it in Windows Azure. Otherwise you may not have licences for the tools, the services may not run well in a designed-for-failure environment (like SQL Server Integration Services), and you will end up re-architecting years of enterprise duct tape for something that could be easily done by existing enterprise resources for a fraction of the cost and hassle.

So while it may be tempting to try and run everything in Windows Azure, it is not always possible or practical. The reasons can be valid technical ones or the result of people unwilling to commit to Windows Azure. When architecting for Windows Azure it is important to consider the broader needs of the organisation and, in that consideration, realise that on premise or co-located infrastructure has its place. The resultant architecture would therefore not be a Windows Azure only solution, but one that is a hybrid of Windows Azure and traditional IT environments.

Business Case

In assessing the costs and risks, the technical team provide valuable input and estimates for the project. Business can then select the best project to undertake and using the information gleaned during the assessment (representing technical input) can go about developing the business case.

Summary

Cloud computing platforms are suited to many different types of applications. The addition of IaaS features to Windows Azure also means that you can run just about any application on Windows Azure. However, some types of applications really shine on the cloud, and others are better suited to a traditional on-premise datacentre.

The qualify process is about picking out the best candidate applications for cloud computing. This is done by assessing the risk, cost and business value across all candidate projects — resulting in the right project filtering to the top. The qualify CALM model helps make sure that the right application is chosen at the beginning of the project. The wrong choice can be a total disaster and scupper the adoption of cloud computing, and the right choice means that the application should deliver to, or exceed, expectations.

Steps

1. Create a list of candidate projects.
2. Perform a business value assessment of each project.
3. Assess the costs of each project.
4. Assess the risks of each project.
5. Narrow down the candidate projects to viable projects.
6. Develop the business case for the viable projects.

Prove

Despite the best efforts in qualification, the most informed technical considerations and the best non-cloud development skills, cloud applications are still risky. The most important part of embarking on the development of an application for a cloud platform is to reduce this risk level as early as possible to what would be considered normal for the development team. This is achieved by making a conscious effort to prove the architecture, approach, and specific technologies.

Most of the proving is done by developing a Proof of Concept (POC) in which code is written, deployed, and run on the Windows Azure platform. Other ways to prove the solution include looking at case studies, getting vendor support, and developing technical spikes, but by far the most important is to run code on Windows Azure. Not only is it relatively easy to run applications on Windows Azure, it is also the only way to get a realistic view of the suitability of the application for Windows Azure, the architectural approach, and the capability of the implementation team to deliver.

The ability to run the POC in a production environment is what makes applications built for the cloud so compelling. On-premise applications cannot be tested early on for suitability to the production platform, because at the stage that the POC is performed no production platform exists, and it would be too expensive to set one up just for the POC. Even the use of lab environments (often hosted at third parties) will not prove the entire stack. With Windows Azure, a POC can be deployed to production, in a production configuration (perhaps with hundreds of instances), and extensively tested as part of the POC exercise. This can last for a short period, possibly a few hours, and simply shut down. This means that the cost of building a POC is not wasted on procuring, setting up or running infrastructure. Budget is rather spent on the most important part, namely the writing and execution of the code.

In addition to the increased need for a POC in an application developed for the cloud, the ease at which it can be done, relative to a traditional application, should ensure that the case for a POC is justified and accepted.

Why develop a proof of concept?

The enthusiasm to build applications for the cloud does not automatically mean that a particular application is well-suited to run on the cloud or on Windows Azure in particular. Perhaps it won't work well within the regulatory environment of the business? Perhaps it has a dependency on a database configuration that cannot be run on virtual machines? These reasons, although they should have been used to qualify the application initially, still need to be double checked. The end of a POC is the best place to finally review the suitability of the application for the cloud.

Even if the application is a good cloud candidate, certain architectural and technical assumptions have been made, and these need to be tested. For example, Windows Azure SQL Database may be chosen as the data store, but nobody really knows how it will perform. A POC either eliminates that uncertainty or uncovers performance issues that need to be addressed, possibly by testing within the POC by the selected alternative data store.

De-risking

The primary role of the POC is to de-risk the project as early as possible. This de-risking is achieved by:

- Ensuring that the assumptions made in qualification are correct.
- Ensuring that the application is indeed a good candidate for cloud computing.
- Confirming that the cost implications are not significantly different from what was expected.
- Confirming that major technical decisions are correct in terms of the requirements (performance, availability, cost, etc.).
- Uncovering areas that require special attention and that need to be architected or planned for.

- Confirming that development effort estimates are reasonably accurate.
- Providing insight into areas that have been overlooked. These areas can be technical in nature, or related to the organisational environment.

A good project manager, together with the technical lead or architect, will start the project with areas of concern. The architect and technical lead will have technical concerns, such as the performance of the database, whether or not instances failover as expected, or how simple it is to debug a service. Project managers will have concerns relating to cost, development effort, and making sure that there are no hidden surprises. Each of these concerns can be red-flagged as risks at the beginning of the project, and the POC should clear those flags, or at least provide further information to be used to manage the risks.

Improved confidence

On projects where there is little or no experience with developing applications for the cloud, there will be areas where members of the team are unsure. This lack of confidence may not indicate risks per se, but at least an air of doubt and vagueness. Individual operators, for example, may have read up on how to deploy a worker role, and how to swap it into production from staging, but have no experience to be sure that it works as described. Maybe there is a missing step, or some particular knowledge that the operator doesn't have, that could take days to resolve.

This lack of confidence can be damaging to the project. There is a lack of morale, reluctant acceptance of the project vision, and no confidence in effort estimates provided. The POC allows all members of the implementation team to get their 'hands dirty' with the environment and allay any personal doubts that they may have.

The POC increases confidence in:

- Qualification — when the application, even in the crude form of a POC, is seen running, the confidence in the qualification of the chosen candidate application increases. This includes some degree of the confirmation of the risk and cost issues.
- Platform — despite seeing presentations, or even running simple applications in Windows Azure, nothing beats the running of a functionally representative POC in a production Windows Azure environment to confirm that it does

work as promised. A deployed POC can be started, stopped, scaled up, monitored, and shut down as if it were deployed in a production environment. The confidence that the platform does work can be fairly simple to achieve, but has a significant impact on the project.
- Design and Architecture — the most important reason for developing a POC is to ensure that the application design and architecture is correct. The first parts of workload decomposition (see workload model) will be seen in action, together with the beginnings of loosely coupled asynchronous services. Tactics developed in the availability model will be tested, and the chaos monkey can be set free in order to test the availability approach (by arbitrarily shutting down instances). The primary data store should be selected by the time the POC starts, as well as some secondary ones (such as blobs and cache), allowing for the decisions made within the data model to be confirmed. For most members of the implementation team (including decision makers), the architectural approach will be unfamiliar, and proof of the architecture is important to get support and buy-in from all members of the team. Teams that are staffed by smart developers will have to explain and motivate their approach, and code running in production is the best way to do it.
- Delivery — Senior members of the team, particularly non-technical members, such as the project manager and project sponsor, need confidence that the application and the team can deliver. The application running on Windows Azure should prove that the platform is up to the task and that the operators know how to deploy and run it. The functions that have been developed within the POC should prove that the developers can deliver.
- Operations — Operational staff are often the most wary of the cloud. They see all sorts of problems that may not exist, including the threat to their jobs. The POC should increase the confidence of operators, about how the platform works, the fact that a cloud platform is not a toy, and confidence in their own job security.

Input into models

Although it is expected that by the time the POC commences, significant work is done with most of the CALM models, at such an early stage of the project the models are far from complete. Some models should be mostly complete (such as the lifecycle model, others will be finalised much later in the development cycle (such as the cost model). The successful running of a POC will provide valuable input to models that need further development. Examples of this input are listed below:

- Cost Model — An application running on Windows Azure consumes billable resources, even if it is just a POC. The amount of resources that are consumed, and their cost implications, can be analysed in detail and fed into the evolving cost model.
- Health Model — The POC will often be the first time that realistic monitoring data is seen in the logs and the portal. A running POC will also not run smoothly and will need to be debugged. How it is determined to be running in a state of diminished health (or not) is useful to the health model.
- Capacity Model — The POC can be tested with various configurations and instance sizes; this is useful information to feed into the capacity model.
- Operational Model — As most operators will be unfamiliar to Windows Azure, the running of the POC in a production Windows Azure environment will give them a good idea of how to operate the application. This is only useful if operators themselves do the deployments and look for problems. Often, during POCs, the developers do it themselves, which may be quicker, but is less useful in terms of contribution to the operational model.
- Data Model — While most of the data model will be complete before a POC runs, vital information such as volume (size of data), throughput and performance may be useful to refine it.
- Test Model — The POC is a good opportunity for testers to try out their test model and test plan on a deployed application. The feedback on the process can be integrated back into the test model.
- Availability Model — Like the data model, much of the availability model will already be complete by the time the POC runs. Since the POC will include simulated failures, this may require an updating of the availability model. At the very least, it will provide useful metrics, such as failover time for databases.

Reach

For enterprises that are used to developing and releasing applications into their own on-premise datacentre, releasing a cloud-based application can uncover previously unnoticed organisational and internal IT behaviour. Deploying a POC, particularly when it has some integration with existing applications, helps towards understanding some of the broader business and IT responsibilities of the organisation. For example:

- The POC may require a hybrid active directory federation, which requires involvement by internal IT.

- Internal IT networking rules and procedures may need to be challenged or adapted in order to, for example, punch holes in the firewall for access to Windows Azure SQL Database, or to set up a VPN. Networking and security people are, quite rightly, unwilling to make arbitrary changes, and need to be properly convinced of the necessity.
- Internal audit and compliance processes may need to be involved before an application (that collects some or other important data) is deployed on infrastructure owned by a different organisation.
- Other architects within the enterprise, or architecture steering committees, may want to validate and approve the design.

Side effects

The focus of the POC should be to deliver as much as possible within the allocated time and budget and to de-risk any architecturally significant requirements (see What to prove? below). There are some side effects in the process of developing a POC, which although should not be the primary reason for the POC, are nevertheless useful in the overall context of the project. These side effects include:

- Training — Since a POC is, almost by definition, work done on something that is unknown, by the end of the POC the members of the team will know more about the cloud and Windows Azure than when they started. A POC is about delivering a short-term project, so there is no time to take it slow and let people take their time learning the details. However, the project can be structured in such a way as to maximise the training benefit. This is why it is important to have testing done by testers, and not developers, and likewise with deployments done by operations.
- Estimating — After running through a full deployment to Windows Azure, from conception to deployed and running code, the entire implementation team will have a much better understanding of what it entails to develop an application for Windows Azure. This understanding should translate into better estimation, after all, most errors are due to the cone of uncertainty[1], and the removal of that uncertainty improves the accuracy and quality of the estimates.
- Re-use of POC assets — A POC should generally contain code that is going to be discarded before the primary development starts, otherwise too much

---

[1] http://construx.com/Page.aspx?cid=1648

time is wasted on a level of quality and engineering that is, at least for objectives of the POC, unnecessary. It is prudent however, to try to make sure that some of the assets are re-usable. It should be possible to harvest some code, deployment scripts, configurations and other deliverables from the POC to give the primary project a kick-start.

What to prove

A POC is not the first sprint of a long project. It needs to be a mini-project that has a scope of work, a set of deliverables and a plan. Rather than just diving in to code, spend some time making sure that the POC proves the correct things and that everybody is clear on what needs to be delivered.

State the constraints and objectives

It is important to clearly state up-front what the objectives of the POC are. The overall objective will be to make sure that the qualification of the project is still valid and that the key risks identified are being reduced and further managed. The project may be assessing the suitability of Windows Azure, in which case the POC should include extensive use of Windows Azure features. The project may be assessing the ability of data stores to cope with the volume, in which case more attention will be paid to building data stores, data access, and subjecting the application to load tests.

The POC will also be subject to constraints, and these need to be clearly stated before commencing, as part of the project plan for the POC. Constraints may include, time, budget, people, access to internal resources (such as IT), and availability of third-party resources (such as consulting services).

Prove all models

Fundamental to the CALM guidance is the need to do up-front design work on the application. It is not practical, nor expected, to have completed all of the models in detail (some models, such as the cost model, are only 'complete' towards the end of the project), but all models will have to be worked through, to some degree, before the POC starts. Starting the POC without spending a few days working through the CALM models will result in a POC that mostly proves the wrong thing. For example:

- The lifecycle model provides important data as to the load that the application will be subject to.
- The workload model will provide necessary insight into the individual services that will need to be built in the POC.
- The data model will provide candidate database technologies and data access approaches that need to be verified.
- The test model provides approaches to how the success or failure of the POC will be determined.
- The health model helps developers implement the necessary monitoring, which is needed to see how the POC is performing.
- The operational and deployment models will help operators determine if the operational environment is workable.

The CALM models contain the design, architecture, approach and processes, all of which need to be proven.

Perceptible business value

Architects and application designers are tempted to focus the POC on challenging or interesting technical issues. The desire to try out new technology can also influence the choice of features to develop in the POC. The POC is funded by the business, for business reasons, and as the customer, they should have something that they can showcase and understand the value of.

While there is significant value in de-risking the project, particularly as it impacts downstream costs and delivery, a checklist of managed technical risks may not be enough to present to a non-technical audience in order to push the project to the next phase. Consider the situation where business has to present the successful project to senior management for their approval in order to commit resources to the rest of the project. In such a situation, it is useful to show a working application, with pages to render and buttons to press, rather than just the output from a performance log file.

The POC, while it is mainly about tackling technical risks, needs to address the needs of the business by delivering something that business can relate to. A successful demonstration, a test of real functionality by a focus group, or an example of integration with existing applications, is crucial to taking the technical successes of the POC and using them to push the project forward. Some time may have to be spent on the user interface development of a major feature, with some UX and graphic design work too.

Avoid low-risk requirements

Although developing something that is business-centric is important, it needs to be balanced against the risk of spending too much effort building features that don't fulfil the need to de-risk technical aspects. If the objectives of the POC are to prove cloud computing, it wouldn't make sense to spend too much time developing the web client; all of the effort spent on the UI may be wasted, as it is not considered a risk that needs to be managed. Similarly, time should not be wasted on implementing the full breadth of data access and trivial features such as sending emails.

Determine the architecturally significant features

Regardless of the amount of time or budget allocated to the POC, it is only ever going to be able to deliver a subset, and probably a very small subset, of the overall application functionality. The choice of the functionality to prove is crucial. Choosing the wrong functionality will mean that the POC is unable to de-risk enough of the issues, reducing the value of the effort. Technical people will want to take a technical component, such as a single service, and to make it functionally complete, with all of the software craftsmanship and quality that we generally expect from them. The choice of functionality may be architecturally significant as it is seen as the component that has the most complexity, or the most issues. They may optimise the performance, make it unit testable, refactor, and make sure that it contains minimal technical debt. This understandable focus on proper engineering and quality could result in a POC that does one thing very well, but is not broad enough to deal with multiple issues, and it may not look like much to a non-technical audience. For this reason, it is important to focus on architecturally significant *features*, rather than components or services.

Feature	Scale	Performance	Availability	Decoupled	Integration	Data complexity	POC Priority
Feature 1	Low	Low	High	High	Low	High	2
Feature 2	High	High	High	High	Low	Low	1
Feature 3	High	Low	Low	High	High	Low	3
Feature 4	Low	Low	Low	Low	High	High	5
Feature 5	High	Low	Low	High	None	Low	4

In order to achieve this we must map high-level features to architectural significance. If this is done for all requirements, the best candidate features will emerge. The table below is an example of how this is achieved. The high-level features are listed, and their need for a more complex architecture is assessed. The architectural needs are chosen based on what emerges from the design work as being the most significant, and should be geared towards cloud-oriented needs.

The POC should deliver end-to-end features, not necessary complete in terms of functionality, but in terms of touching the technical issues in the stack. The choice of a feature also satisfies the need to deliver something that makes sense to the business. The more time that is allocated to a POC, the more features can be developed; bearing in mind that the preference is to cover more features briefly, rather than one in detail.

How do you prove that it will work?

The architecture and application design of projects can only be proven by running code. The development and deployment of code is also the most time consuming and may not always provide the most convincing proof for the effort spent on development. Besides, some parts may be so complex that the amount of code needed to be written to prove a particular aspect may simply be too much for a short project. Other ways to prove an approach, design, or technical choice need to be investigated, as they may answer a lot of questions for a lot less effort.

Some of the ways to prove that the application will work are discussed below:

Functional Proof of Concept

A functional POC, where a subset of functionality is developed and run on Windows Azure, is the most widely understood technique to prove that the application works. This is also the technique that is most commonly associated with the term 'POC'.

Functional POCs have the following benefits:

- They are targeted at risks that have been identified for the specific project.
- They deliver demonstrable features specific to the application.
- The outputs are understood by the business.
- The extensive effort required ensures high degrees of involvement by many stakeholders.

Functional POCs do suffer from the following problems:

- They can be expensive to run. A fully staffed team running for a couple of weeks can burn a significant budget.
- They run the risk of producing a deliverable that cannot be understood by everybody, thus making their value, and the ability of the team to deliver, questionable.
- They require a significant amount of design work to be completed to ensure that the proposed architecture is implemented.

Technical Spikes

Technical spikes are used to prove specific architectural decisions. For example, an architect may want to implement a specific caching technology, but before handing it over to the team for implementation, will want to write some code against it and get it to run in a production environment, just to make sure that it behaves as expected.

Technical spikes are focussed, and generally developed by one person, and offer the following benefits:

- Allow proving to be done at any stage of the project, even when development is well under way.

- Are inexpensive to do, and can often be fitted into the normal workloads of individuals.
- Can be targeted and deal with a specific technical issue.

However, technical spikes are not as good as a functional POC:

- Their specific focus may not address all of the risks.
- They may be done too late to have a significant impact.
- Planned technical spikes may never be done, as individuals run out of capacity to perform them once the project gets underway.

Evidence

One of the easiest ways to prove the suitability of an application for Windows Azure is to look for similar success stories. Within Microsoft enterprise sales, this is a commonly used and frequently requested method of proof. These similar success stories are manifested as case studies that can be viewed and, depending on the nature of the parties, can even involve site visits and demonstrations.

Using case studies as evidence for proving an approach has the following benefits:

- They are inexpensive to perform.
- They are usually quite quick to conduct.

But they have the following well-known disadvantages:

- They will never match the exact requirements.
- They are sales-oriented, so may be embellished.

Vendor support

Microsoft, in particular, is approachable for help when building an application on Windows Azure. Particularly when the application is either large or for a worldwide recognised brand. Microsoft provides many ways to support POCs, which includes direct support from the Azure product group, TAPs (Technology Adoption Programs) for customers using features that are not yet released, and CTPs (Community Technology Previews) for features that are not yet in production. In some cases, a particular business unit within Microsoft may even sponsor the POC by providing resources or funding.

Vendor support, if accessible, is probably one of the best ways to prove an application. Direct support by the people that work on the platform is immensely valuable. This support may include:

- Access to skilled and experienced people who can answer difficult questions.
- Influence on the design in the early stages, so that the implementation team does not go down blind alleys.
- Validation of the design, and recommendations where it may be wrong.
- Insight into the product roadmap, that may mean that architectural decisions should be different, based on inside knowledge of Windows Azure features that may still be in development.

The benefits of support by the vendor include:

- A massive injection of skills onto the team that would be impossible without the vendor.
- Years of experience from successes and failures on the platform.
- Inside information into behaviour of features that may not be quite as they are marketed.
- Funding, if received, can make a big difference to the project budget.

Unfortunately, getting vendor support may not be easy:

- The vendor has limited capacity and cannot help every customer.
- Getting vendor support requires special vendor relationships.
- Extensive vendor support is seldom provided to small applications from unknown brands. The costs taken on by the vendor have to either be offset by revenue from the application or a marketing benefit.

Consulting

Consultants, whether as individuals or as part of a consulting company are a good way of getting skills on board to prove an application, and to build the POC. Reputable consultants come with these skills, experience, and a desire to get things done.

The benefits of using consultants include:

- Experience of implementing similar applications, so consultants can point out problem areas and offer solutions.
- Consultants are especially useful when time is short and your own team is not sufficiently skilled.
- Consultants have networks of relationships with colleagues and vendors that may not exist within the internal team.

Consultants do have some drawbacks:

- Since consultants need to keep finding more opportunities, they may stay on the project too long. This may be problematic if they are only wanted for the POC.
- Good consultants are more expensive than internal resources and fees may be too much for the budget.

When to do the POC

A POC should be done as early in the project as possible, but there are different points in the project that proving work can be done, depending on the means.

- After the project has been validated — Immediately after validation very little design work has been done (across all the CALM models), so proving means are limited to evidence-based proofs, such as looking at case studies. Depending on how much the project can be talked about, bouncing the application concept and the initial architectural ideas off the community may also help validate the architecture. Since no design has been done, the easiest means may be to appoint an experienced consultant who can give the approach the once-over for an initial validation.
- After the initial design — The functional POC should be completed after the first-pass of the design. Once all of the models are complete, enough information exists to state the POC objectives, identify the features to develop, pick the technical areas that need attention, and plan the delivery of the POC.
- Multi-step POCs — For larger projects, it may be unnecessary to prove the entire application at once, and the POC can be completed in multiple steps over a longer period. For example, the consumer web facing part of an application, which needs to be highly available, scalable and cost-effective, may be proven first. Then, once the development is underway, the back-end integration POC can be done, possibly by a different team.

- Just-in-time architecture — Agile methodologies are often interpreted as eschewing up-front design because it smells too much like Waterfall, the arch nemesis of agile. Throughout the project, the YAGNI principle (You Ain't Gonna Need It) delays major architectural decisions for as long as possible. The approach of delaying architecture *may* work, but is highly dependent on the skills of the implementation team, the engineering culture, and the organisational support (e.g. project management acceptance of refactoring). In these environments, proving the architecture and design can be a continuous process that makes use of frequent technical spikes.

Time and effort

Proving an application approach and architecture needs a balance between doing enough to deliver meaningful proof and not taking too long to get it done. Functional POCs should try to address as many of the risks as possible, but at the same time not fall into the trap of being bogged down trying to do too much. Often the scope, time, and effort of the POC will be limited, not by technical reasons, but by deadlines, budget and resource availability constraints placed by the business.

The amount of time spent will vary depending on the team and the project being undertaken, but the following points should be considered:

- POCs should not try and undertake tasks that belong in the development phase. This means minimal high-quality engineering, and incomplete functionality.
- POCs are most effective when completed over a shorter period by a full team. A lone developer taking months to do a POC may not satisfy all of the objectives. A full team can get things done quickly and make sure that there is a common understanding of the architecture before development commences.
- Functional POCs should have a definite end date, with deliverables checked-in and assessed. They should not gradually turn into full-blown development projects.
- A nervous business environment, where there is concern about the viability of the application or the cloud, will need quick results to reduce anxiety. Resourcing and planning a POC to deliver quick results will help secure funding and resources for the development phase.
- High risk projects, such as those that deal with regulations, or where the primary business processes are being reworked into the application, will

benefit from considerable effort spent on proving the architecture and approach. It is more important to make 100% sure on a crucial application than a small 'test' application.

- POCs need to be scheduled so that the full development project can start soon after the conclusion of the POC. This ensures that skills are not lost as people move back to where they came from. If the main development project is not ready to start soon after the conclusion of the POC (for example, by not having funding lined up), consider delaying the start of the POC.

Failure to prove

A POC that fails to prove the viability of an application, approach, or architecture is still a result. Not only did the failure potentially save the business from committing resources to something that was destined for failure, but also lessons are learned along the way. Make sure that the POC does not end up as a project that absolutely has to succeed because of the investment in it by the business or individuals. If the project cannot be proven after a short POC, then the likelihood of long-term success is low, and making it work by changing the scope or measure of success of the POC will not increase the long-term viability of the project.

When a POC fails to prove the application, value is still added. Business is more aware of the implications of the cloud, architects have a better idea of how things work, and developers have more hands-on experience. Failure to prove is an opportunity to go back to the drawing board, either by selecting a different candidate project, by reworking the architecture to make it more suitable, or by starting a programme to change the internal influences on the project (such as internal IT and networking). Try and make sure that the outcome of the POC has value by documenting the lessons, keeping the source code, and encouraging team members to retain and develop their cloud skills. Another opportunity is bound to present itself, and a POC team that has learned what they can from a failure to prove, will be far more prepared, and have more to contribute to the next project.

Summary

As detailed in qualify, some projects are more suitable to cloud computing than others. Too often we see projects started on the back of enthusiasm (often driven by technical people), without clearly thinking the project through. Fortunes can be wasted on applications that simply don't fit on a public cloud platform. Not only is this a wasted money and effort but also ruins the opportunity for other applications that may be perfectly suited.

The purpose of the qualification process is to think through the viability of the project, but it is still subject to optimism and enthusiasm. The development of a POC, with custom code that is deployed and running on production Windows Azure, is where the reality sets in. The POC is the definitive running test that eliminates wishful thinking, positive marketing, and misinterpretation.

The POC is one of the most crucial steps in the early phases of the project, provided it is done correctly and at the right time.

Steps

1. Complete a first-pass run through of all CALM models.
2. Plan the POC (scope, objectives, constraints, time, etc.).
3. Investigate the use of evidence (case studies), vendor support, and consulting means of proof.
4. Develop a functional POC that implements an architecturally significant feature on a production Windows Azure deployment.
5. Perform technical spike proofs as and when necessary during the project.
6. Assess the viability of the application, architecture, and approach at the end of the functional POC.

Workload Model

Traditional n-tier architectures are largely influenced by the underlying infrastructure. Stateless web servers in a web farm, a big application server or two, and a single monolithic database is a recognisable pattern. The physical servers, storage, and networking underlying the application have been primary influencers of the application architecture, where administration of physical devices is costly, hardware within a data centre is standardised, and the same storage, power and networking is applied uniformly across all machines. This infrastructure basis has led to applications being architected to fit the physical model where, for example, certain functionality runs on lower grade web farm servers and application servers sit on higher-grade machines and host unrelated functions.

Cloud computing provides a layer of abstraction where the physical infrastructure, and even the appearance of physical infrastructure, has less of an impact on the overall application architecture. So instead of an application being required to run on a server, it can be decomposed into a set of loosely coupled services that have the freedom to run in the most appropriate fashion. This is the foundation of the workload model because what may be considered an appropriate way to run for one part of an application may be wildly different for another, hence the need to separate out the different parts of an application so that they can be dealt with separately.

When architecting for the cloud, we don't create all of these decomposed services just because the platform allows it. After all, it does increase the complexity and require more effort to build. In the context of cloud computing, this architectural pattern has, amongst others, the following benefits:

- Availability — well-separated services create fault isolation zones, so that a failure of one part of the application will not bring everything down.
- Increased scalability — where parts of the application that require high scalability are not held back by those that do not.
- Continuous release and maintainability — different parts of the application can be upgraded without application-wide downtime.
- Operational responsiveness — operators can monitor, plan and respond better to different events.

Consider an example of an e-commerce application and the two distinct features of catalogue search and order placement. Even though these features are used by the same user (consumer) their underlying requirements differ. Ordering requires more data rigour and security, whereas search needs to optimally scale. A search being slightly incorrect is tolerable, whereas an incorrect order is not. In this example, the single use case of searching for and ordering a product can be decomposed into two different workloads, and a third if we count the back-end integration with the order fulfilment process.

The workload model requires that features be decomposed into discrete workloads that are identifiable, well named, and can be referenced. These workloads form the basis of the services that will deliver the required functionality. The workloads are also used in other CALM models to establish the architectural boundaries of services as they apply to specific models.

The workload model, application architecture and architects

The workload model forms the basis for application architecture fundamentals and the objective is to use the concept of decomposing application functionality into clearly defined workloads. The workload model should not be seen as simply a document, but rather a tool to influence the correct architectural decisions.

Decomposing application functionality is not an easy task and requires the architect to apply their skills and experience. It may involve input from other members on the team, and it may take a few attempts to get it right. Less experienced architects, or those that are not used to thinking about architectural approaches that encourage the use of loosely coupled services, are encouraged to seek help and advice from others. Other architects, whether from the same organisation or external consultants, may be invaluable in reviewing the workload model.

The role of a good architect cannot be understated when developing the workload model. There are no easy metrics to check to see whether or not the defined workloads are correct (unlike the cost model for example, where costs have to be in a certain range). The validation of workloads can only be done by a capable architect able to understand the far-reaching consequences of their decisions. Because the workload model influences so many design decisions, the architect needs to be continuously thinking in terms of the workloads, and even adjusting them as other parts of the architecture are defined.

Decomposing Workloads

There are no easy rules for decomposing workloads which is why it should only be tackled by an experienced architect. An architect with little cloud computing experience will probably err on the side of not enough decomposition. The challenge is identifying the workloads for your particular application. Some are obvious, while others less so, and too much decomposition can create unnecessary complexity. Workloads can be decomposed by use case, features, data models, releases, security, and so on.

As the architect works through the functionality, some key workloads may become clear early on. For example:

- Separating the front-end workloads (where an immediate request response is required) can be easily distinguished from back-end workloads (where processing can be offloaded to an asynchronous process).
- Scheduled jobs, such as ETL, need to be kicked off at a particular time of day.
- Integration with legacy systems.
- Low load internal administrative features, such as account administration.

For example, the diagram below depicts an application that has separate workloads for each (primary) feature of the application.

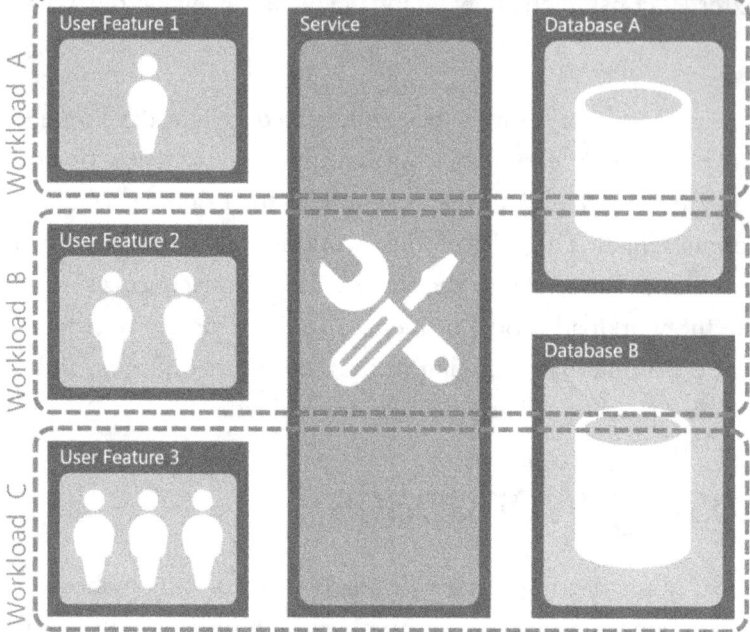

Feature/ Use Case Workload Decomposition

The same application can separate workloads based on asynchronous processing, as illustrated in the example below. The CQRS [2](Command Query Responsibility Segregation) pattern can be implemented this way.

---

[2] http://martinfowler.com/bliki/CQRS.html

Async Processing Workload Decomposition

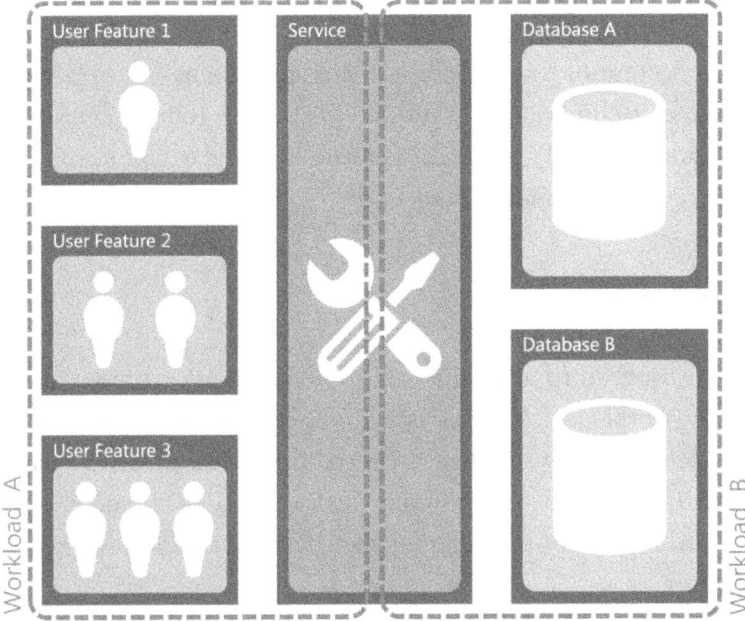

More complex workload separations can be developed. In the diagram below, the same application has a separate front-end workload, as well as separate workloads for each data model.

Data Model Workload Decomposition

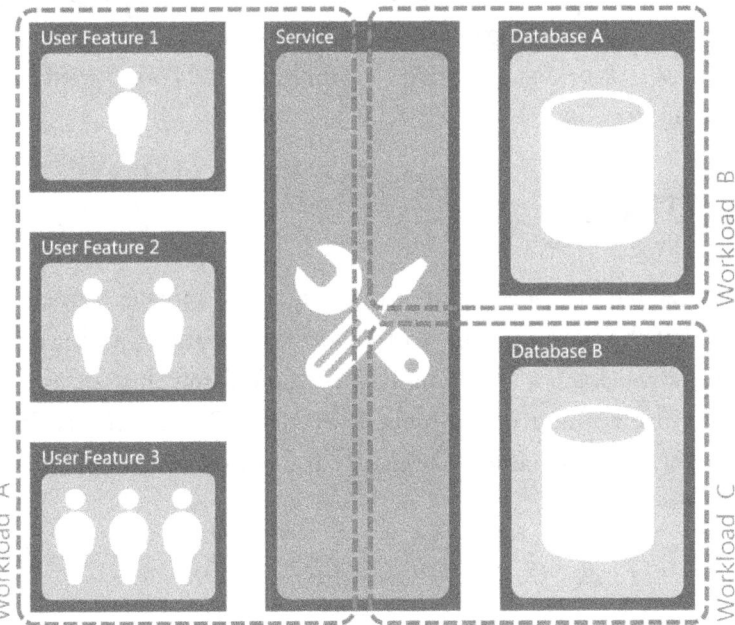

Indicators of differing workloads

Determining how to decompose workloads is the responsibility of the architect, and experienced architects should take to it quite easily. The following indicators of differing workloads are only a guide, as the particular application and environment may have differing indicators.

Feature roll-out

The separation of features into sets that are rolled-out over time are often indicators of separate workloads. For example, an e-commerce application may have the viewing of product browsing history in the first release, with viewing of product recommendations based on browsing history in a subsequent release. This indicates that product recommendations can be in a separate workload to simple browsing history.

Use case

A single user, in a single session, may access different features that appear seamless to the user but are separate use cases. The separate use cases may indicate separate workloads. For example, the primary use case on Twitter of viewing your timeline and tweeting is separate from the searching use case. Searching is a separate workload, which is implemented on Twitter as a completely separate service.

User wait times

Some features require that the service provides a quick response, while others have a longer time that the user is prepared to wait. For example, a user expects that items can be removed from a shopping basket immediately, but are prepared to wait for order confirmations to be e-mailed through. This difference in wait time indicates that there are separate workloads for basket features and order confirmation.

Model differences

The importance of workload decomposition in the design phase is because all other models that need to be developed in design (such as the data model, security model, operational model, and so on) are influenced by the various workloads. Using our e-commerce example, without identifying search and ordering as separate workloads, we would get stuck when developing the security model as we would either end up with too much security for search (which is essentially public data, and has low security) by lumping it together with the higher security requirements for orders, or the reverse, where we are exposed to hacking because orders are insecure.

In the process of working through the models, a clue that workloads are incorrectly defined is when a model doesn't seem to fit cleanly with the workload. This may indicate that there are two workloads that need to be separated out. Whilst it is better to clearly define the workloads early on, it is possible that some will emerge later in the design, or indeed as requirements change during development. The problem, of course, is that when new workloads are identified they need to be reviewed against models that have already been developed, as at least one model would have changed.

Below are some examples where a difference in a model indicates the possibility that the feature is composed of two different workloads:

- Availability model — When developing the availability model, if one feature has higher availability requirements than another, then it may indicate that there are separate workloads. For example, the Twitter API (as used by all Twitter clients) needs to be far more available than search.
- Lifecycle model — The lifecycle model may show that a particular feature is subject to spiky traffic or high load. In order to be able to scale that feature, it should be in a separate workload to those that have flatter usage patterns. For example, hotel holiday bookings may be spiky because of promotions, seasons or other influences, but the reviewing of hotels by guests may be a lot flatter. So, hotel reviews may be in a separate workload.
- Data model — The data model separates data into schemas that may be based on workloads, so getting the workload model and the data model aligned is important. Features that use different data stores indicate possible workload separation. For example, the product catalogue may be in a search optimised

data store, such as SOLR, whereas the rest of the application stores data in SQL. This may indicate that search is a distinct and separate workload.

- Security model — Features or data that have different security requirements can indicate separate workloads. For example, in question and answer applications the reading of questions may be public, but asking and answering questions requires a login. This may indicate that viewing and editing are separate workloads.
- Integration model — Different integration points often require separate workloads. While some integration may require immediate data, such as a stock availability lookup and will be in the same workload as other functionality, the overnight updating of stock on-hand may be a separate workload.
- Deployment model — Some functionality may be subject to frequent changes while others remain static, indicating the possibility of separate workloads. For example, the consumer-facing part of an application may update frequently as features are added and defects fixed, whereas the admin user interface stays unchanged for longer periods. The need to deploy one set of functionality without having to worry about others can be helped by separating the workloads.

Implementing workloads as services

Workloads are a logical construct, and the decision about what workloads to put into what services remains an implementation decision. Ultimately, many workloads will be grouped into the single services, but this should not impact the logical separation of the workloads. For example, the web application service may contain many front-end workloads because they work better together as a single service. Another example is the common pattern to have a single worker role processing messages from multiple queues, resulting in a number of workloads being handled by a single role.

The decision to group workloads together should happen late in the development cycle, after most of the CALM models have been completed, as the differences across models may be significant enough to warrant separate implemented services.

Identified workloads

The primary output of the workload model is a list of workloads, with some of their characteristics, so that they can be used and referenced in other CALM models. For each identified workload:

1. Name the workload.
    2. Provide a contextual description of the workload. Bias the description towards the business requirement so that all stakeholders can understand it.
    3. Briefly highlight relevant technical aspects of the workload that may influence the model. For example, the workload may have special latency requirements, or need to interface with an external system. These aspects should be quick and easy to read through for all workloads when developing the models.

You should end up with enough detail on the workloads to feed into the rest of the design process.

Summary

The brevity of this description of the workload model masks the enormous value that it provides. As every application and situation is different, it is not possible to explain how to decompose individual workloads in this book. It is the responsibility of the architect to figure out how workloads decompose in their particular situation.

Workloads are used extensively in all CALM models and form the basis for many of the architectural decisions. Decomposed workloads are at the core of cloud computing architectural approaches as they mirror the architectural desire to build loosely coupled services. They should be given sufficient attention at the beginning of design and continuously revisited and updated throughout the application lifecycle.

Lifecycle Model

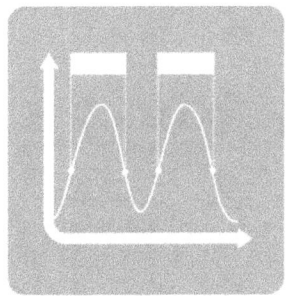

One of the primary benefits of cloud computing is the ability to handle non-linear workloads, as depicted in the well-known diagram below of the four main reasons for irregular load.

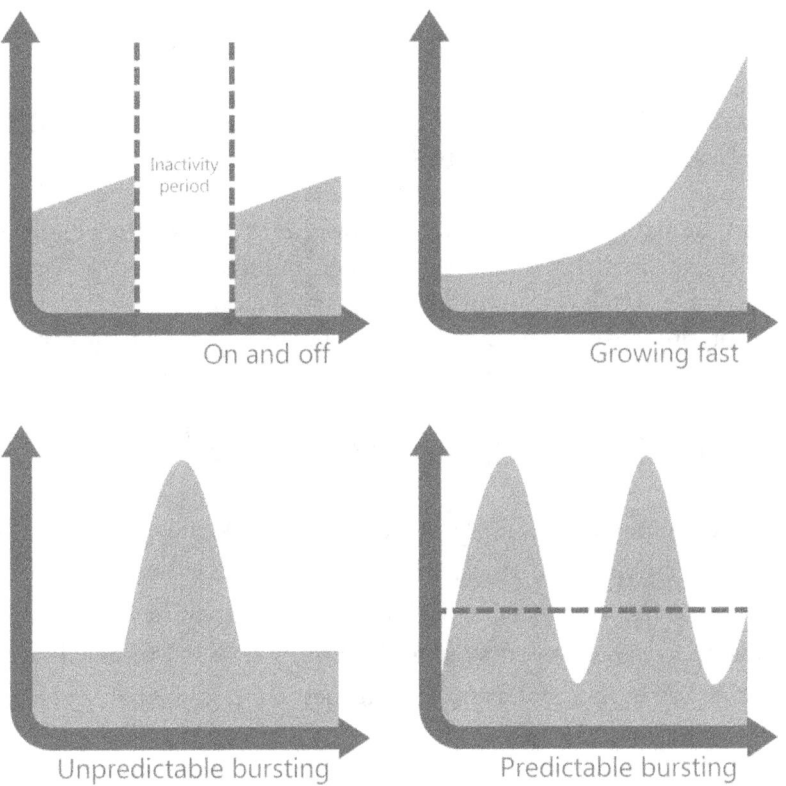

With linear (or slow, steady growth) workloads, the cost benefits of cloud computing over an extended period of time cannot be realised and the TCO model seems to favour more traditional hosting architectures. Since the ability to handle spiky traffic is a primary reason for the move to cloud computing, it makes sense to model the system for the expected load whilst it is operational.

There are many important reasons to develop the lifecycle model, aside from understanding the cost benefits of a pay-per-use model. These include:

- Influence on architectural decisions — developing for 'infinite scale', or some other vague indication of the requirement, may be unnecessary. The architecture needs to be developed with realistic expectations in mind. This greatly influences the approaches of the management of state (within the data model) as it is the most complex part of the architecture to scale.
- Load and performance test requirements — simple statements such as 'the system should handle 10 million page impressions a week with a response/render time less than two seconds' fail to take into account varying workloads over time. This can lead to a testing focus that is too narrow, resulting in unexpected failures when the system goes live. The lifecycle model provides input into load tests that need to be conducted for varying workloads.
- Operational readiness — while a business may understand expected load because it is obvious to them, it may be less obvious to operational staff. This results in a lack of communication (coupled with the myth of instant scalability) and an inability of the system to respond to spikes in demand. A lifecycle model captures demand over various periods of the application's operational lifecycle. It allows operations to plan accordingly by scheduling maintenance, pre-initialising capacity (and the reverse — reducing capacity), staffing the support desk and other measures to prepare for usage increases.

Developing the lifecycle model

The lifecycle model should be fairly simple to develop as most of the information required should exist. It may be difficult to tease out of participants however, not because they are recalcitrant, but because they have not had to consider the impact of business events on applications with such rigour. It is best to sit down with as many people from the business as possible, from various departments, to hammer out the details.

Development of the lifecycle model requires a clear understanding of usage depending on the standard consumption of the product, as well as the effect of events on top of usual business. It is also important that you are able to understand the effect of usage across the various decomposed workloads, as it may not be uniform.

Although it may be simple to list the factors, it can take a while to consider the detail of every single factor, and the impact of a number of factors occurring simultaneously. Rather than getting bogged down trying to think of every possible scenario, try and identify the factors that have the highest impact or which are most likely to occur.

Capturing phases and events

The most important part of the lifecycle model is to capture the phases and events that impact the usage or availability of the application. Most of them will be product based (customer, business or market), such as the daily lifecycle exhibited by users in a handful of time zones. Other phases and events will be technical in nature, such as the deployment of a new release.

Phases

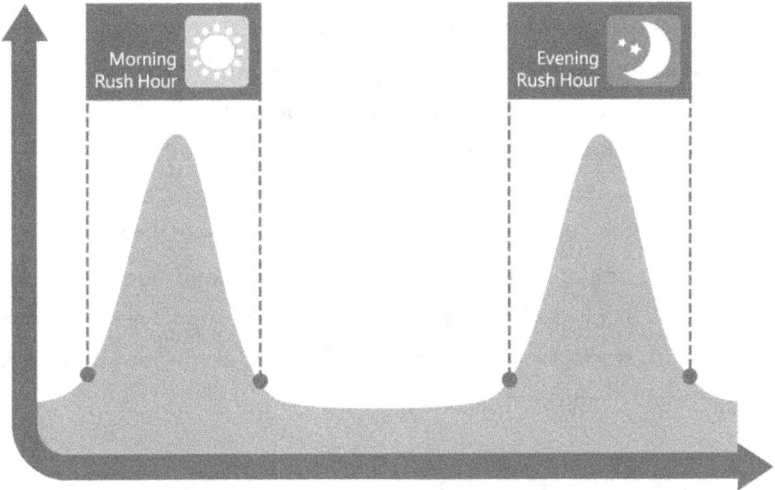

Phases are changes in usage or availability that are spread out over a longer time period. Most applications exhibit higher demand phases depending on when users are most likely to access the application and where they are based. The above example shows two distinct daily phases during peak hours. Some phases are predictable, such as rush-hour events, some may be planned, such as the rollout of a new marketing campaign, and some may be the result of unexpected events, such as a news item that drives traffic.

Events

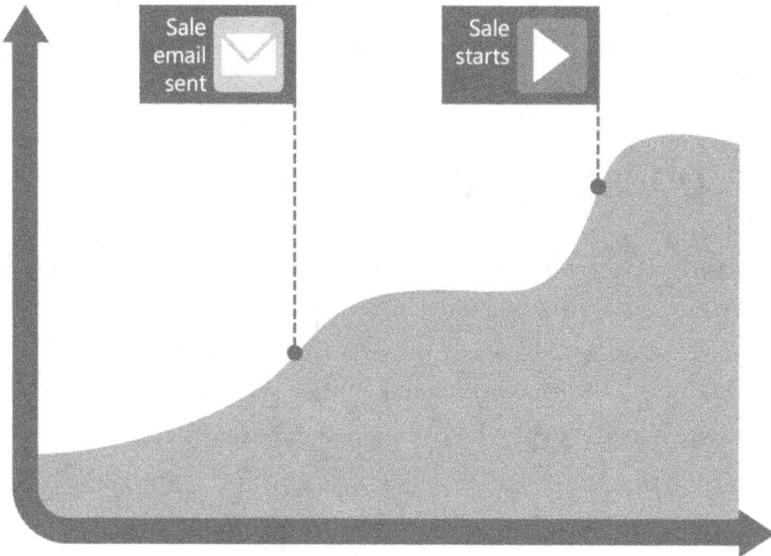

Events happen at a specific point in time and can have either a short or longer-term impact on usage or availability. The example above shows the event of 'Sale starts' will occur at a specific point in time and the application will be subject to additional load as the sale continues. Most events are followed by a phase; the event would be the start of the sale and the phase would be the time that the sale is running. Some events can have a high impact that is short lived, such as a celebrity Twitter mention, which may cause a massive peak load but things return to normal very quickly. Technical events, such as deploying a new release to production, may have no impact on usage and availability at all but still needs to be recorded and planned for in the lifecycle model.

Business factors influencing usage

The application will be measured against business factors and as such they are the most important factors to include in the lifecycle. They form the basis for the domain knowledge on which the business competes and differentiates itself and, to a large extent, they are out of the control of the application designers.

Business as usual

Much of the spikiness of the application can be put down to normal business conduct. Behavioural patterns of target customers, a response to marketing, product launches etc. are all part of what the business is used to or should have uncovered in the research for their new venture.

If the application (or something similar) already exists within the business, valuable data in the form of web analytics will be available. Check the quality, accuracy and validity of the analytics and use it to gain key metrics and insight, rather than relying on it as a single source.

Temporal cycles - Daily, weekly, monthly and yearly

By far the most common lifecycle to describe is related to cycles that repeat over time. This is often directly related to the product of the application itself and when consumers will interact with it. For example:

- Daily cycles — a weather application may be under load in the morning when people are getting ready for work, a news application at the beginning of the working day and a gambling application at night.
- Weekly cycles — a sports application may be more popular at weekends and business news during the working week.
- Monthly cycles — luxury shopping may be under more load after payday and online banking at the cusp of a month.
- Yearly cycles — fashion shopping, gift shopping and travel are highly seasonal, but there are some less obvious cycles, such as academic years, sporting seasons and so on.

Planned usage spikes

Many surprise traffic increases are actually planned by the business but they simply failed to warn IT, either because they 'forget' or assume that the systems will cope. These planned increases in usage can be the result of:

- Marketing campaigns with a specific launch date for print, TV, web or other media.
- Product launches that may or may not have a formal campaign around them.
- Conferences or other events where the product may get coverage.

- Promotions on products, such as discounts to remove excessive stock.

Any warning about planned spikes is better than none. It is easier to prepare for extra capacity, even with as little as one hours' notice, than it is when the application is under excessive load with operational staff potentially misdiagnosing performance issues.

Internationalisation

An application that caters to an international audience will respond differently to one that is local. It may be difficult to understand the behaviours of distant customers, but it could be a worthwhile exercise for bigger target markets.

- Time zones - an international application may have usage that 'follows the sun', with spikes coinciding with different times of the day around the world. While this may average out the usage, it could be compounded where an evening traffic spike in one region coincides with a morning one in another.
- Localised events — a business operating in Europe may not know of events occurring in the United States that affect usage or vice versa. Europeans, for example, are oblivious to Superbowl Sunday.
- Cultural and social differences - it is difficult to understand what a foreign market finds interesting, responds to or even what their patterns of application usage are.
- Platform differences - in one region customers may access the application on a laptop and in another region they may prefer a mobile device. This can affect behaviours and bias usage towards particular workloads.

External influences

While some usage increases may be in the business's control, others may not. Indeed many business models for applications, such as news-oriented applications, are based on external factors. While in most cases it is impossible to predict when these events occur, it is important to identify the types of events and their probable impact when developing the lifecycle model. This will enable the architecture to be tailored accordingly and provide some mechanism for operations to increase capacity in time, or be able to decrease capacity once an identified event has run its course. Examples of events include:

- External media — most obviously news sources, but could include popular TV programmes or sporting events that impact the customer base
- Business markets — even niche applications may need to respond to movements in business markets. This may affect business users as well as consumers.
- Expected events with unknown time — sometimes things are guaranteed to happen, it is just difficult to know when. For example, car insurance claims may drastically increase when it rains; you need sufficient capacity for when it rains, but don't know exactly when it is needed.

Cross workload contagion

In some cases, it may be easy to understand the knock on effects of increased usage. If the application has one web role, any increase in one part of the web application will impact all parts of the web application. Indeed, the reason for workload decomposition is to insulate the impact increases in usage in one workload from the other. For example, a web application that places messages on a queue for processing will not have an impact on the queue reader if the load is high. The number of items in the queue and the length of time each message spends in the queue will simply increase.

In other cases, contagion across workloads is unavoidable and is often related to shared state. The obvious example would be shared database access, but these are usually engineered out of the application anyway. Occasionally we will see business events (as part of a workload) impact other workloads. For example, if an e-commerce application performs a large update to the product catalogue (e.g. increasing prices) the load this places on the catalogue index may impact the searching functionality of the website. This may not be obvious at first glance.

While it is not necessary to try and map out all of these impacts in the lifecycle model, it illustrates the importance of uncovering the events that occur in the business so that the application and the architecture can reduce the contagion of one workload by another.

System events in the lifecycle model

Not all workloads and events that put the system under load, or affect its availability, are from end users. The lifecycle model needs to consider these system events as they can have an impact on the performance and availability of the application.

Releases

With new or evolving applications, new releases may be frequently pushed to production and could influence:

- Increased customer usage because new features are being tried out.
- Variations in the impact on the underlying infrastructure due to code, data model and other changes.
- Instability from insufficient testing or new edge cases requiring developers or other resources to be on hand.
- Version differences between various components
- Schema changes and data migration to new schemas

Upgrades and patches

Perhaps with a lower impact than releases, small upgrades, patches, bug fixes and similar activities can affect the production environment. These cannot be easily predicted and usually have a sense of urgency. It is worthwhile to document the people that need to be available or on call when patches are made within the lifecycle model, as well as follow-on activities such as testing.

Testing

Testing in cloud computing differs from traditional environments in the sense that different testing needs to be done and it is on the same infrastructure as the production environment. For example, testers may want to run tests from a different region on a production environment to see what realistic latencies will look like. The test strategy needs to be considered when developing the lifecycle model so that testing activities do not come as a surprise to operators or customers.

Scheduled maintenance tasks

Although cloud computing applications are engineered to have little need for what would be considered maintenance within a normal data centre, some activities do need to be catered for in the lifecycle model. On Windows Azure in particular, the need for operating system patching, clearing out of log files and similar maintenance tasks are unnecessary. Maintenance tasks that may exist include:

- Database backups and shipping to on-premise site.
- SQL Server specific maintenance such as index rebuilding.
- Cache invalidation.
- Poison message or dead letter queue clean-up.
- Incomplete transaction clean-up (such as expired registration confirmations).

System workloads versus normal workloads

While in most cases it is easy to classify a workload as 'system' or 'business', occasionally 'business' workloads can be lumped together with 'system' just because they seem technical. This means that the lifecycle model can be incomplete because insufficient understanding and planning goes into these workloads. Examples include:

- Integration batch runs — typically run overnight and import data into the system. Importing data using cron jobs is seen as technical, but the business has a need for the data. Some import processes are time dependant, can run for a long time, put the database under load and have an impact on data consistency.
- Data aggregation — a cron job that takes data from the day and summarises it. Again, it can create a high load on the database, but quick access to aggregates information the next day is required by the business.

These types of workloads should already be defined in the workload decomposition, but the scheduling of their execution is part of the lifecycle model.

Describing lifecycles

One of the biggest benefits of cloud computing is the ability to scale and handle any load an application may be subjected to. So why is it necessary to detail the application and workload lifecycles? Cloud computing applications still need to be engineered for scalability and data about lifecycles is vital in order to make the correct architectural and design decisions. In the context of Windows Azure, just because the infrastructure and platform scale well (as provided by Microsoft), it does not mean that the application will do so automatically.

It becomes necessary, therefore, to describe the lifecycles sufficiently in order to provide input for design, development and operations.

Describing load

It is difficult to find a metric for describing load that is meaningful across all workloads, as they will respond differently depending on the underlying components and architecture. For example, a web workload will be linearly affected by the number of users. A cache is not similarly affected by the number of users, but is affected by the number of cache misses, and the database is only affected when users post data to the database. The number of 'users' or 'services' calling the application will be the most generally understood metric.

In some cases it may be preferable to use another metric, depending on what is relevant to the technology or when existing data is available. Web applications may use page impressions, databases may use transactions and in message oriented applications it may be preferable to use the number of messages. It may be necessary, during design, to convert the number of users (as confirmed and understood by business) into more technical metrics. For example, for a particular use case, a single user performing an action may translate into a number of messages, database operations, cache hits/misses and page impressions.

Graphing load

Graphs showing load over time are a useful part of the lifecycle model.

- Graphs can be drawn quickly on a whiteboard.
- Graphs convey a lot of information visually — making them easy to understand and quick to interpret.
- Graphs can be understood by everybody.

As important as graphs are, they should not be over used or overtly relied upon.

- If the source is a scribble on the whiteboard, graphs are likely to be inaccurate.
- They are difficult to redraw in digital form.
- Engineers will try and decode the curve, when often there is no meaning to the curve.
- Graphs should be used in situations where information about load needs to be conveyed quickly, or the source of the graph is real data.

Describing reduced availability

Most lifecycle phases and events will be described and designed for an increase in user load. Reduced availability also needs to be understood, such as increased response times, increased latency or the inability to process certain transactions.

Reduced availability can be caused by:

- Deployments — where parts of the application are unavailable or underperform while the deployment is in progress.
- External services — may not be able to handle the peak load that your application can, either due to infrastructure limitations or even a contractual arrangement that supports a maximum throughput.
- Maintenance tasks — cloud applications should be engineered for automated or negligible maintenance tasks that affect availability. In some cases, such as when there is legacy code, it may be unavoidable to need to run tasks such as database index rebuilding.

Describing capacity

Cloud based architectures are designed to scale and the available capacity should not be a limitation that needs to be considered. There are cases where compute capacity is limited, such as when there is a fixed budget for compute resources, or use is made of bulk purchases of capacity (e.g. Windows Azure 6-month plans[3]).

The biggest limitation on capacity is the available operational resources and their skill levels. Describing the operator working shifts and even their holidays is important; planning a marketing event that increases traffic when operators are unavailable is not a good idea.

Describing the nature of phases

Not all phases are the same; some can be short and abrupt whilst others can be long and drawn out. Describing the primary phases in as much detail as possible will help immensely when architecting the solution.

Load

Describing the load over time is the most important part of the phase. The load should be expressed in a metric that is understood by everyone on the project and can vary between workloads. For example, the web front-end may be described in terms of page impressions per second and a back-end service may be described in terms of messages processed per second. Variations can also be found which are feature specific, such as expressing searches per second or product page views per second. Not all features or workloads need to be covered in broad detail. Pick the ones that are of concern to the business and their targets and those that are likely to place significant load on compute resources, such as image processing or complex database queries.

---

[3] https://www.windowsazure.com/en-us/pricing/purchase-options/

The description of the load should include the peak value, which is ultimately what the application needs to handle. If other values are meaningful, such as average, they can also be provided.

Duration

The duration of the phase needs to be described. This can be in seconds or even months (seasonal businesses have phases that last long periods).

Shape

Not everyone is able to express the shape of a curve in the correct mathematics or using the correct term, but knowing what the shape looks like and being able to express it is important. The example below shows some basic shapes that are significantly different and tell us a lot about the load over time.

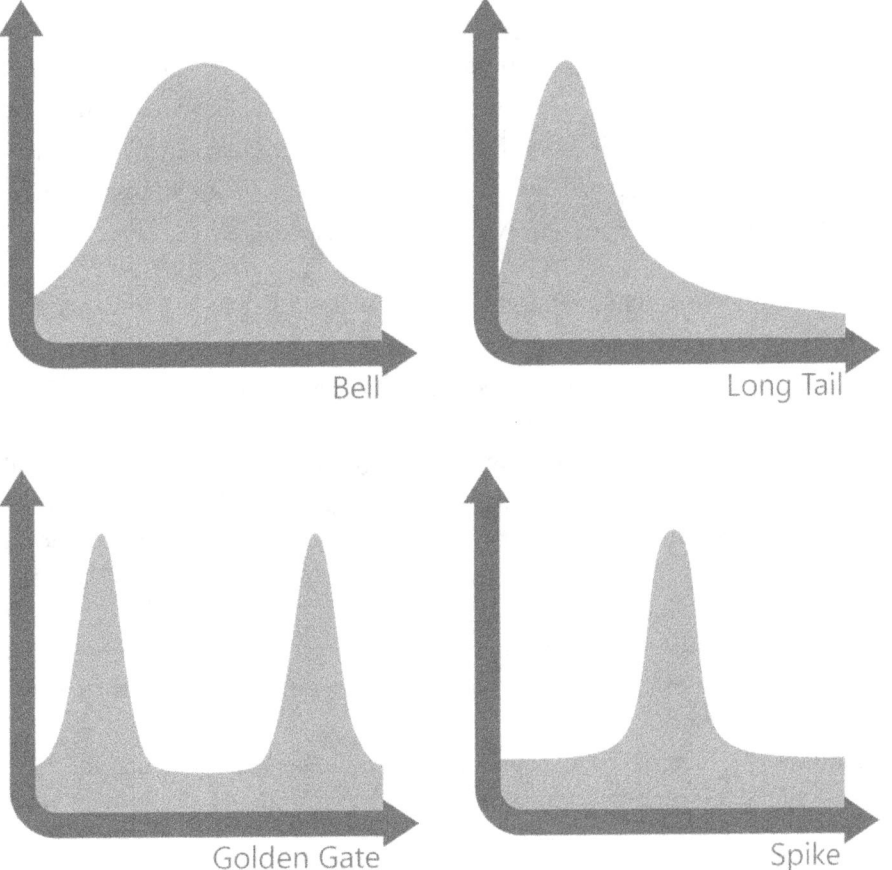

Technical metrics

Describing phases using technical metrics such as I/O stats, cache hits and misses, and CPU load should be used very carefully. They may be useful if the data is available from a legacy application and is well understood, but can lead to confusion and irrelevance because very few people on the project team understand them. The exceptions may be latency (in milliseconds) and bytes transferred, which seem to be well understood technical metrics, due to a higher level of consumer understanding of how they impact user experience and costs.

Describing events

Similar to phases, events also need to be described, but in less detail. Events generally precede a phase (and the phase is the important part to describe) or they are unpredictable, both in terms of when they occur and what their impact will be.

Events that are part of phases can be described as such. An 'annual sales' phase, for example, will have a start event (announcement or time of sale start), a peak (depending on the demand it could be soon after the start or days later if it relies on word-of-mouth), a long tail (as stock gets depleted or most customers have seen the items on sale), and an end (when the sale closes).

Events that are less predictable also need to be described. These events are the result of an external influence, such as a relevant news item or a positive review by an influential reviewer. For less predictable events, try and describe:

- Probability — what is the chance of the event occurring? For some unlikely events (such as being mentioned by Lady Gaga) don't bother describing the event. Other events may need to be described, even if their likelihood of occurring is low (such as your star actor being caught up in a scandal), so that you can be prepared for an application response.
- Event window — when is the event likely to occur? If it is most likely to occur during working hours, then lining up operational staff will be less of a problem.
- Magnitude — events that cause a 5% increase in load are not worth describing. Make realistic estimates on the magnitude of the impact on load that the event will have.

Describing product lifecycles

Product lifecycles are understood by technical members of the team and should be easily pulled together by the Project Manager. The actual application, whether whole or in parts (services) will be launched, fixed, upgraded and eventually decommissioned. This should be described within the lifecycle model as follows:

- Beta release — whether public or private beta, it will be deployed at some point and need to handle load, but availability will not be important and load may not be high.
- First release — depending on the application and the marketing of the launch, the first release can put the application under such high load that it collapses (see the launch of the Pottermore web application[4]).
- Bug fixes — fixing of defects, whether done as scheduled releases or as emergency deployments, can impact availability.
- Additional features — changes that users are waiting for, or UX changes that require users to learn new things, can increase load or support queries.
- Termination of services — while the entire application may continue to exist for a long time, some services may be deprecated from time to time and dependent services migrated.

Example

Consider an example of a web application that takes holiday bookings. This is a fictitious example to demonstrate the questions and outputs of the lifecycle model.

The first step would be to extract long-term figures out of the business plan. The business plan would not be based on page impressions, but on revenue, which would be related to the number of bookings. Some translation between the business metric (bookings) and a technical metric (page impressions) may be required. This example also shows relevant events (launch, added features).

---

[4] http://insider.pottermore.com/2012/03/waiting-for-pottermore.html

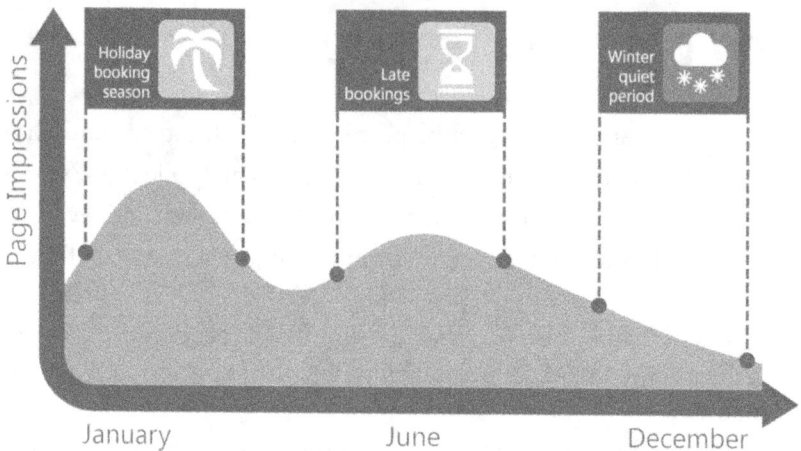

Holiday bookings are seasonal, so we expect to see different phases throughout the year. The vertical axis should depict something that would translate under stable load, such as average number of page impressions per day. The example below shows the annual 'holiday booking season' phase, the 'late booking' phase and the 'winter quiet period' phase, pointing to a need for higher availability during the booking phases.

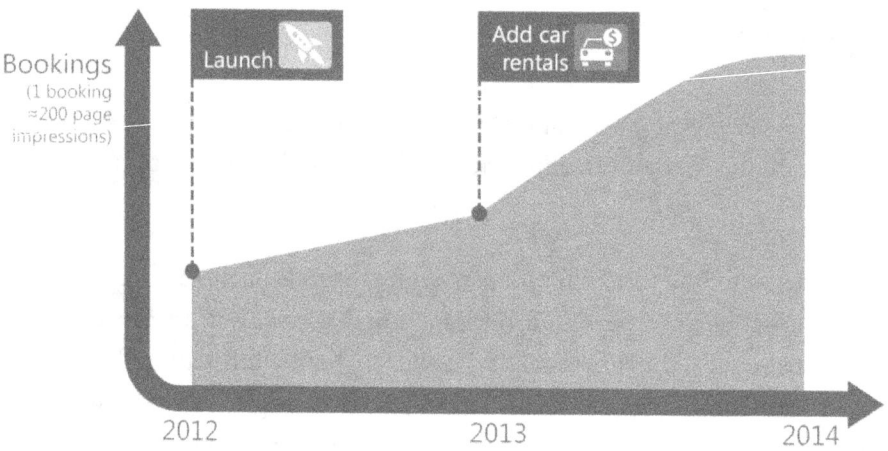

Perhaps people book holidays when they have the Monday blues or when they are planning a last minute weekend away. So there will probably be a weekly lifecycle, as illustrated below.

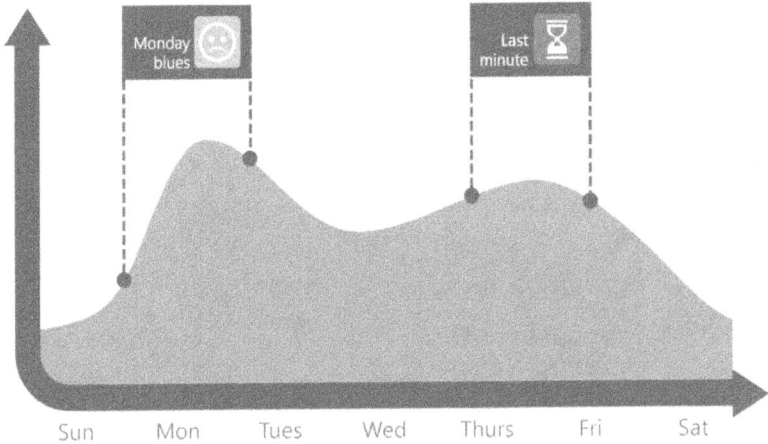

The daily lifecycle is the most commonly seen and understood. In the example below, the application is for the US and has virtually no traffic at night. Additionally peak times for making holiday bookings (such as at lunchtime) are spread across a longer period from the east to the west coast.

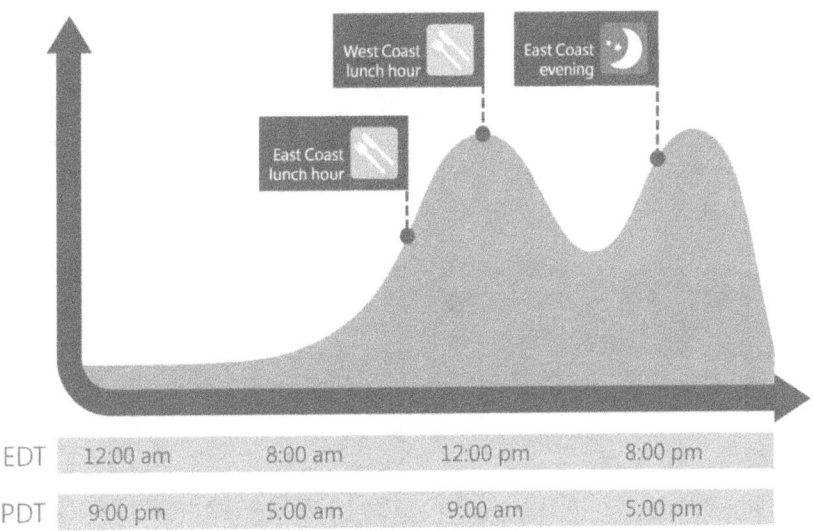

84   CALM with Microsoft Windows Azure

It is good practice to produce views on all of the primary workloads identified in the lifecycle model, as they may have completely different usage patterns. It is not necessary to describe them on the same graph, but it can help to illustrate the differences. The example below shows that bookings mirror searches (but with a lower number) and a data import happens overnight.

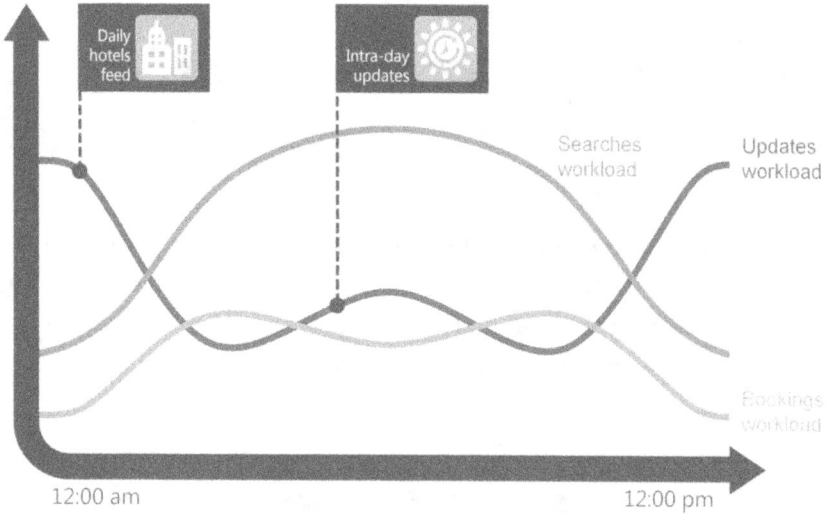

Summary

Too often developers are asked to build an application with only a vague idea of how much load it is going to be under and when. This results in a solution that is not fit-for-purpose, either over-engineered or completely unable to cope with the volume of traffic. While cloud computing solves this problem to a degree, architects, application designers and developers still need ballpark figures to work with otherwise they can land up with a completely inappropriate design. Legacy applications have useful historical data, but new developments have virtually no insight as to the expected load. This lack of insight is often because the business has not thought things through in enough detail. They may have some target figures and 'everyone knows' that traffic will be light after hours, but these loosely defined numbers are not enough on which to base an application architecture. Developing the lifecycle model forces poignant questions to be asked of the business, and how the business finds the answers can help their understanding of the market, their customers and the application.

Developing the lifecycle model early in the design process is a good place to kick-start the architectural approach and provides a meaningful indication of what needs to be built.

Steps

1. Understand the business factors that influence application usage.
2. Understand system events.
3. Identify relevant lifecycles.
4. Describe the lifecycles.

Health Model

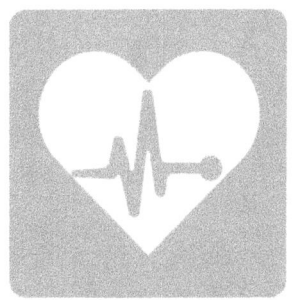

Cloud applications are not monolithic applications that can be considered healthy when you are only monitoring a single metric. Unfortunately cloud platforms are not silver bullets either and cannot automatically adjust to stay in perfect working order. Cloud applications are composed of many loosely coupled and distributed application components and services that, while collectively contribute to the overall health of the application, have individual health behaviours that need to be understood and managed. Well-architected cloud applications are designed for failure and, to a degree, self-recovery or at least tolerance of failure, which masks underlying health issues.

Whilst monitoring every possible metric is useful in debugging and understanding the root cause of problems, health monitoring needs to be more targeted. For example, if a web role puts messages on a queue to be processed by a worker role, the performance counters for both roles may indicate adequate health. But it's the number of messages on the queue that is the best indicator of health. The worker role may be the malfunctioning component, but the immediate recovery solution may be to increase the number of instances in order to get the application to a healthy state as soon as possible.

Health monitoring

The objective of the health model is to provide a platform for operational monitoring of the health of the application. Referring to the diagram below:

88 CALM with Microsoft Windows Azure

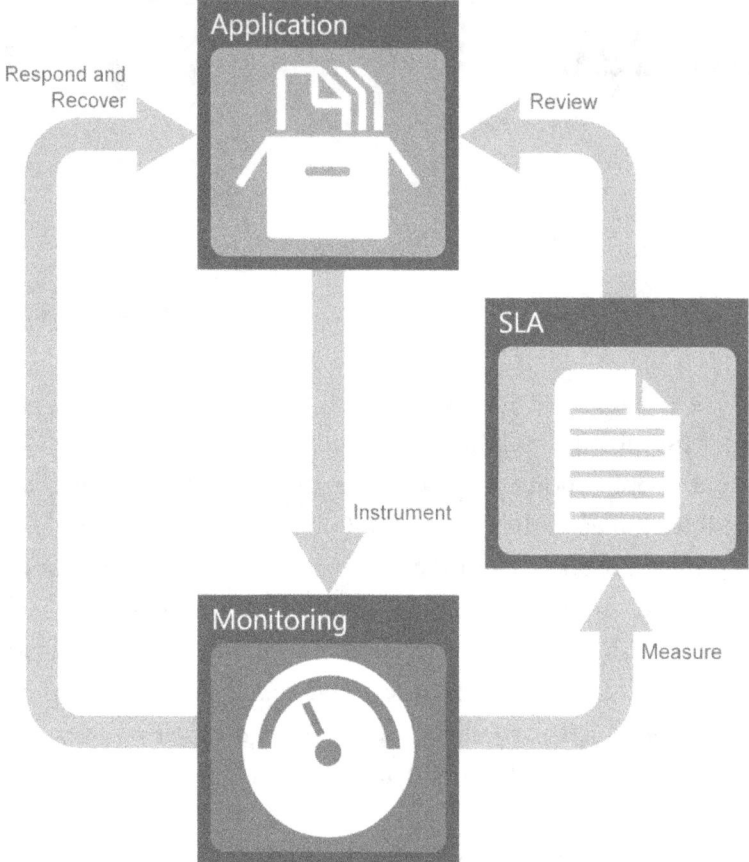

- The application needs to provide data for instrumentation of health metrics that can be monitored.
- The operational processes (manual or automated) use that instrumentation to continuously monitor the health of the application.
- Under normal circumstances the output from the monitoring is compared against the SLAs in order to:
  - determine if the application is in a state of diminished health or,
  - establish any proactive maintenance tasks that can be performed, or
  - provide feedback for application developers on improvements that can be made.

- In the event of an unhealthy application, response and recovery procedures can be followed in order to restore the application to a healthy state.

Developing the health model

To operate a healthy cloud application, a health model needs to be developed during design that will facilitate the necessary business involvement, developer responsibilities and operational needs. The health model should:

- Define the health states of an application.
- Describe how health will be measured and monitored within the application.
- Provide procedures for the recovery of the application to a healthy state.
- Allow for the use of health data within the entire application lifecycle.

Defining the health states of an application

In order to monitor the health of the application, we need to define what is meant by healthy, unhealthy, and diminished health of the application.

Health Indicators

Knowing that a server is up and running is not a good indication of the health of an application. Some of the metrics being monitored need to make sense to the business and this can be achieved by defining health indicators to be measured. These indicators should be set against the decomposed workloads, so that it can make sense within the application architecture and operational model.

List each workload, and at least one operation against each workload. For each operation establish:

- Health indicators for healthy, diminished health, and unhealthy behaviour.
- A possible technical method to be used to measure health. This helps to establish what it is feasible to measure for the business.

The table below illustrates an example of health indicators captured against workloads.

Workload	Health Indicator			Technical Measure
	Healthy	Diminished Health	Unhealthy	
Search - Basic	< 3 sec response	3–5 secs response	> 5 secs response or error	Page load time
Search - Full Text	< 5 sec response	5–8 secs response	> 8 secs response or error	Page load time
Order confirmation	< 30 secs	30 secs–2 mins	> 2 mins or none sent	Approx messages in queue
Sales report	< 1 min	1–5 mins	> 5 mins or timeout	sys.dm_exec_query_stats
Load catalogue	30 items/sec	30–80 items/sec	> 80 items/sec or failure	custom perfmon (items/sec)

Mapping health indicators to the Lifecycle Model

When establishing the health indicators, it is important to establish whether it applies during peak periods or not. Normally one would expect that the application would be designed to be healthy during peak periods, but what about if the load is in excess of what was expected? In some cases, such as batch jobs, peak load may not be relevant, and in other cases, slower processing times (such as order confirmation from the table above) may not be cause for concern.

It is good to discuss the health indicators in the context of the lifecycle model for the particular workload, and perhaps set varying health indicators based on the expected (or unexpected) workload. The (exaggerated) chart below illustrates how a higher load can result in a higher number of requests being considered unhealthy, which for cost/benefit reasons the business may deem to be 'good enough'.

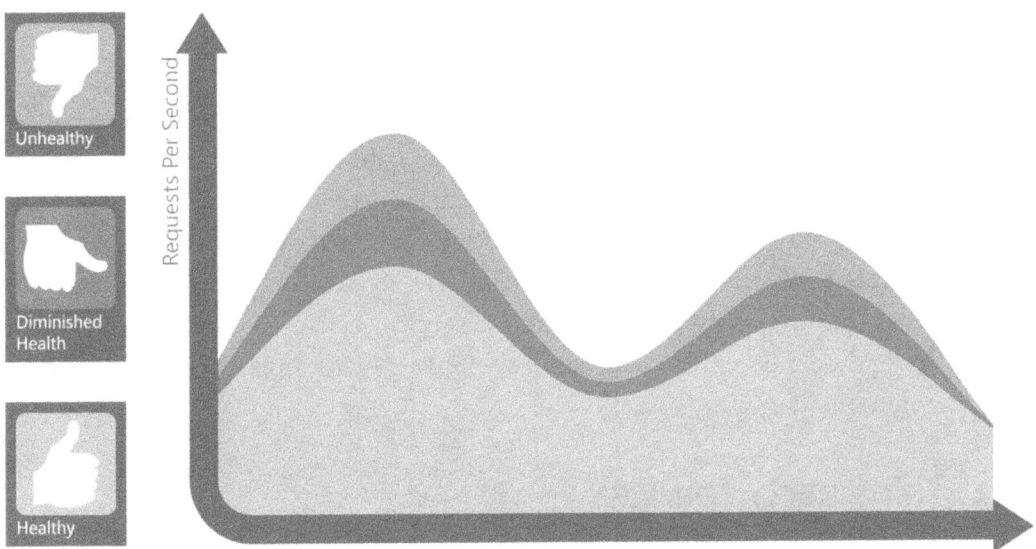

Statistical interpretation of measured data

The SLAs need to consider how the measured data is going to be interpreted. For example, on a web server, recording the measurement of **any** request taking longer than it should is significantly different from the average over a period. While it may seem reasonable to take the worst-case request in a period as a measurement, it does not reflect the behaviour of the system for most of the users. When specifying the health indicators, it is good practice to state the interpretation method. The best place to start would be 90 percentile (90% of the observations must be within the value).

It is worthwhile mentioning that aggregating the data too much can also lead to meaningless results. For example, aggregating across all instances of a web role may not show an underlying problem with a particular instance.

Monitoring the health of dependencies

Most applications have dependencies on systems that are beyond their control, and these need to be monitored as much as the application itself. The monitoring of dependencies is a big part of proactive operational management, as the time needed to restore an external dependency is quite high and detecting diminished health before it impacts customer satisfaction may buy precious recovery minutes.

Windows Azure

A Windows Azure application is dependent on the Windows Azure platform. There are a surprising number of individual (and interdependent) services that a typical application is dependent on, and they all need to be monitored, as a degrading or unavailable Windows Azure service will have an impact on the application. Windows Azure has a publicly accessible service dashboard[5], with service history, to monitor the various services across regions. The deployment model should describe which services are used by the application, and need to be monitored.

Third-party services

Many applications depend on other services in order to function. Examples include identity providers (used by the access control service), analytics, and content delivery. While in many cases, it may be difficult to monitor thirty-party services directly. A process to diagnose their role in health degradation, and support processes for recovery, needs to be developed.

On-premise infrastructure

Enterprise applications that are deployed in Windows Azure may have a dependency on on-premise infrastructure, such as database servers, active directory servers, and even the networking infrastructure used to access on-premise infrastructure.

On-premise applications and services

Applications that have a lot of enterprise integration may have a high dependency on on-premise applications and services. These might include on-premise ERP or CRM applications. Those that are accessed using RPC style calls are particularly prone to impacting the health of an application deployed in the cloud.

---

[5] http://www.windowsazure.com/en-us/support/service-dashboard/

Unhealthy cost

One of the benefits of cloud applications is their ability to scale out and add additional capacity on demand. But what if the demand is the result of an application fault; will additional capacity be wastefully allocated? An application may appear to be in good health against health indicators but is running far too many compute instances, sending too many messages, or using up more storage or bandwidth than initially planned.

The cost model should contain details of expected costs against workloads under various load scenarios. The health monitoring should take this into account, and flag the application as unhealthy if it exceeds the expected cost. However, it may be difficult to extract cost data (particularly at a sufficiently granular level), so other mechanisms of estimating actual cost for a workload need to be developed.

At the very least, check the monthly bill as part of the health monitoring process rather than just being part of a financial check.

Encapsulation within the SLAs

Once the health indicators, dependencies, and cost measures have been defined they should be put into the SLAs for the application. It is only by capturing the health monitoring metrics in the SLAs that they can be used to actively encourage better operations and changes within the application. It should be possible to copy the table of health indicators and the list of monitored dependencies, with few changes, into the SLAs.

Collecting monitoring data

Once the health states of the application have been defined, it is up to the development team to implement mechanisms for gathering the required data as input to the instrumentation tools.

Differences of cloud applications

Gathering data to use in health monitoring is a well-established practice. Effective techniques that work for the application type (e.g. ASP.NET MVC, web services), the .NET environment and the operating system (Windows Server) should be applied; particularly those metrics that the development or operational teams are familiar with. Developing a new way of monitoring, which introduces risk, should only be considered after careful deliberation. When adapting existing practices to Windows Azure, there are some key differences that should be considered:

- Infrastructure is not static — The latency and throughput between various parts of the underlying infrastructure (e.g. between compute and Windows Azure SQL Database) is variable due to the multi-tenant nature of the platform. For example, where existing data collection strategies may have largely ignored a constant latency, some additional data collection in this area is worthwhile.
- Applications are loosely coupled and asynchronous — Windows Azure encourages functionality to be spread across multiple services that are loosely coupled and interact with asynchronous messaging. This means that there is much more to monitor (multiple services) including the points of interaction (e.g. queues).
- Ephemeral instances mean that log files need to be centralised because individual instances can come and go. Log files that are collected on a machine (such as IIS logs) are expected to disappear with no warning. Local machine logging needs to be avoided and integrated into a mechanism that ships local log files to a central storage location.
- Low level monitoring is not available as the base infrastructure (disk, network, etc.) is invisible to operators and administrators of applications. Teams need to wean themselves off a reliance on low level monitoring and choose higher level monitoring metrics.
- Throttling and retries — Windows Azure places limits on the rate at which services can be called (for example, throttling on Windows Azure SQL Database and Table Storage). Knowing when throttling is taking place is an important addition to health monitoring metrics.
- The API for collecting data has changed — although not a fundamental change (Windows Azure still relies on base trace logging), the addition of the Windows Azure diagnostics API requires learning new features and differences.
- DBAs have less information — Windows Azure SQL Database, as a multi tenant database platform, removes a lot of the monitoring that DBAs are used to on an on-premise database. There is no access to the low level metrics of the database server itself (such as disk subsystem performance counters), SQL Trace cannot be used, and many management views are unavailable.

Cost of data collection development

The engineering effort involved in collecting data for health monitoring is often overlooked in task estimates and project plans. Development teams embarking on their first cloud project are advised to make explicit allowances for additional effort to implement health monitoring. For example, while in an on-premise application the IIS log files are not the concern of the development team, some development effort is required to make sure that they are stored in table storage. This is an additional cost to be accommodated.

Viewing monitoring data

The dashboard for viewing health monitoring data is part of the operational model, but is worth cross-referencing. By being considerate of the operational use of health data, developers can provide more appropriate data collection mechanisms.

Types of monitoring use

How data is collected, stored, and the tools used to view it, is dependent on the type of data being collected and the value it has at a point in time. The health model should describe how the data is going to be used in order to meet the health monitoring objectives. The following categories of data monitoring need to be considered:

- Real-time availability — A simple 'traffic light' status of services in order to gauge, at a glance, the general health of those services. While services that are part of the application will often have more detailed views, the monitoring of external dependencies can generally only be viewed as on or off.
- Real-time capacity — A view of the available capacity for a given service. For compute, this may not be relevant as the number of instances available is variable, as with table storage capacity. For other services, this may need monitoring and can include available capacity for transaction throughput and remaining database space.
- Real-time performance counters — Custom performance counters are relatively easy to put into an application, and there are many performance counters available for Windows Server and IIS (web/worker roles). However,

the collection, storage and use of performance counters does require some work before it can be used in a monitoring tool.

- Alerts — Alerts are a side effect of real-time monitoring. The availability of alerts is an important consideration because (automated) alerts work better when they have more (structured) data about the event in order to perform a meaningful action.
- Log file analysis — The eventual analysis, aggregation, and storage of log files is one of the most important uses of health data. Often the amount of data produced in real-time is too much to consume and glean any useful information from. Looking for patterns and trends in log files is necessary to understand murky health issues.

Monitoring tools and platforms

A tool is required to view collected data and present it to operators.

Windows Azure Management Portal

The Windows Azure Management Portal is the primary tool for monitoring the health of applications. Although the detail may not be application specific or fine-grained enough for all health monitoring purposes, it is the only place where information is presented on the exact state of individual instances.

In addition, the management portal also has live graphs on various metrics that can be viewed to monitor the health of an application. While useful, the graphs are displayed per service, and not able to display a higher-level overview, but they are individually customisable, so specific problematic services can be more closely monitored. The addition of live health graphs (viewable on any browser), was a major feature addition of the 'Spring 2012' Windows Azure release, and is expected to increase their functionality over time.

Microsoft SCOM

The Microsoft standard for presenting, managing and responding to health information is Microsoft System Center[6] (SCOM). As Microsoft moves Azure

---

[6] http://www.microsoft.com/en-us/server-cloud/system-center/default.aspx

into more enterprise environments, and consolidates its private and public cloud operational environment, the product story and roadmap of System Center will continue to improve and evolve. With System Center 2012 Service Pack 1 CTP2[7], System Center is able to collect data (performance counters, event logs, IIS logs) and store, manage, and present them as if they were any Windows based service. System Center has the advantage of being able to present cloud based applications within the same operational environment as other on-premise applications within the enterprise.

Third-party tools and platforms

Although the Windows Azure Management Portal and Microsoft System Center are the official tools for analysing data for health purposes, other third-party tools exist.

Cerebrata Azure Diagnostics Manager[8] — Coming out of the RedGate stable, the Cerebrata Azure Diagnostics Manager offers an affordable mechanism to import information logged in Windows Azure. It presents it in a rich client that allows event logs, IIS logs, performance counters, and other useful information in an archived or real-time fashion.

New Relic[9] - While not a tool specifically for Windows Azure (or Windows based applications), New Relic offers a low effort option that works on Azure applications (implemented as a profiler that sends data to a service). New Relic is particularly good for web applications, and also offers support for Ruby, PHP and other platforms that may be used within Windows Azure.

Recovery of unhealthy applications

Applications in a diminished state of health may initially be the responsibility of the operational team, but the sustained health of an application is ultimately the

---

[7] http://www.microsoft.com/en-us/download/details.aspx?id=30133

[8] http://www.cerebrata.com/products/AzureDiagnosticsManager/

[9] http://newrelic.com/

responsibility of the entire team including business, developers and testers. The nature of applications deployed in the cloud is such that the business plan is often based on unpredictable, aggressive load that pushes the application beyond what development, operations and maintenance staff are familiar with. This requires far more inter-team collaboration for recovery and each member has a role to play in the detection of, response to, and recovery from diminished health.

Detection

The first point of detection of diminished health should not be the users, as is often the case. It should be the operational staff that are monitoring the application. Although detection is a somewhat passive activity, operators should be armed with the lifecycle models, and have other information on hand (such as notification of a marketing campaign). This allows them to proactively monitor specific parts of the application or determine if apparent diminished health is the result of expected high load.

Response

The response to an unhealthy system should not be panic, as that is when mistakes are made. The first question about the response is the impact on the users (or processes underway). If users are seemingly unaffected (such as an indicator that the database will run out of space shortly), then the response will be different to one where there is a complete failure across all workloads.

Although operators want a complete document of what to do in all scenarios, it is virtually impossible to put one in place up-front. However, it is recommended that a placeholder document be created which can be expanded in the future. This will create a knowledge base of valid responses to certain health indicators.

Responses for diminished health across the workloads can be documented in an indicative manner using a similar table to that created for the health indicators.

For example:

Workload	Unhealthy Indicator	Impact	Response
Search - Basic	> 5 secs response or error	Serious, catalogue not working. Lost sales	Raise level 1 incident
Order confirmation	> 2 mins or none sent	High, potential lost orders	Check order log. If orders lost, raise level 1 otherwise level 2
Load catalogue	> 80 items/sec or failure	Low. Out of date catalogue is still valid	Investigate root cause

This can be done across all workloads as well as during different times of the day (or availability of second line support). Note that few health problems detected need to have "Panic and get developers out of bed" as a response.

Recovery

If poor health is sustained, where it doesn't stop after automatic recovery or reduced load, or it is recurring, the system needs to be restored to a healthy state. Recovery is not necessarily just an operational function, it may require more effort from other parts of the team (including developers and testers), and take a while to recover.

Automated Recovery

The Windows Azure Fabric Controller takes care of a lot of automated responses without us being aware. Suspect instances may be shut down, databases will fail-over, and many other services will take care of themselves.

Under the banner of 'design for failure', there are many patterns which provide a degree of self-recovery within an application, particularly when the poor health is due to a brief load spike. Implementing such self-recovery does have an engineering cost and may not represent value for money, or even be necessary, up-front. Examples include:

- Feature shaping (service degradation) — where certain features are unavailable, or operate in a less resource intensive manner when the application is in poor health.

- Data stubbing — where personalised data (or other specific data) is replaced with a default.
- Eventual consistency — where data can be persisted elsewhere, such as a queue, and processed once the problems are resolved.

Immediate Recovery

Some recovery may be quite simple, and be part of the standard operational practice for a large number of poor health indicators. There are a few levers that can be pulled, and it is worthwhile spending some time discussing and documenting some of the 'best guesses' for immediate recovery. Examples include:

- Increasing the number of Azure instances for a role.
- Changing the instance size for a role.
- Changing configuration data (that may turn features off).
- Increasing the size of the cache.

Planned Recovery

By far, most of the recovery is not as simple as flicking a switch or waiting for something to magically recover itself. If all goes well, an operational person can quickly run a script or perform a simple action, but often recovery that is not automated or immediate requires input from developers, testers and even business. Actions performed in a planned recovery include:

- Assignment of responsibility for the recovery of the application to good health. This may be the business/product owner not operational staff.
- Assessment of the business impact of declining health in order to understand the urgency of the recovery.
- Diagnosis of the underlying causes for diminished health.
- Formulation and review of a recovery plan for restoring application health. This may include some testing of approaches, scripts and deployments, in order to determine the feasibility of the approach.
- Implementation of an application change, in the case of a defect or a problem that can be addressed in the application.
- Testing of changes.
- Scheduling of changes. Updates may be deployed during off-peak periods to reduce the number of users impacted if the update fails.

- Deployment of updates.
- Testing of deployed changes on the production environment.
- Monitoring of the success of the deployment.
- Rollback of changes in the case of a failed deployment.

The above list requires the involvement of a lot of people over an extended period of time. The recovery of an application to good health is not the sole responsibility of any group, such as operations or developers.

Health review

Monitoring of health is not just about keeping an application healthy at any given moment; it is also a mechanism to improve the application over time by providing raw data for business, development, and operations. The health model needs to encapsulate how health monitoring data will be used to improve the entire application lifecycle.

Measure health against the SLAs

The health indicators are encapsulated within the SLAs and monitored health should be measured and recorded against the SLAs. While there may be a fear of the SLAs being used as a stick to beat operational and development teams with, the flip side is that failure to meet SLAs may not be a quality issue, but indicative of a lack of resources (for development and operations), or usage behaviour beyond what was expected or planned.

Review recovery processes

When deploying a new application, operational staff will probably start with a blank sheet of paper in terms of how to respond to poor health. While panicked responses are inevitable, especially at the beginning, it is important that a knowledge base of recoveries (both successful and unsuccessful) be built up. This helps to ensure that future recoveries are faster and cause less disruption.

Review health behaviour in order to improve the application

In most cases, the development of a cloud based application will be new to the development team and there is sure to be room for improvement. "It is running slow, make it faster" is a common, but unhelpful, request. The provision of detailed health monitoring information is important for improving the application and provides insight into architectural bottlenecks and underperforming parts of the application, as well as into which workloads require attention (health against business value).

Summary

The decomposition of modern applications into services, and the infrastructure on which they run, makes monitoring the health of the application complex. The health model addresses this by establishing the SLAs as the primary understanding of what constitutes diminished health. It also encourages the collection of health monitoring data that is used in operational instrumentation. The health model is crucial to building applications that can deliver on the application availability, scalability, and performance promises of the cloud.

Steps

1. Define the health states of the application using the SLAs.
2. Implement collection of health data in the application and platform.
3. Provide a mechanism to view collected health data.
4. Develop approaches to handle the recovery of a poor health application to a healthy state.
5. Review application health in order to provide feedback into development and operations.

Cost Model

The costs of hosting an application in the cloud are often given a cursory look during assessment, and then largely forgotten about until the big bills arrive. Unfortunately, once high bills start to arrive, it is too late to change the application enough to get them under control. Developing a cost model and an approaches for dealing with costs are integral to the application lifecycle. Traditional applications provide the luxury of being able to work out detailed costs in advance and then forget about them until the application has to be migrated to a new physical platform. The variable costs for cloud applications do not provide this luxury and have to be part of the architecture, implementation and operations of the application.

Costs differences in the cloud

Of all the differences between cloud based applications and traditional applications, the cost differences are the most well known. Virtually everybody understands that public cloud services are paid for as they are consumed. This makes the cost models very different, but also influences architecture, development, operations and virtually all aspects of building and operating a cloud based application.

"No upfront costs. Pay only for what you use."

The pay-per-use model is the most widely known and, at least at a high level, most widely understood aspect of cloud computing. This level of understanding and the description of the pay- per- use model are extensively discussed, documented and analysed all over the web and even in consumer oriented media. It is assumed that the reader is familiar with this model and an overview of this model is not included here.

Service consumption

Beneath the hyped, pay-per-use model is a less understood, but more fundamental, difference. Cloud platforms do not sell infrastructure, they sell services. It is possible to purchase physical infrastructure on a pay-per-use basis, from traditional web hosting suppliers, but this is more a financial arrangement than the purchase of infrastructure or platform services.

Everything that you buy on the cloud is purchased as a service. This means that there are a lot of things surrounding the basic offering that are bundled as the service. Part of the service would obviously be power and cooling, but it might may include operational services to maintain the platform, networking services, storage, billing and other support services. In the case of Windows Azure, services are also included that facilitate the availability of the application, operating system patching, integration services and others.

This abstraction of physical infrastructure to services requires a mind shift for architects, developers, operators and even business. While conceptually it may seem simple, it does have far reaching consequences that are not immediately apparent. For example, a provided 'service' may only have certain network throughput associated with it, and nothing can be purchased to make it faster, because no 'go faster' service exists. This means that implementers need to be acutely aware of the services available, how they are consumed, what their capabilities are, and how much they cost.

Self-service

The self-service aspect of cloud computing has two side effects that are relevant to costs:

- The consumption of services by individuals can get out of hand. For example, developers are able to create implementations that use more roles than necessary because the capacity is seemingly available for them to use. Testers

can spin up hundreds of instances used for testing and leave them running idle for weeks on end.
- Additional costs that would normally be rolled up in internal IT can be incurred by the project. Operational tasks that need to be done on the management portal, or using the Windows Azure Service Management REST API, may need to be performed by members of the project team because internal IT has no interest or skills. These costs could mount up as they may require a dedicated person for the entire project development duration.

Need for understanding of costs

Traditional applications require that only a few people are aware of and understand the costs. Most of the implementation team, particularly developers and testers, have no interest, exposure or use of physical infrastructure pricing information. Yet the costs of cloud applications are far more directly influenced by small decisions made by individuals on a day to day basis. For example, the method that a developer chooses to access objects in storage using a transaction per object or batching a bunch together can have far reaching cost implications. While most of these costs are trivial, costing pennies per transaction, they can add up when the volume is high.

A lack of understanding of costs can also mean that individuals make decisions based on incorrect assumptions on the cost implications, without thinking them through and considering whether or not the effort is worthwhile. For example, a developer may spend days implementing a sophisticated inter-service protocol that compresses data in order to save on data egress costs only for it to turn out to be a cost saving of $5 a day in a live environment; hardly worth the cost to develop and the increased risk associated with un-maintainable code.

Costs need to be understood by all members of the implementation team.

- Architects need to have the best, up-to-date understanding of the costs. Many design decisions have to factor in development and operational costs as trade-offs so a firm grasp of the implications is vital.
- Developers, particularly senior developers and feature leads, need an understanding of costs at the granular level. They should be aware of how much things are going to cost when working with large numbers of transactions (such as Access Control Service transactions) or coming up with designs that spread processing or storage load (such as database sharding)

- Business should have more understanding of costs than they are used to, or are comfortable with. Design and implementation options presented by architects require an understanding of costs in order to assess the long term financial impacts of the trade-offs. After all, it is the business that will pay the monthly bill, so they need to be sure the costs are what they were expecting.
- Testers need to understand the costs so that their results from testing during development are fed back into the cost model. They also need to be able to determine the value or feasibility of conducting long running soak or scale tests.
- Operators need to understand the cost implications of scaling the application in a production environment so that it can be factored into their availability processes. They also need to know how much it costs to get large amounts of data on-premise for backup or integration purposes.

Opportunities presented by cloud cost models

The pay-per-use service method of acquiring, utilising and disposing of compute resources is revolutionising the application landscape. It allows applications to be developed for new markets, with new features and greater reach than ever before. Cost models are fundamental to opening up the opportunities, and most cloud assessments start to become interesting as soon as the hosting costs are estimated.

Cloud computing cost model opportunities include:

Pay-per-use

Pay-per-use is the most important and well-known opportunity. As mentioned under 'differences', the ubiquity of information and analysis of the pay-per-use model means that it is unnecessary to cover it here.

Higher awareness of costs

You would think that the availability of unlimited capacity would mean that people would disregard the cost implications of what they are doing, but it seems that the opposite is true. Every time a developer suggests putting some code in a separate role, they tend to think about the cost of a role, multiplied by the number of instances and the fact that it will cost money. This causes developers to second-guess many implementation decisions. This is not obvious, time consuming or energy sapping, but does seem to occur and is leddriven by senior developers and architects who are always asking the cost question. Perhaps it is because of the granularity of the costs, where they are at a level that developers are aware of their influence, rather than a tiny blip on a huge machine, that makes people aware of the costs. Sometimes the influence is small, and sometimes great, but there is no doubt that the cost models offered by cloud computing have a huge influence on the architecture of the application being developed.

Cost optimised applications

While it may not be desirable to be continuously optimising for cost, some applications do have the requirement to drive down costs. Maybe the business model is based on a resource-intensive, low-margin business, like video processing and storage, and requires that the application aggressively drives down costs. The cost models allow creative solutions to optimise costs, such as making use of resources for brief periods and only when needed.

Price reduction over time

As cloud providers compete with one another and hardware gets cheaper, cloud services are also getting cheaper. While this makes perfect sense, it is common for enterprise IT to have static costs that don't drop for years at a time, due to the long-term leasing of what will soon be outdated equipment.

Problems with cloud cost models

The freedom of cloud cost models brings its own problems.

Immaturity of cost modelling tools

The current state of cost modelling, billing information and other necessary tools to facilitate the management, control, understanding and modelling of costs, is wholly inadequate. Customers are presented with a bill at the end of the month with little insight as to how it came about. Yes they can see the detail of what was billed, but it may not make sense in the context of overall load for the application or revenue generated from the application.

Over time, cost modelling tools have to improve. Businesses are still coming to terms with cloud operating costs at a conceptual level and haven't started asking vendors for the tools that they need. At this stage, we probably don't even know what the real cost modelling needs of business are.

For now, each team will have to make do with a hand-rolled, spreadsheet model and use this to get on top of the costs.

Business case mismatch

While technical people may get excited about the availability of infinite capacity, that enthusiasm will probably not be shared by the business exposed to the risk of an infinitely large invoice.

There is a risk that the implementation team engaging on their first cloud project will build an architecture that is misaligned with the business case. Scaling up of the number of instances may be easier to consider against the business case, after all, increased load should have some business value. Creating a lot of isolated roles with persistent message based interfaces may be architecturally correct in the scenario, but may not be supported. The business case may not want such high availability, fault tolerance, or even performance under load.

Traditional applications, with a largely fixed infrastructure, have long lead times for increasing capacity that are accompanied by meetings and detailed cost/benefit analysis. The absence of such processes, and the degree to which costs are influences, are already coded in and is a problem that needs consideration.

Costly surprises

Unmonitored costs can result in nasty billing surprises. Costs need to be monitored at multiple levels, from the actual code (for example, the efficiency of storage transactions) through to deployment (for example, under-utilised instances). If they are not actively monitored and controlled, costs can build up and become difficult to track and fix.

Cost surprises can also be thrown by unexpected load, or an unexpected type of load. With pay-per-use billing, access to a resource that is unplanned can result in huge bills for little return. For example, if a publicly facing page had a video served up using the applications bandwidth and suddenly went viral, what would happen to the costs? Potentially tens of thousands of dollars would be spent just to serve up something to non-customers, and, if there was insufficient monitoring, would only be picked up in the billing run.

Need to understand detail

The pricing information page on Windows Azure[10] is relatively simple. TThere are less than thirty individual prices across all services, which is a short list, when you consider how many different SQL Server SKUs exist (or any other Microsoft product). But that apparent simplicity hides the truth. The complexities are in the detail. It is not more detailed pricing breakdowns where the complexities lie, but how things are counted. When is a 'transaction' counted or not? How is database storage calculated per hour? Is a staging instance counted? When *this* service talks to *that* service, is the data transferred counted as data out?

These details need to be broadly understood by the implementation team from developers who make lots of decisions every day that affect the cost, to testers who need to reconcile their tests against expected billings. Unfortunately, these details aren't very accessible as there is no single place that describes all of the details. The information may only exist on blog posts that may or may not be found and be up-to-date (see this post on storage billing transactions[11]).

These low level complexities, combined with the immaturity of the cost tools and the inaccessibility of information, mean that a lot of effort needs to be

---

[10] https://www.windowsazure.com/en-us/pricing/details/

[11] http://blogs.msdn.com/b/windowsazurestorage/archive/2010/07/09/understanding-windows-azure-storage-billing-bandwidth-transactions-and-capacity.aspx

invested in making sure everyone understands how the costs work to the right level of detail. This may be a problem for less experienced teams, where even those who should know, are unaware of the details.

Disregard of costs

Developers are notorious for disregarding the hosting costs of the applications they build. A culture exists that more hardware can be thrown at the problem, and in a developers eyes, hardware isn't that expensive. In many ways, it is acceptable in traditional environments for developers to ignore the cost details. For example, in an on-premise datacentre the cost of sending a message across the network is probably not measured, so has an irrelevant cost from the developer's perspective. This disregard of costs, across all team members, doesn't transition well to cloud applications, where the awareness and control of costs is more important. Not only do we have to deal with communicating the complexities of costs, but we have to alter the apathy towards cost concerns.

Reconciliation of billing against architecture

Related to the lack of cost model tools is the difficulty in knowing how architectural decisions impact the cost. Initially it is optimistic to estimate the cost of architectural decisions. The initial assumptions become invalid as the design moves through to development accompanied by scope change, where the view on costs and the architectural view diverge. An architect can look at a monthly bill of services on the one hand, and look at the architectural representation on the other, and fail to come up with a meaningful explanation of the costs against the architecture. If the business is complaining that the costs are too high, or wants to plan a future release, how does the architect address costs if there is no easy way to tally the two?

On-premise, things are simpler, with fewer services, fewer physical machines and an easier way to reconcile the architecture and the cost. Traditional applications have a physical machine, or a few machines, per tier and a database in the back corner, so architects have a fairly good idea how design changes will affect the number of machines required.

The integration of architectural, development, billing and operations tools does not exist, and is unlikely to exist any time soon. This creates additional load on architects and senior developers to try and keep track of the knock-on costs that result from implementation decisions.

Over-optimisation of costs

All this attention on cost ramifications can result in decision paralysis where implications are over-analysed. If you put three people in a room for a couple of hours discussing a cost issue, you should be sure that the savings are significantly more than the cost of having people discussing and assessing them.

Developers can become too focussed on cost and prematurely optimise when it is unnecessary, which takes the focus away from delivery. Testers can decide not to perform a test because of the cost to run it, at the risk of letting a serious defect through the cracks. Operators can delay responses to diminished health, while they work out how much it will cost to scale up, leaving paying customers frustrated.

Team leaders and managers need to make everyone aware of cost considerations, but also strike a balance with what is practical. It is important to remember that the hosting costs of an application are only part of the overall liability. Delivering the best product quickly, for example by optimising for development costs and time to market, is often far more important and financially relevant.

Licensing of commercial software

Many commercial software packages are built for a non-cloud environment and are intended to be hosted on manually configured and stable hardware. Licences don't always translate easily into a cloud environment, where servers have automated installs and run redundantly or in a load-balanced configuration. As a result it can be difficult to license third party software to run on a cloud platform and the costs can be prohibitive, especially where the software itself requires a licence key that is generated for each machine.

Complexity of cost model

Traditional computing environments may require effort up front to sort out the costs, with quotes, payment plans and discounts from various vendors. But this will be based on an estimate of what hardware platform is needed to run a particular load. Once the order is placed, the platform costs for the application become relatively fixed until the application is launched, and implementers do not have to worry too much about cost implications. Cloud applications are far more dynamic and have costs influenced by implementation decisions throughout the development process, as well being directly and discreetly related to load. This is ultimately where the cloud computing cost complexities lie, as the opportunities offered by a pay-per-use cost model are accompanied by inherently complicated fees.

Developing the cost model

An awareness and understanding of cost issues is mandatory. Actively developing, fine tuning and communicating the cost model for the application should be enough to ensure that cost issues receive sufficient attention without stifling creativity, innovation and rapid delivery. The following sections describe the contents and activities for the cost model, which should be seen as a necessary, but not overbearing, part of the application lifecycle.

Clarify the business stance on costs

The pay-per-use model of cloud applications is often the most interesting part of the proposition to business. In other cases, the scalability may be of interest to the business and the costs are secondary, as they will map linearly to their income. The first objective in cost modelling is to obtain a clear and definitive statement from the business about the permissible costs, and how the business case is, or isn't, supported by optimal costs.

It may seem pointless to engage with business to get a statement about costs, after all, business is always going to ask for the cheapest possible. It is necessary to discuss the costs with the business in order to establish a working framework and have business answer the difficult questions on how much they are prepared to pay for features. For example, the business may ask for a level of availability that is impossible without (expensive) geo-redundancy and, when pushed, may actually realise that such high availability is not really required.

Identify the owner of cost model

Cost issues run as a common, yet thin, thread across all disciplines within the implementation team and most individuals have too much else on their plate to worry about backfilling cost-related data. Neither project managers nor product owners have sufficient technical depth to understand the cost model in sufficient detail to take day-to-day responsibility, so a technical person needs to get involved.

A technical person should be assigned as the owner of the cost model, but it does not have to be the most senior person. Someone who shows interest, understanding and enthusiasm can become the cost model owner in the same way that some teams have an application security owner. While cost models may seem drab, there is sufficient technical detail to maintain the street cred of any technical person.

The cost model owner's primary responsibility will be ensuring that it is maintained as development progresses after initially being put together by more senior members of the team. This person will need to keep track of the application evolution (such as when more roles are added), interface with testers to get meaningful data on consumption of resources, and provide an interface to facilitate business involvement in small cost decisions made by developers on a daily basis.

Describe cost influences for all team members

Developing a culture of awareness and interest in the cost model is the most important function to be performed as part of the development of the cost model. Cost awareness should be as common and pervasive as security awareness.

At the beginning of the project there probably won't be much understanding of the costs, especially if the project is the first cloud project undertaken by the team. It is impossible to describe in sufficient detail all of the cost issues, and some of them will be unknown. Even if all of them were known it would be overwhelming to dump them on team members on the first day. Concern and attention to the cost model is a journey that will be different for all team members depending on their particular remit, so communication of the cost issues by describing the influences, is a good place to start. These can be described as a checklist of questions that particular roles need to think about. Example questions are listed below but you will need to develop you own complete list that is tuned to your project.

Architects and senior developers

- Have you considered the data transfer costs of your redundancy strategy?
- Will you implement a role for each endpoint or try and combine processing?
- Does the workload need to be decomposed, or can all the work be done in one process?
- Which is cheaper, reprocessing or serving up from storage?
- Where is the cache stored and how much does it cost to serve when under load?
- Is there a cost for the session state; are there alternatives to reduce this cost?
- Is this service too chatty? What are the cost implications if the service were less chatty?
- How frequently does data have to be synchronised with the on-premise servers? Have you presented the cost implications of high frequency updates to the business?

Developers

- Can this code be moved into a separate role, or combined with another, without significant rework?
- Have you optimised the use of batch operations and continuation tokens of storage transactions?
- Is it worthwhile compressing a message before sending it? Does that reduce the storage cost? What about the cost to compress and decompress it?

- Have you considered copying static data to the local disk when the role is initialised? Is there so much data that it works out as more data transferred than reading from source as needed?
- Do you slow down the polling on queues when they are mostly empty?
- Do you have mechanisms to control how much logging you do?
- Will the browser client call the external service or will you do it server-side?
- How are you optimising the page payload send down to the browser?
- Do you make sure that database queries return as few rows as possible?
- Have you profiled the ORM to make sure that it is not fetching too much data?
- Are you shutting down your development roles running on the cloud when you are finished with them?

Testers

- Do you know how to determine the optimal instance size?
- Do you know what the limitations are on each instance size, such as network throughput?
- If you run the same scripted test day after day, do you know if the costs are significantly different each time it is run?
- Do you have a definition of what would be considered a 'cost defect'?
- Do you have tests specifically for cost overruns?
- Do you know how much it will cost to run a production simulation?
- What is the cost of running staging instances when testing production upgrades?
- Are you shutting down roles when your tests are complete?

Operations

- Have you analysed affinity groups between the database and the applications?
- Are the databases the smallest size? Do you have a process to monitor when they need enlarging?
- Do you delete data, like backups and logs? Is the cost of not deleting them significant?
- Do you have an explicit agreement with business as to how much you can scale?
- Is the instance cost for each role optimal for load and redundancy?
- Do you have a mechanism to scale down instances on a daily basis during off-peak periods?

- Are all the roles that are currently running actually being used?

Business

- Have you been clear to the development team how important or not operational costs are?
- Do you know the financial implications of large traffic spikes?
- Have you instructed operations how much they are allowed to scale when responding to load?
- Have you discussed with internal IT the costs of bringing data on-premise in order to determine the best frequency?
- Do you have a cost model that shows costs for redundancy, backups and other non-critical components?
- Do you know what the cost implications are for implementing your availability strategy? For example the data transfer costs for geo-redundancy.
- Have you assessed the risk of being unable to pay your bill? What happens to the application and data if you can't?

Develop a custom cost model

As much as the pricing calculator[12] on the Windows Azure website is useful and accurate, it is intended for sales purposes and not to be the basis for cost modelling going forward. Various web-based pricing calculators seem to crop up from time to time, but fall into disuse and should be checked for credibility before commitment.

Ultimately it is up to the implementation team to develop, maintain and enhance their own pricing model and it is likely that it will be composed of one or more Excel spreadsheets. The first version will probably be very similar to the Microsoft pricing calculator, which is a great place to start, and then evolve over time to a level of sophistication that's useful to the team.

When developing the pricing model, make sure that the following items are included:

---

[12] https://www.windowsazure.com/en-us/pricing/calculator/advanced/

Current price reference

Windows Azure pricing changes frequently. It is sometimes difficult to keep track of, particularly with all of the services available. The cost model needs to feature the latest prices, and there is no API, so the pricing details page[13] needs to be frequently checked. Announcements of pricing changes are not guaranteed to make it through inbox noise.

Architectural or platform bias

Since the pricing model will be developed specifically for the application, you have the option of presenting it in a way that mirrors the architecture, or keeping it fairly standard. A pricing model with an architectural bias will allow changes to be made, not to the number of instances but to named services, interfaces, specific databases or any other architectural element within the application.

An architecturally biased pricing model will be easier to present and be understood by a more casual user, such as a business user who has little knowledge of the underlying platform, and is useful over longer periods by being a better reference for operators. Unfortunately because the model is fixed to the current architecture it may not be possible to model architectural changes, and it is also likely to be only suitable for a one-off usage.

Make a decision early on whether to stick with an architecturally biased cost model or to develop something more generic. It may be that you identify one during the technical POC, but be aware that it is the model that you will probably end up using for a while.

Price variations during application lifecycle

As Windows Azure pricing changes frequently, make sure that the model allows for price variation. Pricing changes are generally not known far in advance, so don't attempt to model prices months down the line. The model should be able

---

[13] https://www.windowsazure.com/en-us/pricing/details/

to record what prices were in the past, so that historical analysis of cost information is accurate and meaningful.

Inclusion of other models

The Windows Azure pricing calculator is one dimensional and does not allow for different load scenarios. The custom cost model needs to cater for other models and specifically include parts of those models that are relevant such as:

- Lifecycle model — this is the most important model to include, which will require different capacity at different times (more than just daily).
- Workload model — depicting workloads separately on the cost model will allow analysis to be done on whether or not they can be combined, optimised or scheduled differently.
- Capacity model — including scale units as a basis for calculating costs may be necessary to estimate applications that need to scale.
- Test model — will help plan the capacity and associated cost of large-scale testing activities.
- Integration model — integration with on-premise services such as databases and Active Directory needs to be properly modelled as the costs may need to be managed.
- Data model — understanding where data resides, and how services consume the data, needs to be included in the model as it provides input into storage transaction counts, database sizes, data egress and other cost significant aspects.

Record of cost incurred

In order to perform meaningful analysis of costs over time, the cost model should include historical data, and preferably raw data that comes from billing. It may also need to be separated for different uses (development, testing, production) and should, if possible, be at a granular enough level to map it against the lifecycle model. If at all possible, use the 'Service Info' attributes of the billing information to try and reconcile the billing to specific architectural elements; however this may prove to be more hassle than it's worth.

Non Microsoft costs

Without weighing down the cost model with all project costs, consideration should be made for costs that are not billed through Windows Azure. These could include:

- Third party services such as email services.
- Licenses for third party software installed on roles.
- On-premise costs, such as storage or configuration and maintenance of on-premise services.
- Costs for third party application monitoring and alerting, such as Newrelic and PagerDuty.

Use third party cost tools

Due to the current immaturity of cost models, it is expected that tools to help with cost modelling will become available over time, although this will only start once Windows Azure has a billing API. Keep an eye out for tools and assess their value.

Model specific optimisations

Some cost optimisations can have a big impact on the monthly bill and some turn out to have such small savings that it is hardly worth it. When questions about cost optimisations arise, don't always rely on guesswork. Go away and model them in some detail. Be specific about including non-platform costs such as development, testing and deployment. Only once all of the costs are factored in can a definitive statement about the optimisation be made. In many cases you will find that cost differences are negligible and are offset by high development costs.

Develop tactics for controlling costs

A crucial part of the cost model is the approach to getting costs under control (under control does not just mean cheap, but within expectations and estimates). Due to the impact that team members across different disciplines can have on costs, this has to be a multi-pronged approach. Tactics should be developed that suit each role, such as:

- Continuously review costs (see more detail below).
- Measure costs (see more detail below).
- Creating a culture of being aware of cost implications — every person on the project has some impact on the costs, whether it is a senior developer designing complicated service interactions, or a tester running a series of tests. If all team members are aware of cost implications, costs can be brought under control.
- Encourage specialisation — costs implications can be hidden in the detail of the service being consumed and there is no way everybody can know all of the detail. Having 'go to' people, and specifically not just the architect, ensures that the coverage of cost details is high enough, and specialists will endeavour to have all the answers at their fingertips. Individuals can specialise in storage transactions, Windows Azure SQL Database, data egress, staging environments, or any other particular part of the Windows Azure services.
- Involve business in cost decisions — business needs to contribute to the decisions relating to cost optimisations and understand the cost related complexities of the architecture. Ultimately it is the business that will be stuck with the bill and their guidance on whether or not to optimise in a particular case is necessary.
- Align the costs to the business case — if the business generates more revenue from increased load then it makes sense to scale up as much as possible to handle the load, but this isn't the case with all applications. Understanding the business case, and aligning the cost model to it, is a necessary step to controlling costs.
- Allow testers to create cost defects — testers should be able to identify a piece of functionality as being functionally correct and performing adequately but being too expensive to run. Making this part of the testers' mandate, and allowing them to generate test cases specifically for costs, will generate a huge amount of coverage for cost control.
- Don't make assumptions about costs — all too often things are more expensive, but detailed modelling shows it as being a dollar or two a day, which may be hardly worth the discussion or development effort. "Show me the numbers" will be a useful retort to make sure that costs are under control as awareness about actual costs will tend to increase.
- Scour the web for cost saving tips — people are always running into cost issues as their assumptions on costs are challenged. The details of these observations, often blogged by developers, provide valuable input data. See

these examples: Unveiling the Unforeseen Cost and Tips to Cost Effective Usage[14] and Five ways to reduce Azure Costs[15].

Ensure that costs are continuously reviewed

Cost models are often built during the initial project assessment and then shelved, resulting in shock at the first bill. It is necessary to continuously review costs, in order to keep them under control, and update the cost model on an on-going basis. This should go hand-in-hand with the maintenance and development of the cost model described above.

Detail of the cost related activities at various stages of development are described below:

Qualify

- Model costs in a basic fashion using the Windows Azure pricing calculator.
- Include the calculations as cost factors for the viable projects.
- Check the cost estimated against the business case.

Prove

- Develop a cost benchmark for the subset of functionality being proven as part of the overall business case.
- Measure the costs incurred and extrapolate to a production simulation

Design and Development

- Develop cost model details for services, data transfer and storage.

---

[14] http://wely-lau.net/2011/12/02/unveiling-the-unforeseen-cost-of-windows-azure-storage-transaction/

[15] http://www.opstera.com/blog/bid/136402/Five-ways-to-reduce-Azure-Costs

- Develop team-wide patterns for solving particular problems that have a cost implication and align those with the cost objectives of the application.
- Model costs for availability decisions made.
- Make cost a part of code review processes.

Test

- Develop tests specifically for cost defects.
- Continuously measure costs during testing and feed back into the cost model.
- Create a meaningful schedule of expensive tests (load, scalability) that deliver the most value for the costs incurred.

Production

- Continuously check that monthly bills are in line with the estimates provided by the cost model.
- Establish processes for approval of extra capacity for scaling.
- Develop maintenance tasks that clear up unneeded or unused resources (e.g. backups, staging roles).
- Use monitoring tools to ensure that instances are not running idle. Max out the CPU, memory and bandwidth wherever possible.

Measure costs

Unfortunately, the lack of tools and a billing API for Windows Azure makes it difficult to measure costs. It is then left to the business to pay a monthly bill they do not understand and with no clear idea on how costs can be managed. The cost model, perhaps in the custom spreadsheets developed, should include discreet methods to measure costs. This measurement will initially be based on importing the CSV exported by the billing interface and performing some analysis on it.

- Try to combine the cost analysis with other data, such as activity logs, so that costs can be determined to be anomalous or a natural extension of the load that the application is subject to.
- Compare the measured costs against planned costs if possible. This is particularly useful immediately after the application has gone live, where cost anomalies need to be detected quickly.

- Try to map the measured costs to specific workloads to identify their value. This will allow changes to workload configuration, scheduling or combining of workloads after release.

Document implementation and arguments

The final step in the cost model is to document specific aspects of the implementation that have been influenced by cost issues. This helps to:

- Develop cost patterns that can be used by future projects
- Store a record of the argument for a particular optimisation when it is queried in future.
- Provide a basis for targeting changes, where either the cost of the service has changed or the business rationale for the optimisation no longer exists.

Summary

The primary sales pitch for cloud computing relates to the pay-per-use nature of the costs. In order to realise the benefits, a clear understanding of the cost complexities is needed. With cloud computing applications, costs are directly related to code that is written, which creates opportunities for costs to get out of control. This may be the result of decisions being made that are inconsiderate of costs, or defects that run up costs undetected.

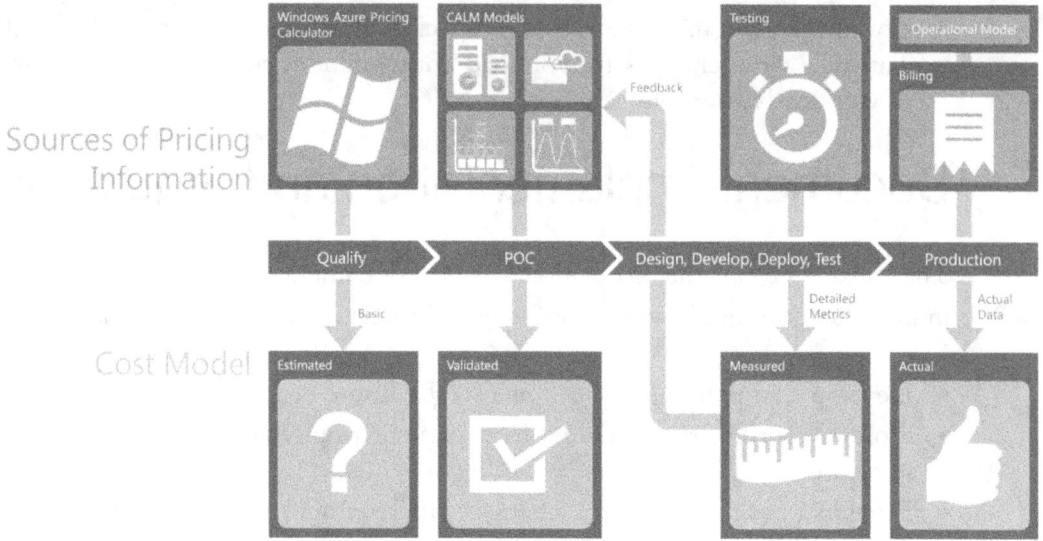

As illustrated in the diagram above, the cost model is never fixed and changes over the application lifecycle. This adaptation of the cost model as more data becomes available, such as from architectural changes or test billing results, is the most important aspect of the cost model. Too often costs are estimated upfront and never touched again. While this may work in traditional environments, on the cloud it can create serious problems.

Steps

1. Clarify the business stance on costs.
2. Identify the owner of cost model.
3. Describe cost influences for all team members.
4. Develop a custom cost model.
5. Model specific optimisations.
6. Develop tactics for controlling costs.
7. Ensure that costs are continuously reviewed.
8. Measure costs.
9. Document implementation and arguments.

Security Model

Security concerns about the public cloud are one of the main obstacles for enterprises when building cloud applications. It is also one of the biggest red herrings, as there are few fundamental differences between cloud security and traditional security. After all, traditionally deployed applications still have vulnerable, public endpoints.

While never an excuse for lax security, whether that is leaving a flash drive on a train or having a public website vulnerable to SQL injection attacks, public cloud projects are subject to extra scrutiny, and security breaches are less acceptable. Most cloud projects are new, paving the way for further applications that can be deployed to the cloud, and the first application, as a flagship test case, should not have security problems. If the first application is subject to an attack, it will be jumped on by the sceptics and derail any future endeavours.

The opinion that 'the public cloud is insecure' is generally unfounded, and even the position that 'the public cloud is more insecure than on-premise' is also probably false in most cases. The security of individual cloud platforms is well implemented, understood, and documented. The same cannot be said for most private datacentres (not all, of course, some private data centres are really good at security). It's more likely that a hard drive that holds important data would be ripped out of a server in a private datacentre than from the Windows Azure datacentre. Apart from physical access, where would you even start looking for a specific hard drive in a Microsoft datacentre? Windows Azure applications are less vulnerable to flaws for which Microsoft has issued a patch, as the underlying operating system is always patched for you by Microsoft. The same cannot be said for the millions of un-patched servers in private hands.

We can go back and forth about which is more secure. Arguments about wanting 'to keep my data in my datacentre' get complicated and are fruitless. The one big difference with public cloud applications is that the attack surface is bigger. There is little in the way of perimeter security, and poor security practices cannot be ignored based on the assumption that a firewall is going to restrict public access to a service that is full of holes. Everything on the public cloud is accessible, even Windows Azure SQL Database. The moment you allow Windows Azure connections to Windows Azure SQL Database anybody can fire up a virtual machine and try to connect to it. All (most) ports are open across all regions, for any amount of data. On the public cloud you need to make sure that good security practices that apply to all applications are applied consistently and rigorously.

The development of the security model within the context of designing for the cloud is about:

- Understanding the differences between cloud-based security and on-premise security.
- Asserting the need for good security practices.
- Developing a plan for building a secure application.
- Inviting early security assessments and audits.
- Understanding the specifics on how Windows Azure supports the development of secure applications.

Developing the Security Model

Understand cloud security differences

A web role running in Windows Azure is pretty much like any other ASP.NET application running on any other hosted or on-premise platform, and subject to the same security concerns and solutions. There are still some differences to be considered when developing the security model.

Attack surface

As mentioned above, the attack surface of an application hosted on Windows Azure is higher than a traditional application. In multi-tier applications, it is common to put the web server outside the firewall and the application and database server inside the firewall, thus restricting access to traffic from the web servers. Windows Azure applications are not architected in the same way (the multi-tier pattern is seldom used) and all services are generally publicly accessible. If the consumer portion of the application needs to communicate with an 'internal' WCF service, even if only intended for use by the application, that service is publicly accessible and needs to be secured.

Enterprise infrastructure

Experienced enterprise developers take a lot of things for granted; firewalls, active directory, secure storage, certificates, DNS, and many more. Some of these are specifically unavailable on Windows Azure (such as firewalls), and some are provided as part of enterprise IT, where developers don't have to think about them too much. In enterprise IT, developers fill in a requisition for a certificate to be installed by IT. As well as architecting and building for the lack of physical infrastructure, Windows Azure implementation teams also find that they need to do a lot of things by themselves.

Governance

Enterprise IT generally has well-established governance processes to ensure that applications deployed within their data centre meet certain requirements. These processes can range from extensive security audits, to making sure that the SQL login passwords are strong enough. Public cloud implementation teams tend to work outside the existing IT processes (at least initially), and may not be aware of the importance of governance, however irritating and draconian they may seem. Windows Azure implementation teams may need to develop their own governance processes, or at least find a way to leverage existing enterprise governance.

Identity

Identity is becoming more complex in modern applications, as attacks become more sophisticated and frequent. It is no longer sufficient to have simple username/password pairs or AD trust. Users want to be able to authenticate using other credentials such as Facebook. REST based services are becoming widely accepted, particularly on mobile platforms, so the issue and acceptance of security tokens becomes necessary. All of this needs to developed within a set of standards (such as SAML) where authentication and authorisation between different security domains and different providers, need to be implemented.

This is not specific to applications deployed in Windows Azure. The types of applications currently being developed need to handle identity properly, and an application being built for Windows Azure may be the first time that an implementation team has run into these issues.

Windows Azure SQL Database

On premise SQL Server has, over the last few years, added extensive security features, such as data encryption. Windows Azure SQL Database does not support the same features (although it can encrypt connection data), and needs to be dealt with differently from on-premise SQL Server. For example, some data may need to be encrypted by the application before being stored in the database.

Storage Keys

Windows Azure Table, Queue, and Blob storage are publicly accessible REST services that use a key for authorisation. There are only two master keys, and keys cannot be generated for general use. This means that access to Azure storage is limited because keys cannot be given to the client application/browser (Blobs have shared access signatures which differs slightly). It also means that if these keys are accessible, or sent down to the browser, all storage can be accessed. Azure storage keys need to be aggressively protected.

Compliance and Regulations

Although Windows Azure supports some compliance standards (ISO/IEC 27001:2005 certification, SSAE 16/ISAE 3402 Attestation and HIPAA BAA), it does not support PCI-DSS or any number of varied and international compliance standards. As the acceptance of the cloud develops, so too do regulations and laws. Microsoft does not explicitly conform to all regulations, even though it may be possible to build a compliant application on top of

Windows Azure. In some cases, like PCI-DSS, it is impossible to comply without some part of the application running on-premise. It is up to the implementation team to understand the regulations, and ensure that their application can support those regulations.

Adopt a security assurance process

Due to the importance of security on Windows Azure, and the need to ensure that the number and severity of vulnerabilities in the application is as low as possible, a security assurance process must be adopted for the project. These processes are rigorous and take effort to implement, but in the long-run reduce development and maintenance cost by the early implementation good quality secure code.

The Microsoft Security Development Lifecycle[16] is a process used by Microsoft to ensure security within applications. The process and supporting tools are publicly accessible and available for use. Other methodologies exist, and it is up to the implementation team to use the most appropriate one (perhaps there is an existing internal process).

Project Managers need to ensure that sufficient budget and capacity is available for implementing a security process, and should embed security documentation, quality gates and other aspects into their software development project plan.

Plan for specific security implementations

A security assurance process encourages the practice of implementing secure applications but it doesn't actually describe the platform and application-specific details required. Security needs to be implemented throughout development and cannot be added just before delivery. It makes sense to get started early by addressing practical, security implementation during the design stage.

The security model should indicate at a high level how the application is going to be secured. This ensures developers can be made aware of development tasks

---

[16] http://www.microsoft.com/security/sdl/default.aspx

related to security, so that they can be included in estimates and planning. Typical areas include:

- Identity - Using ACS and federated identity.
- Authorisation - Claims based identity.
    - Securing ASP.NET - Open Web Application Security Project[17], OWASP Top 10 for .NET developers[18]

- Database security.
- Securing Services - e.g. Securing REST Services[19].

Engage with audit and governance

One of the advantages of using a cloud platform is the ability to bring an application to market quickly without having to wait for the procurement of infrastructure. With all that speed of delivery, it would be frustrating if an internal audit group stalled the project for a few months while they conduct a thorough investigation.

Depending on the level of executive support for the cloud project within the organisation, the stage where internal governance and audit processes get involved can be tricky to determine; too early and they have a panic attack and derail the project. Too late and it takes so long for them to understand that they panic anyway and stall delivery. One thing is for certain, governance and audit processes fulfil an important role and should not be ignored. They need to be engaged on the project as early as possible so that you can sail through any governance gates further down the road.

---

[17] https://www.owasp.org/index.php/Main_Page

[18] http://asafaweb.com/OWASP Top 10 for .NET developers.pdf

[19] http://msdn.microsoft.com/en-us/library/hh446531.aspx

Understand Windows Azure specifics

Due to security being a major concern with cloud platforms, there is a wealth of information on security within Windows Azure; provided, sponsored, and supported by Microsoft (probably more than any other part of Windows Azure). With so much available, there is little point in covering the detail in this book. As part of the design process and establishment of the security model, it is imperative that at least one member of the team is assigned the subject matter expert on Windows Azure and reads all necessary documentation.

Below are *some* resources for Windows Azure Security specifics:

- Windows Azure Trust Centre[20] - The Windows Azure Trust Centre contains the latest details about security, compliance and privacy on Windows Azure. It includes details of all certifications and links to the latest downloads on security documents specific to Windows Azure.
- Microsoft Global Foundation Services - Securing Microsoft's Cloud Infrastructure[21] - A paper introducing how Microsoft manages security within its data centres.
- Windows Azure Security Overview[22].
- Windows Azure Security Notes[23] - at 121 pages it is more than 'notes'.
- Security Best Practices For Developing Windows Azure Applications[24].
- See MSDN and the Windows Azure SDK for information on:
    - Access Control Service.
    - Windows Azure Active Directory.
    - Windows Azure Connect.
    - Windows Identity Foundation and Security Token Services.
    - Installing and using certificates on Windows Azure.

---

[20] https://www.windowsazure.com/en-us/support/trust-center/

[21] http://cdn.globalfoundationservices.com/documents/SecuringtheMSCloudMay09.pdf

[22] http://go.microsoft.com/?linkid=9740388

[23] http://go.microsoft.com/?linkid=9741707

[24] http://download.microsoft.com/download/7/3/E/73E4EE93-559F-4D0F-A6FC-7FEC5F1542D1/SecurityBestPracticesWindowsAzureApps.docx

- Securing Windows Azure storage.
- Windows Azure SQL Database logins, certificates and firewall.
- Windows Azure Virtual Network.

Summary

The security of cloud applications is of critical importance and is echoed in the vast amount of material available, references, and specialisation on cloud security in general, as well as Windows Azure specific information. Due to the availability of security information and processes, and the rate at which security has to change, CALM is not prescriptive about the security model. CALM recommends that a security process and methodology be adopted that is specific to the application, and is complemented by Microsoft's security endeavours on Windows Azure.

Steps

1. Understand cloud security differences.
2. Adopt a security assurance process.
3. Plan for specific security implementations.
4. Engage with audit and governance.
5. Understand Windows Azure specifics.

Availability Model

The demand for high availability is a driving force behind the architecture for modern applications. Users and consumers are always connected using a multitude of devices and expect all applications to behave the same way as the large scale social media applications they consume on a minute by minute basis. Increased connectivity and discoverability of applications means that demand can spike unexpectedly, but has to be handled. With the income per user so low (or completely non-existent), architects cannot throw money at the problem and need to implement innovative ways to achieve high levels of availability on the cheap.

Cloud computing is a popular base solution for high availability for most applications. While the top 1% of applications may build their own datacentres economically, the cloud provides a platform for availability that is more accessible and as affordable as the rest. Cloud computing is no availability silver bullet and there are two catches to getting the most out of availability in the cloud. Firstly, cloud platforms are based on commodity infrastructure and availability is provided by architecture in the application. This means that application architects and developers need a better understanding of how to implement availability, as getting the infrastructure to go faster is not an option. Secondly, most organisations have little experience in availability and skills, neither amongst their own staff nor in the market. This extends from planning, to development, to testing, to operations — where the business need for availability cannot be easily matched by delivery capability.

The simple requirement for an application to work when needed and perform adequately makes availability the most important non-functional requirement. This, in turn, means that availability needs a lot of attention and, when cloud computing is chosen because of its perceived availability characteristics, requires that specific attention be given to the availability model. The availability model process is actually fairly simple; develop the SLAs, establish the business rationale for spending on availability, and choose the appropriate technical approaches. Yet these simple steps mask a depth of necessary understanding. What is needed is a clear brief from the business detailing their realistic requirements against the implementation costs, a well-defined understanding of the required effort, other related costs, and the risk of technical approaches to availability.

As a result, developing the availability model is an extensive process that requires a degree of depth that can be glossed over in some of the other CALM models.

The cloud computing availability myth

When cloud computing platforms are discussed, availability is one of the hot topics. On the one hand, there are those that see cloud computing as a mechanism to solve availability issues by handing responsibility to the cloud providers with the scale, skills and funds to do it well. On the other hand, there are those that point to frequent and significant cloud outages (whether they are more frequent or significant than non-cloud outages is a different matter) to illustrate that cloud platforms are not the availability panacea that is promised. Wrapped up in this are the businesses that are building applications on the cloud that, by the very nature of being modern applications, must deliver the rapid scale that is promised by cloud computing.

Despite outages, the myth persists that cloud applications have higher availability than traditional applications. There is, of course, an element of truth to this perception. Looking at Windows Azure compute, for $30 per month you can have two extra small instances (two are required for the availability SLA) that run with an availability guarantee of 99.95%. There is no way to self-host and get that kind of availability for that price. Likewise with databases ($5 per month for 99.9%), storage and any other services. Despite this guarantee, it is both possible and highly probable that a developer will build an application so badly that it is always falling over, crashing because of errors, deleting data by mistake and is generally not as available as the underlying infrastructure.

The most important and generally overlooked aspect of building highly available applications on cloud platforms is that the availability guarantee is relevant only to the infrastructure. The availability of the application is, from the perspective of the cloud provider, someone else's problem. That problem then becomes yours, where you are provided with a reasonably highly available platform and challenged to build an application on top of it that satisfies the availability requirements of the business.

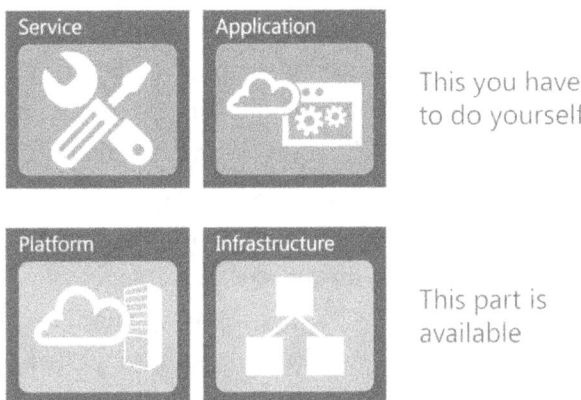

Availability empowerment of cloud platforms

It may be disheartening to discover that cloud platforms only provide availability for some part of the application. It is also difficult to break the news softly to a business that has been convinced by the (narrow) promise of availability. But it is not all bad news; the availability of infrastructure offered by cloud platforms can be significant in terms of the overall application lifecycle and costs to the business.

The degree of significance depends on the amount of availability needed down the stack. For example, an application that relies on the database for availability would get a big chunk of availability, for little cost and effort from Windows Azure SQL Database. Applications that have a high dependency on external services would not benefit much from the availability offered by a cloud platform.

When comparing PaaS cloud platforms with IaaS platforms, the benefits offered by having the availability at the platform level of the stack, are worth considering. Windows Azure Compute availability for the platform includes the infrastructure below it, and is why the availability assumes more than one instance is running. Amazon Web Services EC2 availability is for the infrastructure (underlying VM, OS and networking) and does not cover any part of the application that runs on it (Elastic Beanstalk, the AWS application platform, doesn't seem to have a very clear SLA).

Ultimately the benefit of the availability of the underlying platform is the ability to use this as an affordable building block for the rest of the application. While the overall application availability is still the responsibility of the development team, a large part of it is provided for 'free' (in a sense that there is no development cost or other capital expenditure cost associated with it). This means that an application of reasonable availability can be implemented a lot cheaper than a self-hosted solution. At some point this cost advantage is lost up to the point where the availability exceeds the 99.95% guarantee, where the only option on Windows Azure is a geo-distributed architecture with additional cost considerations.

The diagram below illustrates that self-hosted applications can provide higher availability than public cloud platforms, but only at the high end of availability, where costs are prohibitive, whereas Windows Azure provides higher availability for a lower cost at the lower end of the availability scale.

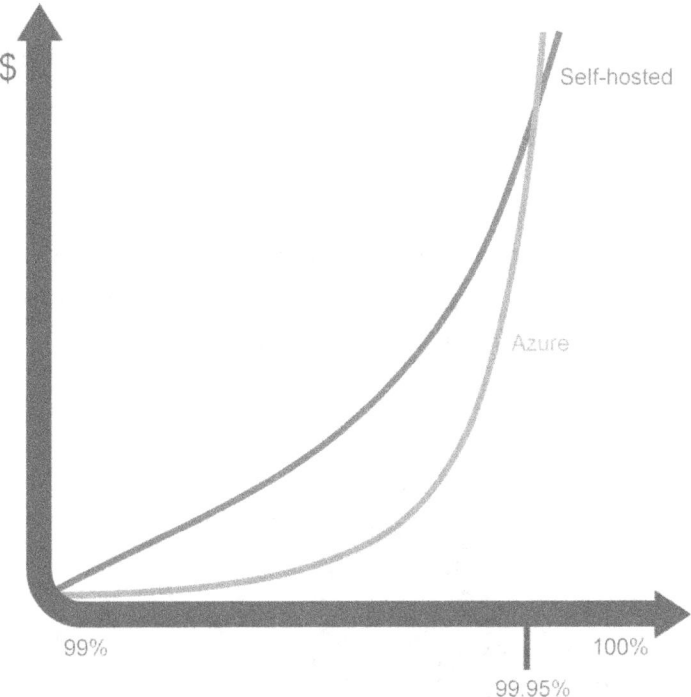

How these costs are incurred also differs on cloud platforms and again depends on the services used, how much availability has to be built into the application layer of the stack, and how much load the application will be subject to. Although, as described earlier, it is possible to achieve relatively high availability for extremely low cost on very small applications, for larger applications the underlying nature of the platform may mean that more is spent on development for availability than traditional applications.

With a database, for example, if we disregard the cost of the actual database itself (hardware, licenses and storage) it is cheaper to develop for an on-premise database than a cloud one, as certain assumptions can be made. The on-premise database may have high availability, sufficient bandwidth and be reasonably fast, where simple database code can be written against it. On the same sort of database in the cloud, more code has to be written to handle throttling, latency and other issues endemic to a cloud database.

While for a particular application (or part of an application) the development cost for availability may be higher, the on-going operational costs may be lower. A platform that has a lower on-going maintenance cost (OS patching, backup, configuration) or has a better model for performing tests, may prove to have a better cost benefit over the full application lifecycle. If the on-going costs associated with availability are largely in the platform and infrastructure layers of the stack, the cloud platform may work out more cost effective over the long run because those costs are largely taken care of.

The charts below illustrate that on the cloud the development costs consume most of the budget, as the upfront platform costs are minimal. However, the pay-per-use model of cloud computing means that running applications will spend more on the platform than the maintenance of the application.

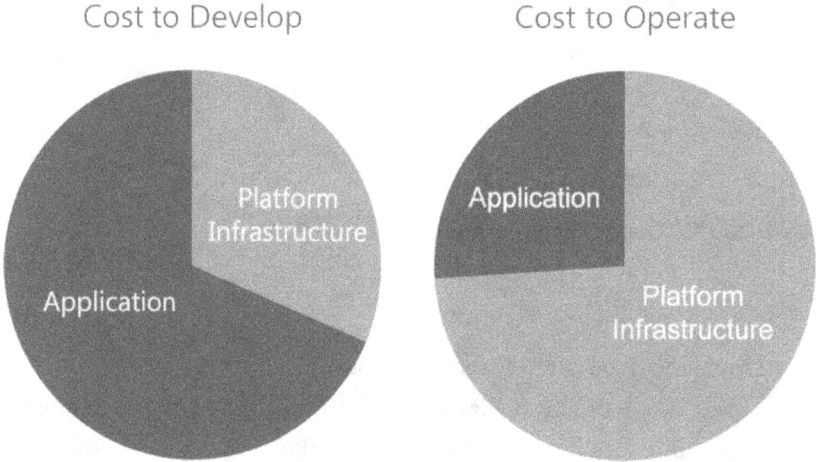

What is availability?

Availability is a term that is so widely used in different contexts that it is very difficult to define in a way that satisfies all audiences. At its most basic, availability is the ability of a system to provide the expected functionality to users. This means that the application needs to be responsive (not frustrating users by taking too long to respond), and reliably able to perform those functions. But that is not enough to understand the full story about availability.

Availability is simplistically viewed as binary; the application is either available at a point in time, or it is not. This leads to a misunderstanding of availability targets (the 'nines of availability'), the approaches to improving availability and the ability of salespeople to sell availability snake oil off-the-shelf (see 100% availability offered by Rackspace). Application availability is **influenced** by something and has a visible **outcome** for the consumer, as discussed below.

Availability outcomes

The outcome, or end result, of availability is more than just 'the site is down'. What does 'down' mean? Is it really 'down' or is that just the (possibly valid) opinion of a frustrated user? A user that, for example, is trying to capture a claim after arriving at work late because they crashed their car, is bound to be frustrated enough to deem a slow web application to be 'down'. The outcomes of availability are those behaviours that are perceived by the end users, as described below.

Failure

The obvious visible indication of an unavailable application is one that informs the end user that something has failed, and no amount of retrying will make it work. The phrase 'is down' is commonly used to describe this situation, which is an obvious statement about the user's perception and understanding of the term 'down', rather than a reasonable indication of failure. The types of failure include:

- Errors — where the application consistently gives errors. This is often seen on web applications where the chrome works but the content has an error, or garbage.
- Timeouts — an application that takes too long to respond may be seen as being 'down' by the user or even the browser or service calling it.
- Missing resources — a '404 - Not found' response code can have devastating effects on applications. Beyond missing image placeholders, missing scripts or style sheets can 'down' an application.
- Not addressable — a DNS lookup error, a 'destination host unreachable' error and other network errors can create the perception that an application is unavailable regardless of its addressability from other points. This is particularly common for applications that don't use http ports and network traffic is refused by firewalls.

Responsiveness

While it may be easy to determine that a switched off application is unavailable, what about one that performs badly? If, for example, a user executes a search and it takes a minute to respond, would the user consider the application to be available? Would the operators share the same view? Apdex (Application

Performance Index[25]) incorporates this concept and has an index that classifies application responsiveness into three categories, namely: Satisfied, Tolerating, and Frustrated. This can form a basis for developing a performance metric that can be understood, and also to acknowledge that in some cases we will experience degraded performance, but should not have too many frustrated users for long or critical periods.

Reliability

In addition to features being snappy and responsive, users also expect that features can be used when they are needed and perform the actions that they expect. If, for example, an update on a social media platform posts immediately (it is responsive), but is not available for friends to see within a reasonable time, it may be considered unreliable.

Availability influencers

While the availability outcomes receive attention, simply focussing on these by saying "Don't let the application go down", fails to direct effort and energy to the parts of the application that ultimately influence availability. Some of these availability influencers are discussed below.

Quality

The most important, and often unconsidered, influence on availability is the quality of the underlying components of the system. Beyond buggy (or not) code, there is the quality of the network (including the user's own device), the quality of the architecture, testing, development and operational processes, data and many others. Applications that have a high level of quality, across all aspects of the system, will have higher availability without it being specifically addressed. An application hosted in a cheap datacentre, with a jumble of cheap hardware, running a website off a single php script, thrown together by copying and pasting from forums, by a part time student developer, will guarantee low availability.

---

[25] http://apdex.org/

Fault tolerance

Considering that any system is going to have failures at some point, the degree to which an application can handle faults determines its availability. For example, an application that handles database faults by failing over to another data source and retrying will be more available than one that reports an error.

Scalability

If a frustratingly slow and unresponsive application can be considered to be unavailable (not responsive or reliable) and this responsiveness is due to high load on the application, then the ability to scale is an important part of keeping an application available. For example, a web server that is under such high load that it takes 20 seconds to return a result (unavailable) may be easily addressed by adding a bunch of web servers.

Maintainability

If a fault occurs and an application needs to be fixed, the time to recovery is an important part of availability. The maintainability of the application, primarily the code base, is a big part of the time that it takes to find, fix, test and redeploy a fixed defect. For example, applications that have no unit tests and large chunks of code that have not been touched in years wouldn't be able to fix a problem quickly. This is because a large code base needs to be understood, impacts need to be assessed and regression tests performed, thus turning a single line code change into days of delays in getting an important fix deployed.

Serviceability

Modern web based applications don't have the luxury of downtime windows for planned maintenance that exist in internal enterprise applications (where planned maintenance frequently occurs on weekends). The ability of an application to have updates and enhancements deployed while the application is live and under load is an important aspect of availability. A robust and high quality application will have low availability if the entire system needs to be brought down for a few hours in order to roll out updates.

Recoverability

Assuming that things break, the speed at which they can be fixed is a key influencer of availability. The degree of recoverability in an application is largely up to the operational team, including support/maintenance developers and testers, to get things done. The ability to diagnose the root cause of a problem in a panic free environment and to take appropriate and effective corrective action is a sign of a high level of operational maturity and hence recoverability.

Detectability

If availability is measured in seconds of permissible downtime, only knowing that the application is unavailable because a user has complained, takes valuable chunks out of the availability targets. There is the need not only for immediate detection of critical errors, but for the proactive monitoring of health in order to take corrective action before a potential problem takes down the application.

Build a consistent understanding of availability

Whether you use this definition of availability, or source and adapt one that suits your environment, it is important to build a consistent understanding of availability across the team. Too often we state that something needs to be highly available without considering the different interpretations of "highly available". The web developer's idea will be completely different to the telecommunications engineer and they will go their separate ways and build completely different solutions.

While a common understanding of what availability means in general discussions is important, it is not enough to assume that it is sufficient to build an application. The availability understanding needs to be translated into something that can be understood by the entire team, from technical to business bias. This translation and understanding needs to be captured in the availability SLAs.

Developing the SLAs

In most cases, availability is expressed as a percentage of service uptime, and even Windows Azure expresses availability this way. There are benefits of having a simple percentage statement of availability, but it is generally difficult to measure and meaningless in a business context. Often these percentages are expressed for a specific component and the entire user experience is neglected. Also, the time period that they apply to is disingenuous to the need for an application to be available during critical periods. Indeed, some providers make a mockery of service availability by promising an unachievable 100% availability and relying on SLA credits if the target is not met, leaving the customer to measure and argue the downtime.

In order to architect, build and operate a cloud application properly, it is important to express the SLAs in a manner which makes sense to the business, can be reasonably measured, and is attainable within the budget.

Heterogeneous availability across workloads

Not all workloads are equally important to the business. If increased availability comes at an increased cost, it makes business sense that the less important workloads have less money spent on their availability and therefore a lower availability target as a requirement.

Examples are easy to uncover, such as the primary web application, where an hour of downtime is headline news, versus the monthly reporting workload which, if it sent out reports an hour late, nobody would even notice. Others are less obvious and in some cases the differing availability requirements may be irrelevant because the rest of the application already provides higher availability than is required.

Places to look for differing availability requirements include:

- Significant lifecycle models or phases. The lifecycle model may uncover times when availability is high — for example, a retail site may have a high availability requirement for the start of Boxing Day or Black Friday sales.

- Back office processes, such as order fulfilment indicate that a particular workload's unavailability is offset by the time that it takes to process transactions manually.
- Third party integration. Some third party services may have a lower SLA and the availability of our application cannot be higher than that of the third party service.
- Administrative features. An application will always have features available to the administrative users of the application and generally these users have a lower availability requirement, where they can do something else if the application is down. For example, an application may have a high availability requirement for the reading of content on the public pages, but the content management functions will be lower.

Availability influence on workload definition

Part of the reason for putting effort into decomposing workloads is because different workloads have different availability, operational, data and other requirements. But workloads may be defined in a specific way because features that have distinctly different availability requirements in a single workload, may be decomposed into different workloads in order to take advantage of the reduced availability requirement for a particular feature. This is often seen where asynchronous messaging via queues is used to isolate a single feature into different workloads. For example, the emailing of an order confirmation may be seen as part of the ordering process, but the lower availability requirement (email confirmations don't have to go out immediately) results in the architecture being changed to put email confirmations in a different workload.

Part of the design process of cloud applications is to be able to revisit existing workload decompositions as the design evolves. Architects may find that the development of the availability model causes their workload decompositions to change slightly.

Expression of Availability in SLAs

The traditional means of describing availability using the "nines" (99.99% = four "nines") is open to interpretation and doesn't adequately communicate the availability requirements of the business. An availability expression of 99.9% allows for 43 minutes of downtime per month, and if those 43 minutes take place one minute at a time at 3am, then it is probably good enough availability. But if they happen all at once on Black Friday, it may not be good enough. Availability expressed over a long period such as a year or month, as the "nines" generally are, creates an unintended bias towards applications that are highly available when not needed and do not allow for reduced availability to perform maintenance tasks, or free up resources for other workloads that may be more important at the time.

It is better to express availability in a business context that can also be understood by the development team. These statements about availability are expressed in the following formats:

- When *<event>* the *<workload>* should handle *<load>*
- During *<phase>* the *<workload>* should always respond within *<response>* for *<percentile>* users
- The *<workload>* can be unavailable available during *<phase>* for up to *<time>*

These formats suggest that the lifecycle model and workload models are required in order to sufficiently express the availability.

For example, consider the following lifecycle models and their corresponding availability statements.

The above e-commerce example illustrates heterogeneous workloads that have different availability requirements at different stages of the lifecycle. Product search is used consistently throughout the day with additional load during the day. The catalogue update is done at the end of the day, but early enough for administrators to address problems. The availability can be stated as (this is not a complete list):

- When the catalogue update starts at 4:30 pm, it needs to complete by 5:00 pm.
- The catalogue update can be offline at any time except between 4:00 to 6:00 pm.
- During the day, the product search should respond within 0.5s for 90% of users.

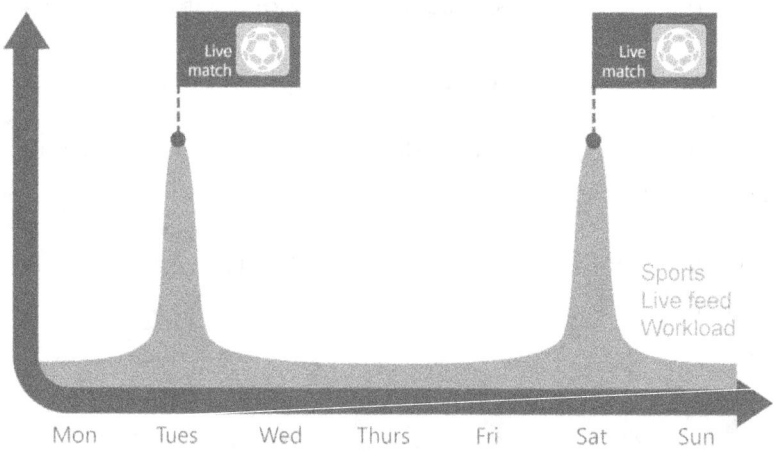

The above example shows a live sports event where the primary feed is only used during live matches. Example availability statements include:

- The live feed has to be available for up to 100,000 concurrent users for 30 minutes before the match and until 30 minutes after the match.
- When under load, the frame rate can drop by 10% and latency by 2 seconds.
- When live matches are not being played, the workload is not used at all.

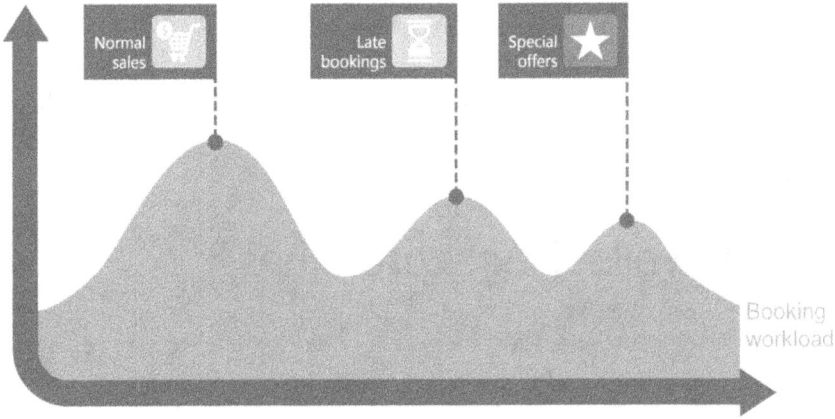

The above example shows a workload that has a predictable seasonal pattern and illustrates how reduced availability can be planned based on business knowledge. The availability requirements can be stated as:

- From October to February, when people are booking holidays, three times the annual average load needs to be handled.
- The application can have reduced performance during any period except for daytime during the normal sales, late bookings and special offer periods.

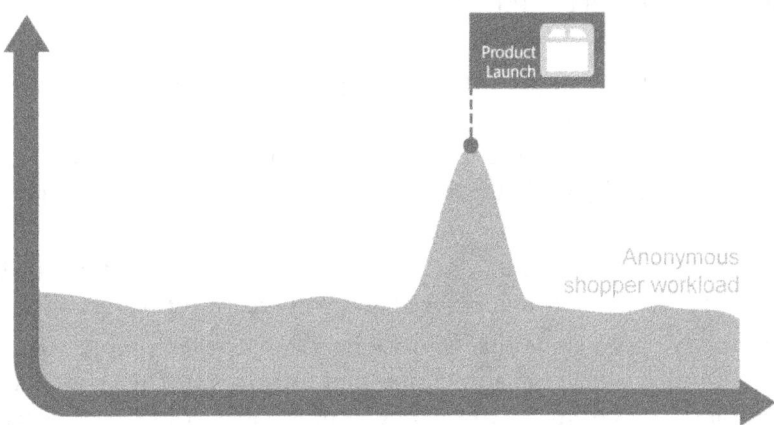

This example illustrates statements about availability in the scenario where an application needs to be prepped for a specific event, such as a launch.

- Anonymous users need a page response time of <0.5s for 80% of requests during normal periods where there will be 200 requests per second.
- When a product is launched and for five days after the launch, the application needs to handle 1000 requests per second with a response time of <0.5s for 70% of requests.

Meaningful availability expressions

As can be seen from these examples, it is easy to create expressions of availability. However you should consider that too many availability expressions in the SLA can become problematic:

- Too many different availability expressions may conflict with one another, making it impossible for all of them to be achieved.
- Members of the team need clear goals and too many availability expressions can dilute the value of having goals to work towards.
- If the availability SLAs are not met then corrective actions need to be developed to resolve the underlying problems. Attempting to unravel too many expressions can complicate the process.
- Too many expressions about availability could add unnecessarily to the costs as every single one of them, including the less important ones, is attempted to be successfully met.

When developing the availability expressions:

- Keep the number of expressions to a minimum. Two or three for each primary workload and/or lifecycle. Obviously for very large and complex projects, there may be many parts and accompanying expressions, but for a project to be developed by a small team in a few months there should be less than ten.
- Make sure that availability expressions can be measured. Using phrases like "up most of the time" cannot be measured and will create confusion.
- Develop availability expressions that lead to practical architectural discussions and decisions. Do this by having something that can be tested (e.g. simulating a load), technologies chosen (e.g. a latency expression leading to a decision about the cache), or developed against (e.g. expressing that a message needs to be delivered within a certain time).
- Make the availability expressions accessible to the entire team. Put them up on the wall if it helps and constantly ask individuals, when they are making a decision, how it impacts the availability targets. SLAs that are hidden away in the contract are only of use to lawyers.

Cost of availability

High availability costs money and time, and it is the main factor in all architectural discussions relating to availability. It is important that this simple fact is understood by both business and the technical team. Business needs to be careful about asking for too much availability, as the costs will increase. Architects need to be careful about committing to too much availability without asking for extra budget.

Availability costs can be demonstrated with a simple non-IT example.

Consider a simple requirement of lighting an area. The cheapest solution that satisfies the lighting requirement may not satisfy the availability requirement. A simple solution has a single light wired to the mains and will give sufficient light once switched on. But the light bulb itself may need to be of high quality so that it burns out less frequently, and putting in a higher quality bulb costs more money. Obtaining high availability with a single bulb will be difficult, as a failed bulb would need to be detected quickly and replaced. So it would be better to have two bulbs, either sharing the load, or with electronics to switch the spare on when one goes off. This adds cost in both the extra bulb and the additional electronics. Since the source power can fluctuate, we don't want spikes in external power to burn the bulb prematurely, so we add the cost of additional electrical components to smooth the power. Relying completely on a single external power source may not be good enough so we add the cost of building in batteries so that the light is on when the power fails. We can go on adding costs to something that has a simple functional requirement but a high availability requirement. The more available it has to be, the more we have to spend on taking care of possible reasons for failure. That is why there are completely different approaches to having a light in an attic versus an emergency exit light on an oil rig.

The same process of adding costs in order to achieve higher availability exists with applications. The increase in costs is not necessarily simple or linear. Using the lighting example, you can buy a cheap emergency lighting unit with LEDs, electronics and batteries that you just plug into the wall and get high availability for a low cost. Likewise, applications have similar affordable off-the-shelf high availability solutions, such as the platform provided by Windows Azure. But, to refer again to the lighting problem, such an affordable, high availability solution may not exist at your local hardware store if you want to light an airport runway.

The answer as to why availability costs more is a complex one, but has to be provided in the specific cases of your proposed architecture. The articulation and investigation of costs and options is fundamental to the availability model. Some of the factors that contribute to the increase in costs are discussed in more detail below.

Skills

People need to know how to build available systems or at least have the ability and capacity to learn them on the job. These skills are expensive if they are acquired through consulting or recruitment. It is also costly and risky to develop these skills on the job, as a lot of new technologies and techniques need to be learned. The skills required broadly fall into the following three categories:

- Architectural skills — the knowledge as to how to approach solving a problem that implements a scalability pattern. For example, when to separate processes with a message queue. Included in these skills is the ability to rapidly evaluate the suitability of a particular technology or pattern to solve problems in the way that is expected, without negative side effects.
- Specific technology skills — availability is delivered using specific technologies, be that a message queue or NoSQL data store. These technologies, many of which will be new to the team, from installation and maintenance to learning a new API and discovering hidden problems, can only be learned through experience.
- Implementation skills — many developers are unfamiliar with the basic implementation skills necessary to actually code available systems. For example, developers tend to save data to a database without thinking about timeouts and retries. While web developers may be more used to building stateless code, other developers have implementation skills that make assumptions about the state of the host process.
- Operational skills — as discussed in the operational model, operators need to learn a whole new way of working with applications that have high availability. Particularly if those applications involve complex data models or various out-of-phase deployments taking place and all while monitoring that the application is still available.
- Planning and estimating skills — with a lack of architectural, technology, implementation and operational skills on the team, the ability to plan the

project suffers. Without having the basis and experience, it is difficult to apply planning and estimating techniques that people are familiar with. Skills need to be developed to plan and estimate unknown technical challenges.

Engineering effort

Building available systems takes more engineering effort from the developers who write the code. The additional technologies, complexities of distributed architectures, the general slower pace of writing quality code (with all of its supporting processes of reviewing and refactoring) and many other day-to-day tasks required to build features, takes more time and effort when availability is important. The actual difference in effort depends on the approach taken to availability and the difference between 'normal' and 'high availability' in the code quality and patterns that the development team is comfortable with. The section below on [development approaches for availability](#) indicates some of the engineering effort involved with each approach.

Testing effort

A fundamental principle of cloud oriented architectures is that of 'design for failure', where the application should be able to cope with, and recover from, failure. There is an accompanying incorrect assumption that testing has a decreased role because the application can cope with failures, so testing all possible failures is not important. The effort required in testing cloud applications is extremely high, and availability places extra demands on testing. Looking at the [availability influencers](#) above, each of the influencers (Quality, Fault tolerance, Scalability, Maintainability, Serviceability, Recoverability and Detectability) needs to be explicitly and exhaustively tested. Without adequate testing, there is no way to determine if availability targets can be met or to provide feedback to the team in order to make necessary adjustments.

Operations effort

The operation of a highly available application takes a lot more effort than an application that is backed up weekly and left to itself the rest of the time. Operators need to develop processes and tools that allow them to keep the application running within the agreed SLAs. With cloud applications, this is further complicated by unfamiliar architectures and relationships with cloud suppliers (such as Microsoft) that work differently, thus requiring extra effort to establish operational processes.

Resource consumption

Building higher availability applications usually involves building a distributed application with some redundancy. This means that more processes run that are spread across more machines, connected by a network that consumes more bandwidth. Simply put, high availability systems need more resources. Those resource can include more machines, more bandwidth and more storage.

Complexity

Building applications that are highly available generally increases the complexity. Availability patterns such as message orientation and caching, add to the overall complexity. Complexity increases the cost; particularly if that complexity results in reduced failure (usually increased complexity increases the likelihood of failure because there are more places for defects to develop).

Non-linear cost increases

Building an application that is 50% available is fairly easy and cheap. Building one that is 80% available is not that much more expensive. Even building one that is 99.9% available is not significantly more expensive than the 80% one, especially when using a cloud platform. But building an application that is 99.9999% available is significantly more expensive than the 99.9% one. The increase in costs is non-linear and sometimes to gain a tiny bit of availability you need to spend a large chunk on technologies and code to support it.

For example, consider needing to display the current user profile on a page. Let's say that direct database access takes 0.25s when there are 1000 concurrent users and 1s when there are more than 1000 users. Let's also assume that the rest of the page render time is 0.25s. Consider now two availability expressions:

- The page must display the user profile within 0.5s for 80% of the users during normal load (when there are 1000 concurrent users).

- The page must display the user profile within 0.75s for 70% of the users during the peak lunchtime hour (when there are 1500 concurrent users).

Based on the constraints of the database it may be decided that the only way to meet the second availability expression is to add caching as increasing capacity will not solve the database bottleneck. Adding of caching is not a simple task and significantly adds to the cost. In this example, increasing the load by 50% for a brief period (1 hour), while also compromising on performance expectations (which is a fair and seemly minor adjustment to availability) still has a major impact to the overall development cost.

It is good to train your eye, when looking over availability expressions, for those which trigger a solution that increases cost, so that they can be discussed and ruled out if possible. It is also important that capacity and availability be tested early on in the development and decision process, so that you can feedback to the business with reliable cost implications.

Availability business rationale

Knowing that increased availability increases cost or time, the availability model seeks a balance of what costs are acceptable for what availability. The project sponsor is ultimately responsible for finding the balance and making the necessary trade-offs, but has to be assisted by the architect and development team.

Before engaging with the technical team for detailed solutions, it is important that the business is clear about how much they are willing to spend, or how much time they are willing to take (cost and reduced time to market) in order to achieve availability goals.

Assessing business value of availability

Having a highly available application has to have some benefit to the business, otherwise there is little point in building an available application. This may sound obvious, but many implementations are done in the name of availability but are actually done because a technical person thought it was 'cool' and wanted to pad their résumé with the latest shiny new technology.

The business benefits can be varied, and are not always clear in terms of the ability to handle normal business load and transactions. Some of these possible benefits are highlighted below:

- Customer experience — even if customers are not buying products using the application, they still expect an experience that works, is snappy and usable. For example, a major bricks-and-mortar retailer may still want a web application that enables customers to find their nearest store quickly and easily.
- Sales and revenue throughput — applications that generate revenue have a clear need for availability. After all, if no sales take place when and outage occurs, then it is obvious that outages need to be reduced.
- Paid for service — while people may tolerate sluggish web applications when they are free, if they are paying for the service they expect it to work a lot better than the rest of the free applications that they may use. This may be unfair as some of the free applications that we all use are also some of the most sophisticated and available. Apart from SaaS type applications that are paid for, there are others, such as the schedule or live news and streaming for a cable sports channel that require subscription.
- Response to unprecedented demand — no application should be over-engineered on the basis of wishful thinking and hoping that the product will go viral. But, if there is a valid business reason and expectation that the application needs to handle unprecedented load, then it may justify spend on availability in order to cope with the load. Cloud computing platforms, by allowing the rapid provisioning of capacity, make this a significantly smaller investment than traditional hosting platforms.
- Reputational risk management — an established brand that may not use a web application for any transactions may still want to ensure that their application is always available, so as not to reflect poorly on the brand.
- Development of skills — the implementation of costly availability approaches for no other reason than to give developers a chance to play with something new, sounds nonsensical at first. If the application being developed has been chosen because it is low risk, and will be used as a test of Windows Azure before embarking on bigger projects, then putting in engineering that is unnecessary for the current requirement in order to get a feel for the technologies and develop skills, is a valid longer-term business benefit.

Special considerations when assessing the need for availability

Variation of availability requirements across workloads

Stating availability needs that broadly apply to the whole application, will result in additional costs being applied to parts of the application where it is unnecessary. For example, a customer facing workload such as placing an order may have a high availability requirement The same application may have a separate order fulfilment workload that has a significantly lower availability requirement (fulfilment of orders can easily be delayed by a few minutes). This should become clear when the detail of the availability expressions are worked out for the SLA, but it is worth considering when communicating the business rationale. This consideration allows for budget to be allocated for high availability of specific parts of the application, without significantly adding to the overall cost.

Architectural input is required because workloads share platforms, technologies, tools and even skills. Although the availability targets may differ across workloads, the end result will tend towards the highest availability common denominator because of the integrated nature of the application and teams. Using the order placement and fulfilment example from above, although the database availability for fulfilment can be low, when implemented, where the order placed is stored in a shared database, the fulfilment workload will benefit from the availability requirement of the order placement workload.

The option of decreasing availability

Most availability discussions are about increasing availability, and responsible architects make sure that questions about high availability are addressed. But the option of decreasing availability can also be investigated. We don't necessarily want to discourage availability as it can be interpreted as an acceptance of low quality, yet in some cases reducing availability can result in significant savings.

For example, FTP is commonly used as an integration tool, and it is surprisingly difficult to build a highly available FTP endpoint. It is worthwhile questioning whether or not a highly available FTP server is required as it may be possible that the client service that uses the integration point has sufficient capabilities for retries and resends, negating the perceived need of availability.

Disregarding baseline availability during assessment

Assuming some basics are in place, a degree of availability can come for 'free', where the request for availability comes at no additional cost. A stable platform such as Windows Azure, has established development practices that have a positive influence on quality, and the right mix of skills. When assessing the business support of availability objectives, this degree of 'built in' availability can be disregarded once the baseline has been established. It doesn't decrease the importance of the availability required or delivered, but allows conversations to focus on specific key aspects of availability.

It is often specific workloads where the baseline is simply 'good enough', such as administrative or back office workloads. In these cases, specific components of the application, such as the availability of web roles, can largely be disregarded.

Assessing the business impact of reduced availability

Before being able to determine how much business is willing to pay for availability, the risk of reduced availability needs to be determined. This is potentially quite a complex subject and is, particularly within enterprises, a highly specialised function that falls under a broader banner of business risks and contingencies where availability of specific IT components is only a small part of the overall picture. If your environment has an approachable and helpful risk management practice, you are encouraged to make use of it where practical and possible.

The likelihood of reduced availability

Determining the likelihood of outages occurring is an industry in itself and assessing the risk, with any authority, shouldn't be undertaken by amateurs. Experienced technical people can make observations about what is more or less likely to go wrong, and these can be fed to the business to include in their overall risk management plan. It is worthwhile to document some of these in the availability model.

The table below provides examples of causes of outages simply classified as to whether or not they are more or less likely.

More likely	Less Likely
Failure of application due to edge-case bug	Complete network infrastructure failure
Degraded performance due to memory leaks	Complete disk failure
Database throttling/performance issues	datacentre off line
Things deleted 'by mistake'	Unable to provision new instances
Degraded performance due to unexpected load	Loss of long-term storage (backups)
Network throughput problems	
Network latency problems	
Single region partial Azure outage	
External service unresponsive	

Without getting into the detail of how frequently these reductions of availability may occur, it encourages focus on causes that are more likely. These examples coincide with some of the fundamental principles and practices in cloud application architectures. For example, we will put effort into designing an architecture that allows for poor database performance because it may occur frequently and is reasonably easy to design for. But we won't do the same for complete network loss, which is both highly unlikely and difficult to work around. The 'less likely' outages are also specific to cloud providers than they might be with private datacentre. Windows Azure storage, for example, has fairly sophisticated and trustworthy geo-replicated mechanisms as well as the engineers in place to ensure that the likelihood of data being lost is close to zero. This cannot be assumed by storage within a private datacentre which may not be highly available in every case,

The high dependence on base cloud infrastructure is of valid concern to some people. If most applications assume that the network works, then the failure of the network, due to hacking and other sinister means, can cause massive economic and other damage. So while we make assumptions about infrastructure, don't forget that there is a risk, and be thankful that there are networking, security and other specialists continuously working to keep our infrastructure available.

The business impact of reduced availability

Knowing the likelihood of reduced availability is one aspect of managing the risk; the other being the impact on the business when this occurs. For example, a web server falling over may happen quite frequently, but having stateless web servers behind a load balancer will mean that the impact to the business in negligible. However, a system with a single database that is unavailable for days can have a massive impact on the business. As with assessing the likelihood of failures, you should make use of existing risk management practices if they are available in your business.

Impacts on the business can be loosely grouped according to those that have a direct financial impact and those that impact the business reputation or customer perception.

Direct financial impact

Financial impacts are generally the easiest to measure, but the reality of actual losses incurred may not match what the business believes the losses will be. How much this is reconciled or adjusted may be worth discussing in particular situations. Often it is the perception of loss that is the greater driver for availability than actual losses, which may influence a business to spend more on availability than they need to. The most common financial losses incurred are:

- Lost revenue — Applications that generate revenue per transaction, such as e-commerce websites, an outage can mean that customers don't make the purchases. Depending on the type of product and the value of the brand, the calculation of losses is not as simple as average revenue per minute multiplied by the number of minutes of downtime. Not only does it depend on when the system is available (at what point in the lifecycle), but in some cases customers will return (as Apple customers do when the store is offline for the latest product release), where in others the customers may go elsewhere to make the purchase immediately (such as airline reservations).

- Penalties - some applications, particularly those that provide a service for other businesses, have SLAs with penalty clauses. In some environments, regulatory or government penalties may also apply.
- Refunds - if an application has paid for customers, such as subscribers to live news or sports, downtime may contractually necessitate some sort of refund. Even Windows Azure, as a supplier of application services, is subject to customer refunds if it is not available.

Reputational damage

Large, established brands that have web applications for lead generation to traditional channels (brochureware) or investor relations, can suffer serious reputational damage if the application is unavailable. Nobody really cares if coca-cola.com is available, as consumers don't turn to the web when buying coke or make purchasing decisions based on the companies' home page. But a sustained lack of availability could become a mainstream or investor news item that can tarnish the brand's reputation.

Lost loyalty

Loyal customers are not easily swayed, but frequent lack of availability of their favourite services can turn the most loyal customers over to the competition. Not only are loyal customers lucrative, they are expensive to develop and can take others with them when they leave. A good example is the sustained outage of Blackberry messaging services in 2011 that was severely damaging to the brand. Loyal customers who had kept with the less trendy handsets vowed to leave in droves when their upgrade was due.

The cost of mitigating reduced availability

The cost of availability is discussed above and ultimately that cost needs to be weighed against the impacts to the business of reduced availability. The availability model should contain the business rationale behind expenditure on availability mandated approaches, technologies, infrastructure and skills. Apart from direct costs to implement a specific approach, the availability model needs to present detail on the following:

- Costs for the entire application lifecycle — The cost of availability needs to be considered in the broader context of the application lifecycle which includes development, testing, operations, maintenance, and decommissioning.
- Capital costs and operating costs — Rarely are costs incurred in a single budget, and the application is likely to have costs associated over a number of years. Upfront development costs may be taken off a CAPEX budget, reducing the on-going costs if availability is addressed later. Conversely, reducing development costs may allow the business that sponsors the application to generate revenue, which can be used to fund future availability endeavours.
- Costs of maintenance — Too often we focus on the direct costs to implement a specific technology and disregard on-going maintenance costs. Enterprises are familiar with the problem of dealing with high maintenance costs, mostly due to the brittle nature of applications that have been built. A focus on availability, with the associated development approaches, can have a positive effect on reducing maintenance costs. This, of course, is only relevant in cases where the application is intended to have a long life.
- Costs of skill retention — Once the development is complete, the skilled individuals that put together the solution may move onto something else or leave the organisation altogether, which could introduce significant risk. Business needs to consider the cost of retaining key individuals, or having access to a skills base, as part of the long-term costs of implementing availability.
- Sharing costs with other projects — In larger organisations it should be possible to share skills across projects or business units. These skills can be used during initial development and on-going maintenance. This is an important aspect of increasing the relevance of internal IT in an environment where applications are moving away from the on-premise datacentre and onto the cloud.
- Use of third-party consulting services — Some of the costs of providing higher availability can be reduced by making use of third-party consulting services. They can provide resources and patterns that would otherwise take a lot of time and trial and error if left up to a development team unfamiliar with aspects of high availability on cloud platforms. Consulting services can also be retained during on-going maintenance, further reducing long-term costs associated with high availability.
- Long-term predictability of availability requirements — availability requirements for launch may be different to ongoing future requirements.

They could be higher, if the application is a success, or lower if the adoption is not as high as planned. Business needs to make an informed decision on availability for the longer term. Putting in high availability after development is complete may be cost prohibitive and maintaining a high availability application that doesn't need to be could cost a lot over time.

Assessing the business impact of increased time to market

Much of the focus on availability cost relates to direct costs of people, man hours, resources and so on. One of the biggest costs of building high availability is the impact that it places on the project schedule. The scarcity and specialisation of skills required mean that implementing high availability cannot necessarily be implemented faster by increasing the size of the development team, and it is likely that a high availability application will take longer, in terms of calendar time, to implement than a low availability counterpart. One of the benefits of cloud computing is the ability to bring an application to market quicker, because capacity is instantly available and the provisioning of hardware is not on the critical path. It is a benefit that business places a high value on and it would be a wasted opportunity to squander that benefit by taking too long in development.

The availability model needs to assess and communicate the impact on the project duration that availability introduces, in addition to the direct cost. Business may opt for lower availability in exchange for shipping the application. This also requires some architectural and design input into the viability of adding availability later.

Investigating the staged implementation of availability

If high availability is not necessary at product launch, can it be implemented later, saving upfront costs and time? There is no simple answer. The degree to which you can defer engineering for availability depends on:

- Engineering practices and maturity in the team.

- Different approaches taken to building for availability.
- Specific technology choices that force the application down a particular architectural path.

For example, redundancy is generally easy to add later in the development cycle or during application maintenance. The idea being that adding another instance is simply a configuration task. This is only true for specific parts of the application. Adding redundant databases can prove tricky, whereas adding redundant web servers is fairly simple. But this, in turn, is only true if the developers have followed the practice of implementing stateless web servers.

At the other extreme, fixing scalability of databases late in the application lifecycle is virtually impossible. The data model and approaches to data have to be engineered to cope, at the application level, with availability. This is particularly relevant in the cloud. On-premise database performance is frequently addressed by adding expensive hardware to the database server, and this option is not available on the cloud. If SQL causes a performance bottleneck for your application, there is nothing that can be done to the infrastructure that underlies Windows Azure SQL Database, and no quick fixes to increase the application availability.

If application architects and designers insist that all the future availability is engineered upfront, it is likely that the project will fail; if not because the proposal is undercut or shelved because it doesn't match the business case, then it will fail because of the time taken to deliver or the risk associated with building complexity into the first release with an inexperienced team. A balance is required between implementing enough availability upfront to reduce further cost and risk, versus scrimping initially with the intention to increase availability later. Architects need to take a look at their longer-term 'to be' architecture and implement the foundations. The process will be along the lines of the following:

1. Select the appropriate availability approaches for the long-term architecture.
    2. Define ways that the implementation can be skipped in the current release. This can include creating necessary abstractions or stubs of availability functionality but not actually implementing it, selecting a less available version of a specific technology or implementing a different technical solution to be swapped out later
    3. For each approach perform an assessment of the implementation costs in the current release versus later releases.

4. For each approach determine the risks involved with implementing the approach later, particularly as it applies to extensive rework or instability.
5. Determine the 'have to have' approaches based on the cost and risk assessment.
6. Establish 'have to have' principles and approaches that are absolutely required, regardless of perceived cost savings. Examples include code quality, retries and exception handling. These are more programming principles which, if not implemented from the beginning, greatly devalue the application and make general operation, never mind high availability, a difficult task.

The end of this process should result in a workable plan that is architecturally sound and can be used by project management to plan execution, delivery and budgets.

Obtaining accurate availability expectations from suppliers

It is often overlooked that 'advertised' availability from suppliers may not match up to what is realistic or even possible. Internal IT frequently makes statements about availability that is anecdotal, not audited, and difficult to measure. So in building a cloud application that is compared with on-premise applications be wary of availability statements that are apocryphal. In many cases on-premise IT states their availability targets or SLAs, which are often not met but not called out because it is not noticed or measured. Similarly, cloud providers can make availability claims that are blatantly untrue. Rackspace has a well-known "100% uptime guarantee" which is impossible. What they do offer is a discount if the service is unavailable but a 5% discount on a few minutes of hosting is not going to make any difference if the financial impacts of an application being down are large.

It is important, when working through the business rationale, to remember that openness and honesty about availability, risk, cost and time may not be reciprocated by others. You will ultimately land up with a better solution but may feel that you are not doing it as well, easily or cheaply as others say they do.

Development approaches for availability

The following approaches for availability summarise the most common patterns used in cloud computing applications and more specifically in Windows Azure. It is not, by any means, a complete list of all approaches. Availability is influenced by so many aspects of the technology, team and processes, and they can't all be discussed. If availability is so dependent on code quality, then the pursuit of high quality code, with all of its variations, disciplines and processes, is an important approach to availability. Similarly, all the solutions and approaches to performance, as a key part of availability, are not discussed here either. Read and understand these approaches in the context of being complementary to availability that your environment already adopts.

Trusting the availability of infrastructure

Developers of applications on Windows Azure (or any other cloud platform) need to place a certain level of trust in the underlying infrastructure. Although low level hardware engineers need to make allowance for power or cooling failures in order to build available systems, developers of applications do not. Many availability decisions require some level of trust or assumption about availability, otherwise solutions can become unnecessarily complex or costly.

For example, when using persistent messaging as an availability approach, a degree of trust is placed in the persistence store. On Windows Azure you would place a message on a Windows Azure Queue, which you know is persisted, and assume that it is delivered. Distrusting the availability, and more importantly, the durability, of the message queue would mean that you would need to build a solution with an alternative persistence mechanism, and preferably one that is at least as reliable. Most architects would, quite rightly, scoff at the idea of having to make provision for an alternative for Windows Azure queues, but this is an obvious example; others are less so.

Failure and bottlenecks

Available systems need to cater for throughput (maintaining availability even when the application is under load) and failures (maintaining availability even when something fails in the application). Approaches to availability generally favour one at the expense of the other. For example, modern databases like Windows Azure SQL Database seldom fail but are the source of availability problems because of their inability to handle the load, where it is the performance of the database that is the bottleneck. The solution to database performance is to put something in-between to buffer the bottleneck, such as a cache for reads or messaging for writes. This results in more moving parts that introduce more defects and more components that can fail; generally reducing the high availability offered by the database in exchange for the ability to handle the required throughput. Conversely, in-memory cache can handle a high throughput, which may be critical in rendering web pages quickly enough to achieve availability SLAs, but is unreliable and prone to failure (cache misses, inconsistent data, termination of process, long warm-up).

Most availability approaches deal with failure rather than throughput. It is important to remember that performance will be prominent in availability expressions and should be given considered attention. It is also necessary to understand the performance trade-offs whenever an availability approach is chosen that favours reliability.

Failure points

Logic bugs do occur, but they affect the behaviour and output of an application and are seldom the cause of reduced availability because of failure. Most failures occur, not at arbitrary points in the application logic, but at failure points. Part of the engineering process of developing for availability is to try and identify failure points within the overall architecture and specific points in the application.

Failure points are typically design elements that are subject to external change or are dependent on data from external sources. Identifying these elements is an effective way of identifying failure points. Examples include database connections, web site or service connections, configuration files and registry keys.

There are common areas where failure points can be identified, typically where processing crosses a physical boundary or an application or system domain. These areas include ACLs (Access Control Lists) and identity services, database access, external web site or service access, configuration, and network capacity and latency.

The identification of failure points is critical in decisions relating to the implementation of other availability approaches, such as resiliency.

Failure modes

In systems engineering, the observing and understanding of the root cause of a failure is known as a failure mode. A failure point is *where* the failure occurs, and the failure mode is *why* it occurs. Failure modes are not:

- Product defects — bugs in the code are more specific and dealt with more directly.
- Symptoms — failure modes are about understanding the root cause of failures.
- Informational — failure modes have to result in an actual failure, not the inability to handle warnings or other information data.

The table below illustrates some examples of common failure points and their matching failure modes.

Failure Point	Failure Mode
Database Access	Excessive writes to the database
Configuration not found	Configuration file not in the default place
Slow page render time	Too much traffic on web servers
Storage inaccessible	Storage keys changed

You can see from the above examples that the root cause of the failure is important to resolving the problem and preventing future failures.

Understanding failure modes is a vital part of designing for failure and if you don't get a handle on likely root causes, then it is unlikely that you will be able to implement the design artefacts for coping with failure.

Assessing failure modes

Determine common failure modes that apply to the particular type of application and technologies used. For each failure mode assess the likelihood of this failure mode occurring in a live application. If the likelihood is high enough to have a significantly negative impact on the ability to meet availability SLAs, mark it down as a failure mode that needs to be specifically addressed. Identified failure modes can then be addressed through the availability approaches such as resiliency, isolation etc.

Determine the appropriate actions

Once failure modes have been assessed, the actions to handle the failure modes need to be established. Different failure modes will have differing actions, and with many failure modes it becomes clear that some approaches are not practical or feasible. For example, the failure mode of invalid credentials is unlikely to be resolved by retrying (in fact it may make it worse), whereas the failure mode of throttling is likely to be resolved by a retry.

Testing

Testers need input from architects and application designers in order to develop tests for availability. The identification of failure modes and the actions employed to deal with them is vital for testers to develop plans. These plans may include simulation, load testing, and the actual replication of a failure mode (such as the forced changing of credentials). Testers need to provide feedback so that the application responds or recovers as expected when a failure mode occurs.

Stable storage

One of the fundamental building blocks of any availability solution is stable storage. Stable storage should be available (there when it is needed) and durable (never loses data). Many availability approaches involve the handoff of data between processes (e.g. asynchronous processing), or at least keep modified data in memory as briefly as possible. This needs to be underpinned by stable storage in order for them to achieve their availability objectives.

Storage on cloud platforms works a bit differently to traditional datacentres. Local machine storage is considered ephemeral and not stable at all. Apart from the inability to share local resources, any data stored on the local disk on a Windows Azure Role will be deleted when the role recycles. While there may be marginal performance benefits of using the local disk (which is, after all, not physically on the machine and subject to network latency), the base stable storage on Windows Azure is Windows Azure Storage (which includes tables, queues and blobs). Windows Azure SQL Database is for relational data and doesn't qualify as being a stable storage building block because it doesn't support any binary or file operations. The performance of Windows Azure storage in practice is better than the two-second response time commitment made in the SLA[26]. The performance latency[27] of Windows Azure Storage is around 100ms for small objects. The real advantage is the durability as there are six copies of each object[28], across three fault domains in two datacentres.

Using Windows Azure Storage requires that developers become familiar with a new API[29] which is encapsulated in .NET within the StorageClient[30] library. This means that developers need to become familiar with I/O operations which do not behave like the file system, adding some cost and risk. It doesn't take much for developers to master, and applications will have minimal need for persistence that is not to a database or queue.

Design for failure

The 'design for failure' mantra has been borrowed from the design philosophies of distributed computing and has become popular in designing applications for

---

[26] http://www.microsoft.com/en-us/download/details.aspx?displaylang=en&id=6656

[27] http://blogs.msdn.com/b/windowsazurestorage/archive/2010/05/10/windows-azure-storage-abstractions-and-their-scalability-targets.aspx

[28] http://blogs.msdn.com/b/avkashchauhan/archive/2012/02/09/how-many-copies-of-your-blob-is-stored-in-windows-azure-blob-storage.aspx

[29] http://msdn.microsoft.com/en-us/library/windowsazure/dd179355.aspx

[30] http://msdn.microsoft.com/en-us/library/windowsazure/microsoft.windowsazure.storageclient.aspx

cloud computing platforms. Central to the idea of 'design for failure' is to expect that everything is going to fail at some point and ask questions and develop approaches accordingly. The key point is that *everything* can fail, and the chaos monkey testing technique is about randomly and arbitrarily turning things off to test this principle.

'Design for failure' is good to use as a core philosophy in development teams but is no substitute for solid availability design and engineering. It does not address non-failure availability problems, such as the inability to handle load or code quality. Neither does it address the problem of whether or not designing for failure in each particular case is practical, valid and supported by the business rationale.

Redundancy

The simplest approach for building availability is to have two or more mostly identical components running where, if one fails, the other is able to take the load. Using redundant components is a popular availability technique because it is fairly simple to configure (as the redundant components are simple and the complexity is in the load balancer). Also, redundant components can simultaneously be used for load balancing and all resources are utilised.

The aim of redundancy is to avoid failure of a single component by having more than one available. By having identical copies of the component the load can be taken up by one if the other fails. Redundant components are generally put in place across all levels of the application stack, from individual hardware components such as power supplies, to physical infrastructure units such as servers (instances), to application infrastructure such as IIS Application pools.

The problem with redundancy as an approach to availability is that while it supports the failure of individual components, it won't prevent failure due to defects. Because all components are identical, a failure due to a defect can result in failure of all components because they are exactly the same and share the same defect. This is particularly relevant in redundant software components where a buggy code, such as a leap year bug, is shared and executed simultaneously. This means that while there will be fewer failures, because a failure of an individual component does not affect availability, when failures of redundancy occur they have a much greater impact. Most of the well-publicised cloud outages have been a result of software bugs in the redundancy systems. Redundancy is also problematic where the components are widely distributed (across datacentres), as the network latency and cost of data transfer, influence whether or not it is practical. This is covered in more detail in multiple locations below.

Windows Azure has multiple levels of redundancy built in to the hardware platform and different Azure services support redundancy in different ways. Windows Azure Compute, for example, allows for redundant roles that are monitored by the Fabric Controller, whereas Windows Azure SQL Database replicates data to redundant databases. The Windows Azure development approach, and indeed the SLA, encourages building applications in a redundant manner. The approach of using stateless (redundant) roles in Windows Azure Compute is the most common method of implementing redundancy that Windows Azure developers need to consider.

The success of redundancy implementation can be measured by recording the mean time between failures of components. In a stable redundancy solution, failures should be infrequent as any particular failure should go unnoticed.

Resiliency

Assuming that failures do occur, a system needs to be able to recover back to a healthy state as soon as possible. Resiliency is about the ability of the application to 'spring back' after a failure in order to ensure that the service is available. The important aspect of resiliency is the automated ability to detect failures and respond to those failures. Examples include:

- Detection of failed redundant components and the automated recovery of those components while others are taking the load. For example, in Windows Azure Compute, the roles are resilient in that when a single instance fails, the Fabric Controller detects the failure and recycles the role. During recycling the application may be in a degraded health state (as fewer instances are handling the same load), but the recovery of the failed instance is fairly quick.
- Detection of failure and fail-over to an alternative as a response to the failure. This is common with ACID databases where two redundant servers cannot run simultaneously. Once a failure has been detected an alternative database is brought online to serve data. The monitoring and fail-over is non-trivial and even when automated, needs to take care of data consistency. This is why fail-

overs on database clusters typically take minutes, rather than seconds, to restore availability.
- Detection of failure and queuing up of processing until the failure has been restored. Message oriented architectures rely on this solution, where the failure of a component is not an immediate problem and processing simply backs up until the failed component has been restored.

Windows Azure has a lot of resiliency built into the platform, such as with Windows Azure compute and Windows Azure SQL Database. Application developers can use other Windows Azure services, such as Windows Azure Queues to implement other types of resiliency.

Resilient systems assume that failure will occur and can respond accordingly. As a result, failures may be more frequent, but the impact is low. There is frequently a cost benefit of building resiliency rather than stability, and this is common on cloud platforms where commodity equipment is used. Although it may be more prone to failure than high-grade equipment, the overall resiliency of the platform makes it an acceptable compromise.

The measure of a resilient application is the mean time to restore i.e. how quickly it can 'bounce back' from failure.

Scalability

As much as there is significant focus on scalability when discussing cloud computing, this release CALM doesn't have a separate model for scalability. Scalability is part of the lifecycle model (the demand for scaling), the operational model (the ability to respond to scale events), the cost model (the cost benefits of scaling, rather than having under-utilised resources), and the availability model. Scalability, in the context of availability, is the ability of an application to respond to load and maintain availability expectations, in particular performance expectations.

Scalability is an approach whereby certain parts of the application can simply be 'scaled out' as a response to load in order to maintain availability. Not all parts of the application can be scaled-out and databases are particularly problematic, but where it is possible it can be a highly effective and affordable approach to availability.

The success of a highly scalable application is measured by the ability to rapidly respond to increased (or decreased) load, using the minimum amount of resources, for the minimum about of time.

Future releases of CALM will bring together other models (availability, deployment, operations, and others) for a clearer view on how scalability is specifically addressed within the application.

Reduce dependency

Dependency of components on others is the most common cause of failures and dependency should be avoided where possible. This applies to components within a single application and those that are external. In the application layer, a process that calls another process, through a service API or similar, and has to wait for a result, is prone to the failure of the external process it is dependent on. This process could be on another machine, across the world, or owned and operated by a completely different organisation, so is susceptible to network problems and general availability, in addition to defects that may cause it to fail.

The most common approach to reduce dependency is to interface asynchronously using shared durable state. In this case, one process persists the data that needs to be worked on, and sends a message to the other process to deal with. Once the data is saved, and the message sent, the process has nothing further to do and continues. The second process is free to receive the message and process the data, and if it fails at some point, the first process is not impacted.

The Windows Azure practice strongly supports the reduction of dependencies by using messaging and provides highly available underlying services that make it simple within the Windows Azure environment. The pattern, using a typical e-commerce scenario, works as follows:

- The web role during the checkout process saves the incomplete order to Windows Azure SQL Database.
- The web role, on receiving the 'place order' request, adds a message containing the unique order number to the 'new order' (Windows Azure Storage queue) and returns an 'Order successfully placed' page.

- The 'New orders' worker role that is polling the 'new order' queue receives a message of a new order.
- The worker role uses the order number to retrieve the order from Windows Azure SQL Database.
- The worker role performs necessary operations on the order, such as validate, send email confirmation, and add to fulfilment queue.
- The worker role deletes the message from the new order queue once it has completed.

In the above example, the web role is isolated from any failures that can occur on the 'New orders' worker role. Any that exist can be many, including failures of services that need to be called (such as shipping), email service failures and others. The persistent message queue is also an important part of the fault tolerance, by allowing the message to be reprocessed if the worker role fails to process it correctly.

Windows Azure supports this approach by:

- Providing a clear distinction between web roles and worker roles and encouraging the use of both.
- Providing a number of shared state options to work with data across processes, including queues, blobs, table storage and SQL.
- Providing a reliable messaging service in Windows Azure Queues which means that as soon as a message is added to the queue it is guaranteed to be processed at least once.
- Providing various APIs that are REST based with .NET wrappers that allow easier implementation.

The problems with this approach to dependency reduction are:

- Process decomposition - in order for dependencies to be reduced, processes need to be decomposed as much as possible. The above 'order' example may be fairly easy to decompose because the end user is not concerned about the back-end processes. But a complex process that is highly dependent on back-end processes, such as payment authorisation, may be more difficult to decompose.
- Notification of completeness — the problem with asynchronous processing is notifying the calling process that work is complete so that it can continue with other processes. Generally we try to avoid waiting for this completeness notification and asynchronous callbacks, as it defeats the idea of reduced dependency. Asynchronous processing that uses callbacks is good for

reducing the *appearance* of waiting, but doesn't actually reduce dependency. It is possible to marshal completeness checks on the front-end with technologies like SignalR[31], and is emerging with more sophisticated front-end applications (within the browser).
- No distributed transactions — Distributed transactions, two phase commits, and sophisticated mechanisms in traditional TP monitors are generally not used in the cloud and not supported by Windows Azure. The Windows Azure Queues (and Service Bus to a lesser degree) are fairly simple messaging systems. While this has the disadvantage of having to hand code compensating transactions, distributed transactions rarely work with the type of applications developed in the cloud, due to the underlying technologies that don't support rollbacks.

Asynchronous processing

Rapid scaling where resources are added when demand increases, and removed when demand drops, is an important aspect of availability. The ability to respond is necessary to ensure that the application performs regardless of the load that it may be under at a point in time. Windows Azure supports the ability to scale rapidly by allowing the required instance count to be changed and the Fabric Controller to automatically spin up an instance and slot it in to the load balancer. Rapid scaling is not without its problems:

- The time from detection of diminished health (as a result of the load) to provisioning of resources is measured in minutes, so there may be a period of reduced availability.
- Very spiky traffic, where the high load interval is less than the granularity of billing (one hour in the case of Windows Azure) removes some of the benefit of scaling.
- Monitoring the need for scaling is not simple — it may not just be average CPU or another metric that determines the need to scale.
- Some parts of the application may not be able to scale. Scaling out front-end web servers, for example, may put excessive load on the database, which cannot scale, and availability is impacted.

The implementation of asynchronous processing allows the load that various components are under to be smoothed out. Using the order processing example

---

[31] https://github.com/SignalR/SignalR

from reducing dependency as described above, the front-end order web role can be scaled up and down as needed, but the back-end 'New order' worker role can be left to run at its maximum throughput at a lower scale. When the front-end is under load, messages on the queue simply wait a bit longer before they are processed. This allows the maximum (and therefore optimal) use of the available resources on the worker role, while at the same time reducing the load on downstream components, such as the database or external services. The diagram below illustrates how the back-end process picks up the load and 'flat-lines' while the front-end process responds to the variable load.

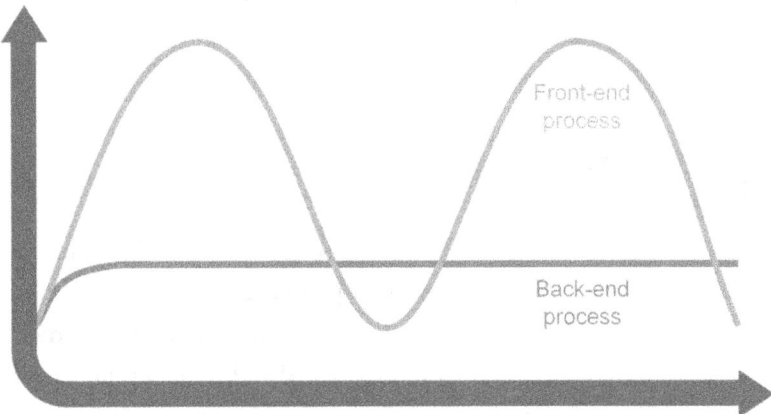

On Windows Azure, the implementation of asynchronous processing (across different machines) is the same as the implementation of reduced dependency using Windows Azure Queues. This is a valuable double use of queues to resolve availability and one of the reasons why the use of Windows Azure Queues is such a fundamental paradigm within Windows Azure.

The diagram below illustrates asynchronous processing using persistent messaging. The separation of work into separate, independent processes allows the data to be persisted (in messages) as it flows through the processes. A failure of any of the processes should not result in data loss as it has been safely saved to a queue.

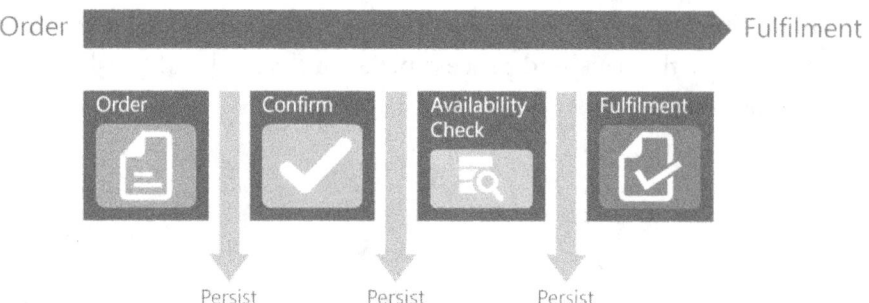

Deferred processing

Asynchronous processing also supports the approach to handling failures of deferred processing. Deferred processing is a retry that allows for long periods between the initial failure and the retry. Asynchronous processing using message queues is well suited to deferred processing, as all of the design artefacts needed for deferred processing exist and may be well used in the application already. In deferred processing using queues, if a failure occurs, a message is added to a queue for later processing. The later processing can perform the same action or, based on information about the data, perform a slightly different action. Unfortunately, Windows Azure Queues do not support delayed delivery of messages so it is possible that the message will be delivered too quickly for the failure mode to be resolved.

Fault tolerance

Failures are bound to occur — what is important is what the application does when failures occur. The first step in the context of availability is to at least make it look like failures are either not occurring or not causing significant problems. This can be done by:

- Ensuring that it is only the failed process, thread, or whatever is the smallest unit, which is impacted. Failures should not bring down the entire application

by corrupting data, typing up the request pipeline, or overloading external services.
- Having alternatives when failures do occur, such as retrieving from the database when the cache fails, retrieving static or inconsistent data when live data requests fail, or redirecting to a stable service.
- Storing the input data in an alternative store, such as a queue, for later processing when the dependant service is available.
- Providing alternatives to the user in the event of a failure that cannot be resolved, such as a telephone number to assist with urgent transactions.
- Hiding error messages. These are largely useless to the user, cause panic and are a potential security risk.

Fail early

Fault tolerance is not the same as fault recovery. Developers believe that it is possible to write code to recover from errors, but beyond a few simple options (such as reading static data when a database error occurs) it is seldom successful. A fundamental principle of building high availability systems is to fail as early as possible and not try to recover. Recovery can become complex, result in corruption and inconsistencies and seldom addresses the underlying problem, so it is likely that failure will occur on the next part of the operation anyway. It is also impossible to specify all failure scenarios, so building recovery for 'unknown unknowns' is virtually impossible. Note that this advice doesn't apply to applications that are responsible for life support, Mars rovers, weapons or other applications where more recovery rigour is mandated.

Retrying on transient faults

Sometimes processes cannot be decomposed into isolated services separated by asynchronous processing. A web page, for example, may need consistent data immediately in order to render a page correctly and has a synchronous dependency on services. In other cases, it may be decided that the increased effort or complexity of decomposing a process is too high, especially when the required service is deemed to be fairly reliable. In these cases, part of fault tolerance is the ability to retry an operation.

Retry is not an attempt at active recovery, but rather waiting a bit before trying the same operation again on the assumption that the fault is transient. Transient faults are faults that are likely to last for a short time and are generally the result of timeout or capacity related failures. Retries should only be attempted on transient faults where there is an expectation that a delay will change behaviour. For example, there is no point retrying a database operation for a key constraint error, but it may be worthwhile if the error is because the database has been actively throttled (as with Windows Azure SQL Database). There are cases where availability may be easily restored by retrying an operation. It is worthwhile retrying at least once if it is not an expensive operation and does not make matters worse.

Scenarios where retries are applicable include:

- Failure from short-lived outages.
- Cases where a service has failed and is in the process of recovering (fail-over).
- Failure due to unreliable or congested networks — this may be a common occurrence when integration with on-premise services.
- Throttling that has been enforced by the Windows Azure platform. Windows Azure SQL Database throttles[32] to prevent the overuse of resources on a machine by a single tenant. Similarly, Windows Azure Storage also imposes limits on throughput[33] for partitions, accounts, queues, etc.
- Calls to services that do not give error codes that indicate a transactional fault.

Retries are a programming technique that is generally applicable and only explicitly supported by Windows Azure through meaningful error codes, such as the throttling specific error codes returned by Windows Azure SQL Database. Separate from the Windows Azure SDK, the Microsoft Patterns and Practices group has produced a library called the Microsoft Enterprise Library Transient Fault Handling Application Block[34] that allows the developer to select an incremental, fixed interval or exponential back-off retry strategy when accessing Windows Azure SQL Database, Windows Azure Service Bus, Windows Azure Storage or the Windows Azure Caching Service.

---

[32] http://msdn.microsoft.com/library/ff394106#throttling

[33] http://blogs.msdn.com/b/windowsazure/archive/2012/11/02/windows-azure-s-flat-network-storage-and-2012-scalability-targets.aspx

[34] http://msdn.microsoft.com/en-us/library/hh680934(v=pandp.50).aspx

Here are some implementation points to bear in mind when retrying transient faults:

- Retry a finite number of times — sticking with the availability principle of failing fast, do not keep retrying indefinitely as the fault may not be a transient one and the application should move to a failed state quickly.
- Make use of back-off strategies (such as exponential back-off). There may be no point in retrying an operation ten times with a 100 ms delay if the failure lasts for two seconds.
- Include logging and instrumentation in record retries so that adjustments can be made, either to the called service or the component that always has to retry.
- Make sure that operations are idempotent. In some cases, the failure is because the called service is running slowly, so it takes a long time to return a result, but the operation is performed. In this case, the retry will perform the same operation, and idempotent data is needed to ensure that the operation does not result in multiple transactions or duplicate data.
- Ensure that if all of the retries fail, the failure is handled correctly by making sure that the data is in a consistent state and that errors are properly handled. Don't let retries run in the background assuming that they will never fail.

Fail Whale — failing with style

During the massive growth of Twitter in the early years, failures were common. The 'fail whale' page that was displayed when Twitter was unavailable became a pop culture icon. The fail whale is well-designed and somehow allowed dedicated fans to develop an affinity for a service that was struggling. Twitter managed to resolve their availability issues, users seemed to stay, and the fail whale was influential in developing that loyalty. This success has been replicated in different forms as humorous, well designed and apologetic error pages that users are more tolerant of.

Spending time and effort on failure error messages that graciously acknowledge a fault, has proven to be worthwhile and can go a long way to retaining users who would otherwise become frustrated and click away.

Isolation

Isolation is a key principle in available systems — whether that is isolated storage, network infrastructure, processes or services. Isolation works for components that fail, by making sure that they don't bring down other healthy components. It also works for healthy components, ensuring that other failing components do not affect their health. Isolation goes hand in hand with 'autonomy', where components exist in their own place and are blissfully unaware and unaffected by rogue components around them.

Modern applications have the additional problem of frequent, out-of-band releases of some parts of the application, resulting in potential problems when one component is being shut down for release while others are under load. This is not technically 'failure', but can result in the unavailability of stable components from being knocked out because of the deployment of another. Cloud applications that have components in various stages of deployment, staging and testing, are particularly susceptible if they are not sufficiently isolated.

When developing applications on Windows Azure, isolation is primarily implemented by building distinct services that have very little interaction with one another. Isolated services only interact asynchronously, where the success or failure of the interaction is irrelevant, or by using stable and reliable shared state, such as Windows Azure SQL Database.

Windows Azure supports the paradigm of isolation by encouraging the use of distinct services. The web and worker roles are the obvious examples, but the Windows Azure model goes further by supporting the implementation of many distinct services due to deployment and cost models. For example, a web application may be comprised of a number of different services, deployed across many roles of varying sizes and varying instance counts depending on the need. It is no longer necessary to be concerned with the physical machine resources available, when architecting the granularity of services in the application.

Feature Shaping (Service Degradation)

One of the key concepts in scalability is the ability to allow for graceful service degradation when an application is under load. But service degradation can be difficult to explain and 'degrade' has negative connotations.

The networking people overcame the bad press of degradation by calling it 'traffic shaping'[35] or 'packet shaping'. Traffic shaping, as we see it on the edge of the network on our home broadband connections, allows some data packets to be of a lower priority (such online gaming) than others (such as web browsing). The idea is that a saturated network can handle the load by changing the profile or *shape* of priority traffic. Key to traffic shaping is that most users don't notice that it is happening.

Feature shaping is the ability for an application under load to shape the profile of features that get priority, or to shape the result to be one that is less costly (in terms of resources) to produce. This is best explained by examples:

- Farmville degrades services when under load by dropping some of the in-game features that require a lot of back-end processing, thus shaping the richness of in-game functionality.
- Email confirmations can be delayed to reduce load. The deferred load is either by the generation of the email itself, or the transmission of the email.
- Encoding of videos on Facebook is not immediate and is shaped by the available capacity for encoding. During peak usage, the feature will take longer and the difference in time taken is generally not noticed by users.
- A different search index that produces less accurate results, but for a lower cost, may be used during heavy load, thus shaping the search result.
- Real-time analytics for personalised in-page advertising can be switched off when under load, shaping the adverts to those that are more general.

Feature shaping can be defined as:

- Feature shaping allows some parts of an application to degrade the normal performance or accuracy service levels in response to load.

---

[35] http://en.wikipedia.org/wiki/Traffic_shaping

- Feature shaping is not fault tolerance — it is not a mechanism to cope when all hell breaks loose.
- Feature shaping is for exceptional behaviour and features should not be shaped under normal conditions
- Shaped features will be generally unnoticeable to most users. The application *seems* to behave as expected.
- Feature shaping can be automated or manual.
- Feature shaping can be applied differently to different sets of users at the same time (e.g. registered users don't get features shaped).

Like with performance requirements it is best to extract the feature shaping requirements as simple statements, for example:

1. Page render time can drop by 100% (2 seconds to 4 seconds)
    2. The most popular 10% of items can be cached without being refreshed for 5 minutes.
    3. Personalised content can be unavailable
    4. Processing of external feeds can be suspended
    5. Administrative functions should still be performant and accessible.

Unlike performance requirements, where it is easier to deal with as few points as possible, when degrading due to load it is probably better to list as many functional parts of the system as possible. Business needs to be given the opportunity to communicate the core features, or minimum viable product, of their application. By listing each of the major features, and how they can degrade under extreme load, architects will build accordingly.

Multiple locations

Distributing an application in multiple locations is a common approach to availability. The main reasons this approach is chosen are either to reduce the latency to end users, or to provide an alternative datacentre in the event of a major outage.

Where an application has users around the world, particularly if they are outside the US or Europe, the response times of the application can have a severe impact on availability as users perceive the performance of the application to be poor. The most common solutions to this problem include the replication of the entire application and its data to a more localised datacentre, but it does have drawbacks associated with having shared data across multiple datacentres (as discussed below). Simpler options include the use of CDNs (Content Delivery Networks), such as the Windows Azure CDN, which facilitate the placement of static data at edge locations, where latency to end users is lower. Strategies of moving particular workloads to other datacentres, while keeping core data centralised, can also be employed and facilitated by using technologies available in Windows Azure such as Windows Azure Queues.

In cases where applications have regional variations, such as language, an entirely different product catalogue or regional fulfilment provider, it may be preferable to build, operate and deploy the application as a completely separate one. Code can be shared across the two projects, and shared data can be handled as integration between two disparate services, rather than a common data source. It may also be that the regional variation has a different lifecycle model, different availability requirements and, because it is owned and operated by a different organisation, has a unique profile that bears little resemblance to any other region.

Major cloud computing outages are generally restricted to a single datacentre. Not because of regional disaster that brings down communication or power, but because of the management, operations and deployments specific to that datacentre. In the event of a single datacentre outage, the only way to ensure availability is to ensure the entire application can run in a separate datacentre. While the risk of a datacentre outage exists, and it is technically possible to address the problem, the cost of geographic redundancy needs to be well understood. Windows Azure helps by providing rapid scalability, where the fail-over deployment does not have to continuously run at full capacity, but there are still on-going costs. Identical replication of data will incur data egress costs from the primary datacentre, and with large datasets this may not be trivial. Costs will also be incurred by the overhead of having to deploy and monitor a second deployment.

Replication of data across multiple datacentres is challenging. These challenges include:

- Data volume — the volume of data could saturate the network, or at least carry a significant cost.

- Latency for non-replicated data — it may be determined that some data cannot be replicated for regulatory or data consistency reasons. Applications that are deployed in different datacentres may have performance problems at key points where centralised data is queried.
- Data consistency — a requirement for high data consistency may not be able to be satisfied with replicated data, as the time taken to replicate the data may result in inconsistent queries.
- Operations — replication of data carries an extra operational overhead. Not only must both systems be highly available, schema changes need to be synchronised and the recovery of an identical dataset in the event of failures can be a challenging task requiring manual intervention.

If it is determined that data does need to be shared across datacentres, consider the following approaches:

- High read, low write workloads — identify workloads that have many reads and few writes. These are better candidate workloads to run out of distributed datacentres.
- Keep writes centralised — if only one database contains 'the truth' and distributed databases contain read-only data, it is easier to maintain the replication. Consider using Windows Azure Queues and worker roles for writes (such as using a CQRS type pattern)
- Allow for restoration of snapshots — sometimes databases can become so out of sync that it is difficult to reconcile, such as when a slave datacentre has a long outage. It may be easier to restore a snapshot of the central database rather than resolving synchronisation idiosyncrasies by hand.

On-premise data redundancy

One of the myths of cloud computing is the issue around key business data being stored on a platform that is not owned by the business. Business and regulatory reasoning aside, it may be technically simple, and create peace of mind, to replicate data from the cloud to an on-premise datacentre. This provides a sense of control of the data and can offer tangible benefits if BI and other tools are on-premise, where it may be better to have the application data on the local network where it can be used further. If data is stored in Windows Azure Storage, an agent will have to be developed to transform the data to suit the on-premise storage architecture. Data stored in Windows Azure SQL Database cannot be replicated using the built-in SQL Server replication, but Windows Azure does offer the Windows Azure SQL Database Data Sync service to replicate data to an on-premise SQL Server database.

Data availability

The availability of data is one of the most important aspects of availability. This applies to both short-term availability, where the data needs to be available when it needs to be processed, as well as long-term availability, where data needs to be safely stored for long-term use.

The implementation of data availability is contained in, and influenced by, the data model which deals with the performant and reliable persistence and retrieval of data. The broad categories of data availability to be contained within the availability model, as references to the detail within the data model, include:

- Data services — when a service that provides data cannot be connected to, either a service that is part of the application or a third party service, the application availability is affected. Strategies need to be developed for alternative sources of data, such as reading from a cache or another service.
- Data performance — applications that wait for data, whether that is from the primary database, the cache or another service, can perform badly and have their availability targets severely impacted. Database performance is probably the single, biggest cause of poor application performance and therefore needs considerable attention when architecting.
- Data consistency — applications have different requirements for having access to data that is correct and consistent. The reliability availability outcome, where the measure of availability is the accuracy or relevance of the data, may be negatively impacted by inconsistent results. Applications that require high consistency (and there are very few of these) place higher demands on data availability.
- Data longevity — often overlooked by application developers and even business, data that is lost forever can have a significant impact on the business. Ensuring that data can be reliably backed up, restored and accessible, is part of the overall requirement for data availability. Windows Azure Storage, for example, is reasonably durable, unless a defective application deletes it 'by mistake', in which case it will be lost forever unless a backup was made. Most losses of long-term data are not related to any platform failures, but rather defects, operational process problems (like forgetting to configure backups) or administrative issues (like termination of an account).

Multiple copies and multiple paths

One of the core principles of availability is to have multiple copies of data and multiple paths to getting data. For example, instead of just having data in a SQL database (single store) accessible by a web page (single path), have the data in an additional data store (say table storage) that can be accessed by an independent service. This principle can be applied to storing the data in a single format in multiple locations (geo-redundancy), or multiple formats in a single location (such as having data in a search index like SOLR in addition to the primary database). It can also extend to accessing or storing data from applications and data stores that are located on-premise. Obviously, the implementation of this principle can significantly add to costs in terms of data storage, consumed bandwidth, development of alternative access paths, and operational effort. Availability of critical data, such as financial transactions, may warrant the extra cost, whereas less important data such as traffic logs may not, so the principle can be inconsistently applied depending on the requirement.

Skeleton applications

In some cases, failure can be so catastrophic that the application is down for days. This can be the result of a major cloud outage or database corruption that takes days to recover. One of the considerations for availability is to have functionality available in order to satisfy the needs of critical business functions. For public facing applications, this may be the ability to view the catalogue or access account information. For internally focussed applications, this may be limited to capturing important transactions or customer lookup and forgoing analysis and reporting features.

Skeleton applications are those that provide the minimum functionality in the event of a major outage in order to provide some level of service. Skeleton applications should be considered separate (as per the principle of multiple paths) and should be able to run on a completely independent platform (such as on-premise). How these applications are developed and how much is spent on them depends on the business rationale and the impact on the business during a sustained outage. Care needs to be taken to ensure that they are not full featured and expensive to maintain. They could even be simple database enquires using Excel.

The role of UX

The discipline of User Experience (UX) is aimed at providing the best interaction with the application for the users, which can have both a positive and negative effect on application availability. For example, a product catalogue search result may provide stock availability information to the user, but this may require queries against a stock database that is already under load. A sudden increase in searches (even by anonymous users) could bring down the stock database and ultimately affect the availability of the application.

Many examples of application of UX, in terms of availability, are more subtle and could require a significant programme of user testing, analytics from live systems and behavioural analysis to find out if the impact on resources is justified. Some reining in on UX may be quite simple. For example, minimising the number of results returned by a search may have a significant impact on the availability of the search engine and be irrelevant to UX, making it an easy decision to make. In other cases, consulting with UX experts may help solve an availability problem. For example, a resource intensive feature may be inadvertently accessed because users try to 'discover' what it does and a small UX tweak, to help the user understand if they need to access the feature at all, may be all that is needed to discourage pointless use.

Most UX practitioners are unaware of the performance and availability impacts of UX decisions, and while they don't try and clutter the user interface, they do try and increase information density, which can be costly to produce. Architects and application designers need to work closely with UX designers during the early stages of the design of the front-end. Even though the application architecture may not be defined, experienced architects and developers will be able to provide input into what parts of the front-end are resource intensive. This should provide an indication as to whether or not particular UX elements are required. For example, a web page with a search box may require an incremental search (where the results are displayed as the user types) and an architect could point out that every keypress is a separate search. If the average search term is ten characters, satisfying such a search requirement would require ten times the resources as a non-incremental one (this is not quite true as search engines have indexing features to facilitate incremental search, but there are definitely more resources consumed). This could result in a discussion between developers, UX and business as to the value of the incremental search feature and business could decide to either commit the extra resources, or decide that the feature is not important enough. Working together early on also provides input to the application design process, where features that are required by UX have architectural considerations that need to be made as early as possible.

It is obvious that features impact performance and availability, yet reducing features in the interests of availability can be futile because reducing features can reduce user satisfaction and adoption. The role of UX is not necessarily the reduction of features, but the presentation, richness and depth of those features. Well engineered UX can find the crucial balance between them.

Air France — Extreme UX for availability

When the Air France Flight 447 disappeared over the Atlantic Ocean on 1 June 2009 the airfrance.com site was put under excessive load due to people wanting more information. Air France changed their home page to provide current information on the crash, in plain text, with a link to the normal booking website. The Air France response is a sombre example of a UX tweak as a response to load. Features were not shaped as they were still accessible (just an extra click away). The placement of a fairly static page as the 'home page' had obvious and necessary non-technical reasons, yet the impact on system scalability, and resultant availability, was high. The static page, which most of the users wanted to see, was lightweight, unauthenticated, directly served (no database connection), cacheable (even across a CDN) and able to be massively scaled out.

Azure specific features for availability

Windows Azure has significant features that help with availability and are built into the platform, so architects, designers and developers can get on with writing application code and worry less about application availability. These features take care of some availability concerns but still need to be understood by architects; so that what they offer is clear within the context availability and their use can be maximised.

Fault domains

In addition to lower level infrastructure redundancy, such as in routers, switches and load balancers, the Windows Azure Fabric Controller tries to spread roles across an isolated physical infrastructure. This reduces the likelihood of application failure because of hardware failure. The use and configuration of fault domains are part of the datacentre topology and infrastructure, but what is defined as a fault domain is unknown, and largely irrelevant, to consumers of the service. Microsoft does observe that one of the fault domains is the rack in the datacentre. Having your application spread across multiple racks will definitely reduce the likelihood of hardware failure bringing down the entire application.

VIP (Virtual IP) swap

When performing a major upgrade of an application, it can take quite a long time for all of the instances to start up and even longer to make sure that everything is working properly. This can have a major impact on availability because the application may not perform adequately while it is starting up and it may not be safe for public access while it is being tested. Windows Azure has a feature called Virtual IP Address Swap which allows a new deployment to be instantiated in a staging environment and assigned a publicly accessible domain name, which can be switched in seconds with the production domain name. This allows the new version of the application to be running and ready to accept traffic as soon as operators are confident that it is working properly. An important part of the VIP swap is that the previous version switches over to staging so that if, for some reason, the new version is not working, it can be swapped back to the previous version very quickly.

Upgrade domain

Minor upgrades to the application, such as changes to configuration, do not warrant the rigour of a staging environment and VIP Swap. Windows Azure has upgrade domains (also known as update domains, although there is a difference) to make it easier and to ensure availability. When an update occurs, roles need to be recycled, and it would impact availability if they were done all at once. Windows Azure deals with this by grouping roles into upgrade domains (a default of 5). Each upgrade domain is upgraded in turn, while one is being recycled, all the others handle traffic, and once the Fabric Controller is satisfied that an upgrade domain is working properly, it moves on to the next one.

Windows Azure SQL Database

The differences between Windows Azure SQL Database and SQL Server largely exist to enable it to work in a multi-tenant environment and to provide for higher availability. Windows Azure SQL Database doesn't have the traditional concept of a database cluster to support availability (which is largely about shared storage) and instead replicates the data automatically across three databases (explaining the need for a clustered index and other limitations). If a single database fails, Windows Azure SQL Database will take care of making one of the replicas the primary and start-up another to replace the failed database.

Windows Azure SQL Database also has federations[36] which are useful in building available systems by providing a mechanism to scale out the SQL database. Windows Azure SQL Database federations shard (or partition) data across multiple databases and allow queries to be written that access the shards at the database level, rather than having the application know which shards are needed.

Traffic manager

The Windows Azure Traffic Manager[37] allows the distribution of user traffic across Windows Azure hosted services. It is not like a network load balancer as it directs the traffic by applying policies to DNS queries, rather than routing the actual traffic. While it can be used in applications within a single datacentre, the benefits of the traffic manager are realised when the application is deployed across multiple datacentres. The traffic manager can be used in the following scenarios:

---

[36] http://msdn.microsoft.com/en-us/library/windowsazure/hh597452.aspx

[37] http://msdn.microsoft.com/en-us/library/windowsazure/hh744833.aspx

- Performance — directs the user to the "best"/"closest" deployment. For example, directing the user to the "best" deployment between US South and West Europe.
- Failover — traffic is redirected to another deployment if the primary goes down. For example, all traffic is directed to US North and if it goes down send all traffic to US South.
- Geomapping — allows users from defined geographic locations to be directed to particular deployment. For example, all users from US are directed to US North, all users from Asia are directed to US North, and all users from Europe are directed to West Europe.
- Ratio — sends traffic to different deployments based on fixed ratio. For example, direct 20% of user traffic to US South and 80% to US North.

Organisational behaviour

The biggest test of availability is not just the technical issues, but how an organisation responds to outages before, during, and after one occurs. Organisations that scrimp on availability spending and then have senior managers running around looking for heads to roll when something happens, generally do not handle availability problems very well. When applications are under load and system downtime has revenue impacts, even the coolest organisation can crack under the pressure; making mistakes, blaming the wrong people and generally taking longer to restore application health.

How organisations and individuals behave when failure occurs is a big subject and out of scope for this book. The business processes, management practices, training and documentation for fault-tolerant organisations can be a large, complex and specialised field. The aerospace/airline industry is a good example of organisational behaviour during failure taken to (valid) extremes; from the amount of training pilots receive to handle failure scenarios, to the processes of air traffic control and airports to sort things out, to the engineering and safety systems in the aircraft themselves.

If your organisation has established processes for business continuity, or other practices to handle outages or other panic scenarios, then make use of those to start with. Key to the organisational response is being prepared for diminished health, reduced availability and outages by responding correctly and learning from failures, rather than running around in panic during a failure and wondering what to do. The availability model should at least highlight the organisational processes as shown below:

- Plan — the health model and operational model are key parts of the planning for reduced availability. Extensive coverage of these models will enable better recovery and part of the overall organisational drive is to ensure that sufficient effort is put into these models.
- Recover — again, the health and operational models should contain the detail, including both the organisational and technical aspects for recovery from failures. The models don't cover organisational aspects such as ownership, accountability and resource plans (for recruiting, training, coverage of shifts, and so on). These additional aspects may need to be covered, or at least introduced, to existing functions within the organisation that need to deal with them.
- Review — after failures that don't meet the agreed SLAs, a review of what went wrong needs to take place. In addition to root cause analysis and determining a technical reason for the failure, other contributors to failure which are organisational in nature must be looked at. Perhaps key people were not available or had not transferred enough skills? Maybe the increase in traffic was expected by the business, but operations were not notified (see the lifecycle model)? Whatever the reasons, they need to be looked at objectively and lessons fed back into the models, or changes made to the application and operating environment, in order to reduce the likelihood of similar failures in the future.

Operations role

Operational staff are ultimately tasked with the responsibility for application availability. The processes within operations, and their relationships with business and development teams, are critical to application availability. Apart from technical ability, tooling and monitoring, operations needs to be able to respond quickly to diminished health. This needs to be done with a clear and rapid understanding of the business impacts, the root cause and a way of recovering the application without making things worse. Depending on the nature of the fault, this may need to be done within a high-pressure environment that may not be conducive to meticulous planning and the clear thinking (including the consequences of actions) required to respond. While some problems could be fixed quickly by internal operational staff, in some cases operations may need to request help and exert pressure on other parties, such as suppliers or the development teams. The ability to transfer some of the recovery tasks to a third party, while maintaining ownership, buffering others from pressure and co-ordinating the recovery is one of the most difficult skills that operational staff require.

Developer role

Developers have two primary roles in availability. The first is to engineer the required availability, and the second is to be on-hand to fix problems in a production environment. The culture of building availability is difficult to foster in a development team as it may not be seen as the most important. One of the ways to get developers more concerned about availability is to make them 'feel the pain' by increasing the role that they play in day-to-day operations. The practice of developers performing more 'devops', as part of their daily tasks, is becoming common in modern applications. Developers, after all, have the most knowledge about how their part of the system works and are best suited to address problems. Additionally the rapid release cycles of services within an application mean that developers have to take a more hands-on role when rolling out new functionality.

This approach may not work in many organisations that are structured to more traditional principles. In these environments, the interface between operations and developers needs to be clearly defined so that when a failure occurs, developers can be included in the recovery (to determine the root cause or fix a defect). Processes between operations and developers need to be clarified upfront and not made up during a major outage.

Availability as an engineering discipline

The building of highly available systems is not new and has been practiced for decades in other engineering disciplines such as telecommunications, where satellites in space need to be reliable. What is new is that mainstream applications that previously only had to serve a handful of users during working hours, are now having to handle millions of users constantly (and for a significantly reduced cost). Those same users are highly intolerant of application outages or poor performance. As a result, architects, software designers and developers who would normally not have cared much for availability, now have to turn their attention towards it.

Fortunately, availability (and scalability) are becoming widely accepted as core skills. The previous generation of availability principles, such as Joe Armstrong's '6 Rules of high availability'[38] (Isolation, Concurrency, Failure Detection, Fault Identification, Live Upgrade and Stable Storage) are being rediscovered and applied to modern application architectures.

Availability is also emerging within products, particularly NoSQL databases, where principles of availability are embedded within the products. This is also a source of good engineering practice. Many of these databases are built with cloud deployments in mind and cater for scalability, eventual consistency, distributed data, high throughput and other aspects required by highly available systems. The continued innovation and addition of new entrants into the market, accompanied by detailed analysis and discussion, also adds to a wider discussion of availability principles amongst developers.

Massive web properties such as Google, Twitter, Facebook and Netflix are pushing the boundaries of availability of web applications and frequently share their lessons in open forums and developer-focussed conferences. They have also founded open source projects of the products that they have developed to solve their problems. Cassandra[39] comes from Facebook; Hadoop[40] comes from Yahoo (based on Google papers). These projects, with their roots in highly available applications, lend credibility to availability engineering practice. Many of these web properties are seen by developers as 'cool' and their approaches are emulated by developers worldwide.

Summary

Modern applications have a significantly higher expectation of availability due to large, popular applications doing it so well and users increasingly moving towards web based applications for daily work, consumption and social engagement. Applications that fail now have their outages flashed on Twitter and discussed at

---

[38] http://www.infoq.com/presentations/Building-Highly-Available-Systems-in-Erlang

[39] http://cassandra.apache.org/

[40] http://hadoop.apache.org/

length on Hacker News within minutes. This creates serious perception problems for any application or service trying to gain market share. Any application launched needs to pay serious attention to availability to the extent that it becomes one of the primary application features, not just a non-functional requirement added to the bottom of the nice-to-have list.

Cloud platforms such as Windows Azure do indeed provide some of the availability needs as part of the service but only at the infrastructure level, and at the expense of performance and latency. Application developers still have a lot of work to do to build available applications on top of that infrastructure. Building such availability is non-trivial and can be very expensive in terms of development effort and skills required, so the challenge remains to get the balance between availability engineering and cost.

Going through the process of building the availability model forces attention to be placed on the availability requirement; so that the underlying business rationale can be understood and cost-effective techniques and approaches developed to satisfy the availability needs. The involvement of all stakeholders in building the model (business, application architects, developers, testers, operations) ensures that everybody understands their responsibilities and the role that they play in implementing an available solution.

Steps

1. Develop the availability SLAs.
2. Understand the cost implications of implementing availability, so that this can be communicated clearly to the business.
3. Understand the business rationale for availability
4. Select the appropriate development approaches for availability based on their ability to satisfy the requirements within the project budget.
5. Create a focus on availability across the development team and the rest of the organisation, which matches the availability expectations of the application.

Data Model

The capture, storage, processing, and retrieval of data, make up the majority of features of any application. Creating the data model as a work stream focuses the required attention on data handling as a fundamental concern of the application and architecture.

Like other models, the data model should not be seen as a model to be completed and finalised before development commences. It should evolve over time, which makes sense architecturally, but should have enough in the early stages in order to ensure that the correct architectural decisions are made, and so that developers can continue without needing to rework any data access code.

How the data model has changed

How modern applications are built has fundamentally influenced database models, the approaches to modelling data and how resulting data models are implemented within applications. While the public cloud has not been wholly responsible for this shift, the patterns adopted in cloud computing applications, and the nature of applications that run on the cloud, have been drivers for this change.

As little as ten years ago, the de-facto approach to data was to store it all in a single, monolithic SQL database that was strictly controlled, had full transactional control, and was modelled as close to third-normal form as possible. Although non-relational databases have existed for decades, the SQL database had emerged as the standard and looked to stay that way due to trust, stability, tools, and developer adoption and acceptance. The arrival of data-centric applications that handled a different type of data, such as Google's search engine, focussed attention on the suitability of alternative data stores that supported the data requirements of high scale web applications. Google, Amazon and similar web properties were seen as having higher data throughput than the traditional stalwarts of data processing, banking and finance, which have more traditional (mainframe and SQL) data stores. This focussed attention on the architectures that the likes of Google and Amazon were using for data, and brought non-relational data stores (key-value stores in particular) into the mainstream. The well-publicised scaling problems with applications such as Twitter or Craigslist and their solutions that replaced, augmented, or adapted their traditional SQL oriented databases with caches, sharding, document databases, and other fit-for-purpose data stores that were decidedly not a pure SQL RDMBS solution. Over time, large web properties have highlighted specific areas where traditional database approaches have failed, such as the ability to handle the data requirements of social graphs (Facebook). Even non-web applications have felt the pressure of increasing data requirements, from complex event processing to the enterprise application of map-reduce technologies. Application architects have been encouraged by the successes of high profile applications. Their own applications are subject to higher loads, and their existing data models have been compromised or adapted anyway (such as by denormalising data structures or adding caches). This compromise and adaptation has resulted in an appetite for the alternative data stores seen in high profile applications within their own projects.

The context of emerging support for data models that are not exclusively SQL based is important. Problems that have been addressed by large web properties are the same that are being seen by emerging applications and business models. The characteristics of high availability, high load through an increasing number of devices and users, complex datatypes and, importantly, the need to serve content at a very low cost per user, are becoming base requirements for all applications. The lessons, patterns, and technologies of the early adopters of data storage variety are directly applicable, relevant, and are being actively adopted by developers.

Regardless of support for SQL databases in general (often by database vendors), or in specific domains in which they excel, the awareness of the need for alternative data stores is gaining serious and credible traction. Even a wall-to-wall SQL-only environment will, at some point, need to implement a cache in front of the database. This is only a hop, skip and jump from serious consideration of distributed cache, which alters the particular applications database landscape and affects the data model.

The influence of cloud computing on data models

It would be disingenuous to suggest that cloud computing applications alone have been the cause of the changes to data models. It is the style of applications developed for the cloud that have had a significant impact. Whether running on a public cloud platform such as Windows Azure, or in a dedicated datacentre, applications that take advantage of distributed databases on top of commodity hardware have had a profound influence. These modern applications have to serve a huge number of users for marginal cost. They are broken down into discrete services that share nothing but interface contracts. The developers that build them use frameworks that treat data differently; no longer bowing to senior datacentre DBAs but rather wanting active involvement and supporting the 'devops' culture. The nature of the applications, the frameworks, and the developer culture has given rise to NoSQL, which has changed the incumbent data model and supporting database technologies. Despite the proliferation of traditional database technologies on cloud platforms, mainly in an attempt to appeal to the enterprise market, the cloud computing culture will continue to exert influence on how we build data stores to support applications well into the future.

Risks of inadequate data modelling

When it comes to data and databases, a degree of laziness has crept in to general database development practices. SQL databases have been solid, reliable, well understood, and mostly coped with the demands of applications and development frameworks. Data, over time, became less of an issue and has been treated with disdain by developers that have little concern over the 'persistence layer' — trivialising the role that databases play in applications. This has not been solely the result of developer attitudes, but the draconian role DBAs have played in distancing developers from data responsibilities, and the continued improvement in tooling and frameworks which remove the need for developer attention to databases, such as the adoption of ORMs. Continued database performance increases, due to hardware improvement (particularly available memory and disk I/O performance), have also contributed to increased database reliability.

This blasé developer focus results in repeated problems such as poor database performance due to suboptimal queries (often due to an over-reliance on the ORM), or excessive load on the database because it is used as a single store for all shared state. These problems exist in all applications, but a lack of attention to data, and the data model, becomes a serious concern in cloud applications, as illustrated by the examples below:

- Database performance at scale. Shared state is the bane of high scalability. Web servers scale out well and individual servers can serve requests in isolation of any others that may be doing the same. Databases, whether designed to scale-out in a distributed manner or configured for scale-up on a single machine, have to be far more cognisant of other processes. Databases must ensure that they have the latest version of a piece of data, blocking reads while particular updates take place, or making sure that constantly changing data is backed up and fault tolerant. At scale, when thousands of users are trying to access data, for concurrent reads and writes, the data model and underlying database technologies become the single most significant performance bottleneck. Inattention to data concerns, and inadequate data modelling, cause applications to collapse when they are placed under significant load. The result of poor database performance when an application scales may not be solved easily. Applications running on cloud platforms run into infrastructure limitations due to the commodity devices on which the infrastructure is built, as well as other limitations on bandwidth, latency, disk performance, and available memory. The mantra of 'throw more hardware at the problem', which is generally a scale-up solution, is not applicable on an infrastructure-limited cloud platform. The problem is not solved by on-premise infrastructure either, where the provisioning of capacity, with the accompanying cost and lead times of sophisticated hardware, is measured in months, rather than minutes. In either case, the poor performance of the database cannot be solved quickly enough to satisfy users and customers who inevitably move to alternatives with no intention, or likelihood, of returning.
- Shared databases encourage tight coupling. Cloud applications endeavour to separate independent workloads into discrete services. The interface between services should be at a scalable endpoint, not the underlying database. The implementation of a single data model, particularly one implemented within a single database, discourages the use of independent services. This means that the application components cannot be loosely coupled, as the database or data

model forms the basis of the tight coupling and this cannot easily be removed. The result of tightly coupled services is that they are less fault-tolerant, less able to scale, and more complex to deploy and operate.
- Security is a major issue to be dealt with in cloud computing projects. Insufficient data modelling can expose the data to security threats.
- Application availability is one of the primary requirements for all applications, and it is often the database, as a single point of failure, that has the most impact on it. Availability problems can be easily addressed by, for example, replicating data or using eventual consistency models, but availability problems need to be understood, addressed, and modelled in the data model to ensure that availability is as expected.

Data is widely dispersed

The simplistic view of data is that a user captures some data, it is processed and stored in a database, and some more data is retrieved from a database to display to the user. This monolithic thinking, where there is one database that is written to and read from, is a common view and is an oversimplification of the problem of handling data in applications. Even applications that have a single primary database will still tend to use multiple data stores such as caches and client-side data stores.

The example below shows a typical web application and tracks the data stored, generated, retrieved, and presented for what would be considered a simple operation such as a user capturing some data and presenting a result.

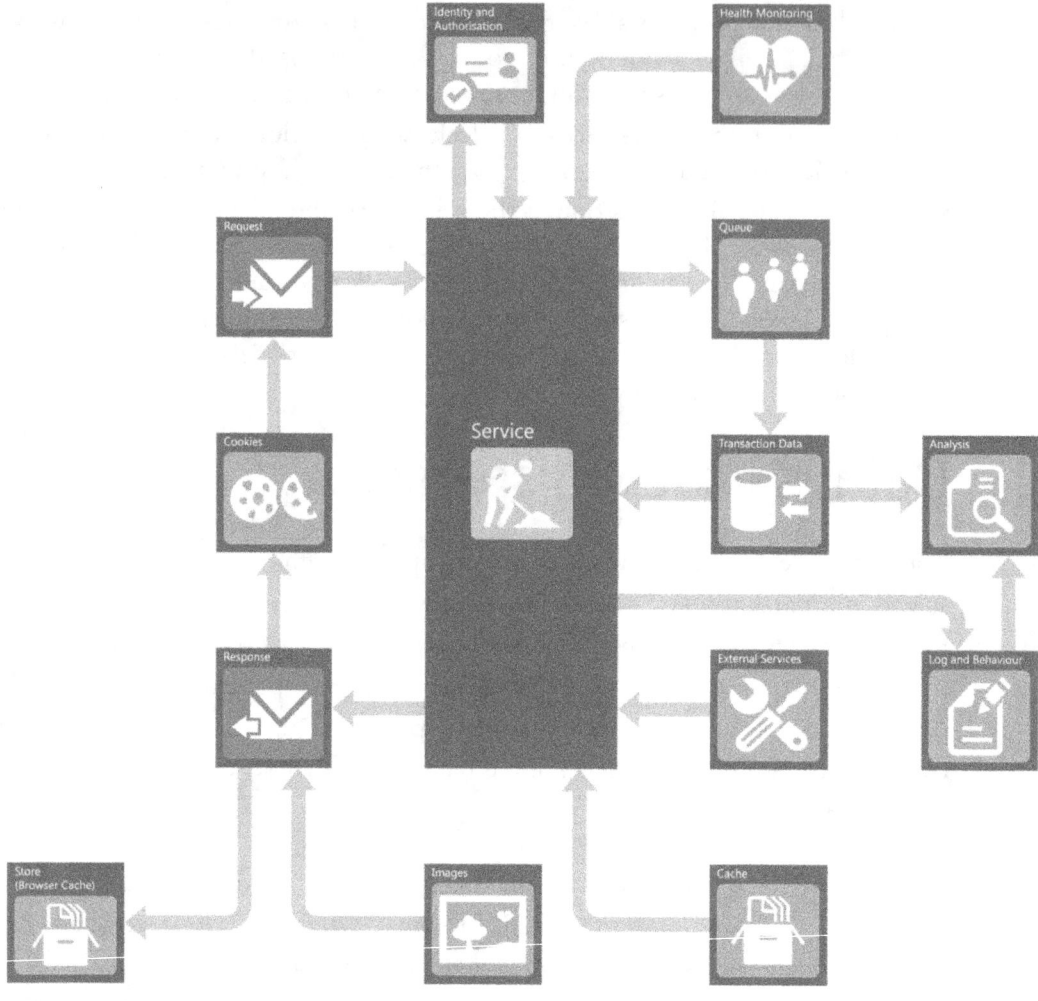

The example illustrates no less than eleven data stores that are used for a simple feature. Some are not considered 'core' databases but are important, necessary, and useful in their own right, such as the log and behaviour data stores. Every one of these data stores needs to be modelled, in the context of the service that they perform, in order for them to be developed properly. All eleven have structure, performance requirements, availability issues, latency, security, operations, deployments and other aspects that need to be considered in sufficient detail.

The following list contains most of the data stores that need to be considered:

- Client-side data — such as client cache, cookies and other state management data stores that are used. Desktops and mobile devices may have more sophisticated stores that need to be modelled in more detail.
- Static content — such as images and even static (JSON) data lists that are accessible by a browser. Static data is almost never perpetually static, and needs to be refreshed, versioned and even secured.
- Session state — whether on the client or the server, session state requires particular attention. Determining what data is part of the actual session, rather than transactional data that needs to be kept beyond the session, is the first step of the data modelling problem.
- Service Contracts - external providers of data, where control over the data is limited, have service contracts for data that need to be modelled and included in the consuming application.
- Messages — messages have structure that needs to be modelled, and most messaging approaches favour reliable messaging, meaning that the data is persisted in a data store. While this persistence is mostly taken care of by the messaging service, it does introduce additional data problems, such as multiple message deliveries, that need to be addressed.
- Business transaction data — the core data within an application, whether stored in a SQL or NoSQL database, needs to be well modelled. Fortunately most architects and designers, backed up by DBAs and IT governance, give this kind of data sufficient attention.
- Function optimised data — some data may be stored in a specific way to serve a single function. For example, data can be transposed into documents that are indexed by search servers (such as SOLR), and these documents need to be correctly modelled in a structure that can be indexed and satisfy the search requirements.
- Blob data — and other 'unstructured' data needs to be modelled, if not for the basic structure that exists, but for security, performance, bandwidth, duplication across a CDN, and other aspects.
- Data analysis — traditional OLAP, data mining, and newer big data approaches using map-reduce, event processing and related tools need to be understood and modelled in detail. The ability to perform analysis as quickly as possible for the lowest storage and compute cost is an important consideration in cloud-based architectures.
- Transactional reporting — the production of reports from the primary transactional database can bring a database to its knees. Modern, high-load scalable web applications need specific attention given to transactional reports so that primary application performance and availability are not impacted.

- Data synchronisation — with applications comprised of multiple, loosely-coupled services, the sharing of data across service boundaries needs to be understood. Where data resides, how the master database is updated, what can be shared, and so on are important aspects of data synchronisation that need to be modelled.
- Cache — the cache is one of the most important data stores as its impact on performance and scalability is significant. Unfortunately, it is often left up to individual developers as to what data to cache, creating scalability problems in production. What data to cache, setting expiry rules, warming up of the cache when a service loads, and so on, need to be modelled in sufficient detail in order to get the most benefit.

The need for multiple data stores

There is no one-size-fits-all solution to data and databases. Models that underlie specific technologies solve specific problems that may not be applicable anywhere else. For example, a cache data store needs to serve up data very quickly, and is less concerned with transactional correctness or data loss than a SQL database would be. That same correctness and concern about data loss makes SQL a poor choice to satisfy the demands of a cache.

The diagram below demonstrates how different database needs, supported by different technologies, have different strengths and weaknesses. SQL, for example, has high consistency and high availability per node, but a low partition tolerance and a low ability to handle flexible database schemas. Whereas the low latency of a cache is offset by its equally low consistency.

Data Model **205**

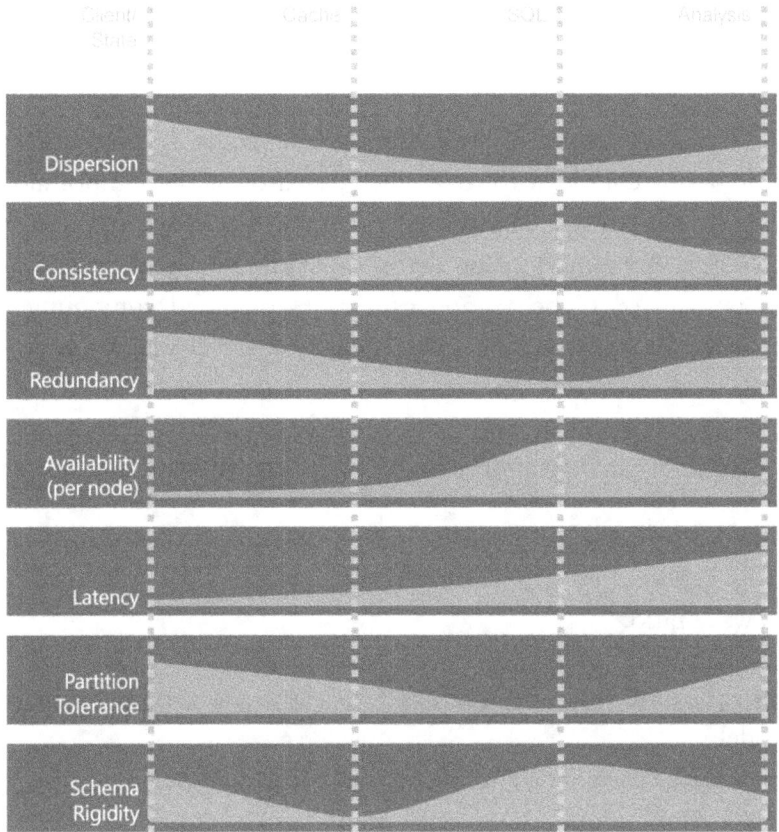

Fundamental to the data model and cloud-based architectures is the realisation that multiple data stores are required to satisfy the varying data demands of the application. The development of the data model is not about finding the single database technology, but about uncovering the application requirements and matching them to technology choices. The subsequent architectural challenge then becomes dealing with the multitude of databases, minimising the effort and skill required to keep them running, and to keep a handle on data flowing between them.

The emergence of NoSQL

NoSQL, probably as a result of the name, is often perceived as an anti-SQL movement. It is not anti-SQL, but is it a movement with significant support from the software development 'hacker' community. NoSQL is about the selection of database technologies that are architecturally appropriate to the task at hand. It just so happens that many tasks are not appropriate to SQL, resulting in what is seen as an anti-SQL position.

NoSQL is beyond the context of this book, but understanding the reason for the emergence of database technologies that are not based on SQL is important, in order to develop an application data model correctly. The drivers behind the emergence of NoSQL are rooted in the demands of modern applications. Any application that is assessed to be a good candidate for cloud computing will exhibit characteristics that make a monolithic SQL database ill-suited. These can be summarised as:

- A business case that cannot support high, up-front hardware and licensing costs.
- A need to minimise operational costs resulting from long-term maintenance agreements and dependency on specialised skills.
- High read to write ratio.
- Little business demand for high degrees of data consistency.
- Unstructured or binary data that does not fit well in a third-normal form relational model.
- High data volumes that exceed the economically meaningful value of single scaled-up databases.
- Developer attitudes, where the SQL database is not considered sacrosanct, result in the acceptance of other technologies to achieve the application objectives.

These are discussed in more detail below.

Commodity devices

Enterprise SQL databases generally run on high performance hardware that is engineered to specifically serve the needs of the database. They contain multiple high performance processors (including RISC-based), significant amounts of high performance RAM, and a storage subsystem that spans high performance NAND storage on the bus (e.g. Fusion I/O[41]) to high throughput networking, and large SAN storage systems. These enterprise database servers can hardly be called 'servers' as they are made up of a sophisticated assembly of high

---

[41] http://www.fusionio.com/

performance servers, networking equipment, disks, specialised software, monitoring tools, and operators with specialist skills and experience.

Such a high performance infrastructure does not exist as a usable unit on the cloud (it may indeed exist to run the platform, but is not accessible to customers). Instead, customers have to make do with relatively small commodity servers that run as virtual machines on a shared infrastructure that can never be optimised (or even analysed) for a specific customer purpose. SQL databases prefer as much processing power and memory on the same bus coupled with a high throughput, low latency, and low collision disk subsystem. Also, high availability SQL is generally implemented as clusters, which share storage systems and require significant network capacity. Few of these requirements can be addressed with a shared, commodity virtualised infrastructure. As a result, applications running in cloud environments have been forced to implement databases that can perform adequately on a relatively low performance infrastructure, meaning that traditional SQL databases are a bad fit.

Cost of procurement

Enterprise IT vendors have made good money from high performance enterprise databases; be those hardware suppliers like IBM, or database vendors like Oracle and Microsoft. The high prices for enterprise software licenses of database products go hand-in-hand with licenses for other components (such as backup and storage), as well as long-term maintenance agreements. Not only do the infrastructure and licenses cost a lot, but installation and setup often needs to be performed by specialised and expensive consultants who assemble the database on site.

This cost of procurement can exceed software development costs, and any budget spent on infrastructure cannot be spent on adding features or attracting customers. Such a bias in cost towards infrastructure can be debilitating for the business plan. The ability of NoSQL technologies to run on commodity hardware (as provided by cloud providers), the ability to scale easily (reducing the up-front infrastructure commitment), coupled with the free license of open source, creates a compelling case to investigate the technical suitability of the significantly cheaper alternative.

The nature of data

Modern applications satisfy varying data needs within a single application, such as:

- Transactional structured data.
- Binary data, such as media, which can be served in blocks or streamed.
- Searching on data which changes infrequently.
- Different data structures contained within a single 'document' structure.
- Data generated as a side effect of normal operations, such as log data.
- Data that spans stores and structures but is grouped within a social graph (or other graph, such as 'those who bought this, also bought that')

Of the above examples, only traditional structured data is well suited to SQL, the rest either do not work at all or are suboptimally addressed by SQL. All of the others require approaches to data that are not strengths of SQL. The degree to which any of these are required may differ from one application to the next, but the crucial point is that a typical, modern application will have multiple types of data that need to be stored and accessed.

Data access patterns

Modern applications have variable data access patterns which are different from traditional enterprise applications. For example:

- Web applications generally have read:write ratios where the number of reads is orders of magnitude more than writes. This necessitates the use of database caches in order to avoid placing excessive and unnecessary load on the database.
- Consumer oriented applications have little need for absolute data consistency. It is tolerable (and not even noticed) if data is a little out of date.
- A single application can have a high read:write ratio (for example, viewing the catalogue) as well as a need for high write:read (for example, logging) or an even ratio (for example, social updates). This requires radically different approaches to data within a single application.
- Consumer oriented applications have very little user customisation for queries (there are no custom reports), so a database query language (and the supporting underlying model) is less important, as queries are purpose built in the application layer.

- Modern applications tend to integrate with other services in real-time wherever possible (such as handing off to fulfilment or querying the social graph for recommendations), and have very few after-hours batch operations.

These variable data access patterns, as well as the introduction of some that are unique to modern applications, heavily influence the application data models, as well as the underlying data stores.

Data volumes

Modern applications, particularly those exposed to consumers, generate significant amounts of data. The data generated may not be in the form of business transactions, but in the data that is generated that has some secondary value. Where applications in the past may only have concerned themselves with dealing with the current operation a user is performing, modern applications need to keep track of past operations (for example, recent items viewed), and derive potential future operations (for example recommendations). These high volumes of data may only be relevant and useful for a short period (for example, trending topics in an individual's social graph), or may want to be kept for later analysis (for example, log files), where value can only be extracted when combined with other data points or datasets.

Storing and querying huge amounts of data in a SQL database, while possible, may not be appropriate or economical. In a world of low margins and free-to-use services, the cost of storing formal transactions in a SQL database may be viable, but storing tens of thousands of pieces of information in an expensive data store for a user that has no immediate business value may not make economical sense.

The cost per transaction and cost per query of a SQL database may not make sense within the business case. For example, the cost of a SQL database (and infrastructure) to run the equivalent of a one hour query on a 1,000 Hadoop cluster weighs heavily against SQL. Similar considerations on write-heavy operations favour technologies like Apache Cassandra[42] over SQL.

---

[42] http://cassandra.apache.org

Developer attitudes

Trying to generalise the relationship that developers have with SQL databases is impossible. Some developers are dismissive and see it merely as a persistence store. Some have significant SQL skills and can get the most out of the database. Others rely on SQL as a crutch to make mistakes appear less costly. One thing that is clear about the relationship between developers and databases over the last few years is that it is becoming more distant. Some developers have embraced ORMs in an attempt to abstract the problem away; others have moved away from SQL wherever possible and adopted alternative data stores. Many enterprise developers have either had their intimate SQL relationship ruined by DBAs, or have been turned into database developers, where stored procedures are where the magic happens.

The developer attitudes and their influence on the database architecture cannot be underestimated. Unless an application already has an existing database and supporting engineering practices, developers are the architects, and their influence on the application data store is profound. Where application architectures drive database architectures, alternative data stores are more likely. Some of the influences on developer attitudes towards databases include:

- The unwinnable ORM war — Developers have been arguing about Object Relational Mapping (ORM) and ORM frameworks for so long that every few years a new generation of developers pick up the gauntlet and argue about it all over again. ORMs are an okay, but not perfect, solution to a difficult problem of mapping between objects and the relational model. After a while, developers get fed up with the effort, compromise, and arguments, and look for alternatives where mapping is unnecessary. They often find document databases a good solution, hence the rise of CouchDB[43] and MongoDB[44].
- Seeking alternatives for database bottlenecks — When applications need to scale, it is inevitably the database that is the most difficult component to scale. Even non-scaling applications spend more time waiting for results from the database (any database, not just SQL) than anything else. Inevitably developers look to profile and optimise these database performance

---

[43] http://couchdb.apache.org

[44] http://www.mongodb.org

bottlenecks and will, at the very least, start looking at what can be cached, so that database round trips can be saved. This leads to looking at distributed cache, cache expiry, eventual consistency, and other principles, techniques and technologies that veer away from SQL as a solution.

- Writing stored procedures isn't cool — As recently as 2005, the 'standard' pattern for data oriented applications was to encapsulate all data access in stored procedures and only interface with the database via stored procedures. This meant that most developers were writing some of the most important code in a stored procedure language rather than the language of the application stack. Over time, developers have moved away from stored procedures, influenced by software engineering principles (too much logic in the database language cannot be tested), advances in languages and frameworks that make application code better and more 'fun' to write (such as LINQ in .NET), and the use of ORMs (a paradigm incompatible with the task specific nature of stored procedures). Modern developers, although they may have good database skills, tend to avoid stored procedures, making the migration to another database platform far easier.

Databases on ACID

One of the most important and useful features of SQL RDBMSs is their support of ACID transactions. ACID refers to the properties (Atomicity, Consistency, Isolation, and Durability) that guarantee that transactions are processed reliably. Mainstream SQL databases fervently support ACID and other principles to ensure that data is always consistent and reliable, and while it is not necessarily the most important part of a SQL database, it often positioned as such. The driving of such features and the knock-on effects of database backups, fail-over scenarios and technologies, tools and operating environments becomes so all-encompassing that the business need for ACID becomes lost in all the sales hype and rhetoric.

When analysed in detail, the actual need for immediate database consistency is very low, and there are few scenarios where it is absolutely necessary. It turns out that the demand for digital perfection is not practically applied to the real world where things get lost, broken, miscounted or stolen. Data architect Pat Helland (from Microsoft and Amazon) spoke about 'Screw-ups and Apologies'[45] where

---

[45] http://blogs.msdn.com/b/pathelland/archive/2008/05/02/link-to-the-video-of-the-irresistible-forces-meet-the-movable-objects.aspx

he observed that even with absolute data consistency, things are bound to go wrong outside the database, and business has to develop approaches to deal with the resultant problems (such as apologising to customers). The example he references is that in an e-commerce scenario, a stock system can have an exact count of widgets available, but when the order is placed for the last item, it may have been run over by a forklift. The response to the customer if the item was run over by a forklift is indistinguishable from the response if there was inconsistent data. In both cases the response would be an apology. The argument being that since businesses have to cater for 'apologies and screw-ups' anyway, why try and aim for the perfection of consistent data (with the associated cost, performance degradation, and potential disappointment)?

Werner Vogels (Amazon CTO) is quoted as saying, "If you're concerned about scalability, any algorithm that forces you to run agreement will eventually become your bottleneck. Take that as a given". This refers to the architectural effort and cost associated with consistency (agreement between nodes). This is important for applications that need to scale, as the first step in building out the architecture is determining the need for consistency. Putting all the architecture in place to support an unnecessary requirement is wasteful and pointless.

If there is a low need for real-time consistency across databases or concurrent connections, how do we deal with consistency problems if they occur? There are a number of techniques, the first being the ability to handle inconsistency within the business model (apology-based computing), or having processes to cope with errors (see Starbucks Does Not Use Two-Phase Commit- Gregor Hohpe[46]), and the other techniques are variations of eventual consistency. Eventual consistency refers to the model where a specific piece of data may not be consistent across nodes at a point in time, but eventually will be. Asynchronous processing and idempotent data, all of which should be familiar in distributed computing (cloud) environments, support this model.

The impact of this thinking on SQL databases is devastating. Even though ACID is not the only good thing about SQL, it is one of the features that have been aggressively marketed for decades as being very important. Dismissing the need for ACID undermines the carefully assembled value proposition of SQL

---

[46] http://www.eaipatterns.com/ramblings/18_starbucks.html

databases and allows other databases to gain a foothold based on their own particular strengths.

Cost of operations

Whether it is in the very nature of the difficulty of the problem that SQL databases are addressing, the sophistication of particular SQL products, the need to understand product idiosyncrasies, or the secret-handshake cabal of SQL DBAs, the cost of operating a SQL database is significant. Not only is the supporting infrastructure costly, but so too are the licenses, on-going support agreements and, most importantly, the cost of specialised DBA skills.

DBAs can have a particularly hard time keeping databases going, especially when those databases are under extreme load. Not only do they need the specialised database skills, but they also need a lot more business knowledge than one would think necessary. An intimate understanding of the business implications and reasons for long running batch operations becomes expensive knowledge to keep around. To top it all, DBAs are paged when things break and are often blamed as the cause; it is expensive to keep highly skilled scapegoats around.

As observed by Werner Vogels - Amazon CTO[47] "Structured data management systems are traditionally served by relational databases but these sophisticated systems have their limitations, especially when it comes to scale and reliability. Often they also require tremendous expertise to operate efficiently and reliably especially when scaling up. Of course, a significant portion of the structured data world does not require RDBMS features such as complex transactions and relations, and can be served by a simpler, much more agile system."

So while something like Windows Azure Table storage has only few features compared to its SQL counterpart, the cost of operating Windows Azure Table Storage is minimal. Most of the storage part is handled by the service, and a database technology that doesn't support indexes or advanced queries leaves little need for a specialised resource for database optimisation. The high differential between the costs of specialised DBAs, and generalist operators that loosely fall

---

[47] http://www.allthingsdistributed.com/2009/10/amazon_relational_database_service.html

under the 'Devops' banner, is significant for the cost optimisation of applications that scale.

Giving up the pursuit of an absolute truth

One of the promises of the relational model supported by SQL databases was the idea that a single database could contain an accurate model of the business. Both in terms of semantic accuracy, with normalised structures properly representing the business domain, and in terms of database accuracy, supported by consistency and application agnostic API. Those ideals of an 'absolute truth' contained within the database have been dashed. Business spans multiple databases in multiple organisations or business units, held together by the duct-tape of integration technologies that have dubious mappings, odd integration schedules, and few reliable ways of ensuring that data is clean and accurate. Under-performing databases have been 'optimised' for application performance, de-normalising data or spreading data across systems and databases. Database professionals have all but given up on having a single model and single database for the business as it is simply unattainable and impractical.

Against this backdrop of multiple data sources for applications, the spreading of data across multiple technologies for a single application is both tolerable and standard practice. It allows for the selection of the correct type of database for different parts of the application, and the 'integration' between different databases.

The case for SQL

The above discussion on SQL versus NoSQL should not be considered an anti-SQL position, and most within the NoSQL 'movement' try and express NoSQL as 'Not Only SQL'. This acknowledges that SQL does have an important, well-deserved, and valuable place in data storage and retrieval. Any overtly anti-SQL sentiment is largely focussed on being against the perception that SQL is the only solution to all SQL problems.

When developing the data model, make sure that SQL is not overlooked, and be cognisant of its strong points and where it fits into the application architecture. The points below highlight some of the compelling benefits of SQL:

The relational model is pretty good

The relational model that sits at the core of SQL is a good one. It allows for the data model to be encapsulated and developed against with relative ease. Other databases may be optimised for a specific purpose and therefore not have as good an underlying model. Document databases, for example, store individual atomic documents, and are unable to support cross collection (or table, or relation) queries with the same ease as SQL.

SQL is a well understood standard

SQL has been used extensively within enterprises for about twenty years, and that time has allowed it to become the entrenched standard. Because of specialised features on different databases, the tools between different database platforms are incompatible with one another (SQL Server tools cannot really be used on Oracle, and vice versa), but many of the skills are (at least developer skills), and database drivers and frameworks have abstracted some of the idiosyncrasies away. Ultimately the basic operations between databases are very similar, including operational processes. Contrast this to other database technologies, where the skills are specific, and generally not transferable. This lack of transferability of skills is not just because the products are different, but also because the underlying model is different. Windows Azure Table Storage and MongoDB, for example, have completely different approaches to data and different underlying models (key-value versus document).

Applications and tools for SQL

Apart from the tooling by database vendors themselves, thousands of applications and tools support SQL. From large scale ERP systems like SAP, to specialised ETL tools, to web application content management systems. Virtually every product that is available, whether off-the-shelf, or custom built, supports SQL Server, or Oracle, or MySQL, or all three. This is not only unavoidable when you need a particular product in your solution (such as CMS), but also when integrating with other tools and applications.

Vendor support

Although the on-going support agreements can be very expensive, the support of SQL databases by vendors is extensive. Well-established documentation, refined over the years, preferential and effective support services, consulting services, migration and upgrade tools, and many other services exist for the mainstream SQL databases. Newer databases, many based on open-source, do not offer the same type of support. While community support may be extensive and paid-for support available, it does not compare to large vendor support (at least for enterprises).

Framework support

Just about every development environment, persistence framework (such as ORMs) and language, supports SQL. From ODBC, ADO.NET, native drivers at the low level, to higher level support of product specific SQL syntax, the support of SQL is extensive. Having to take your favourite framework and find or learn a new database API for another data store may be too much to take on.

Suitability to low scale applications

SQL shows its cracks at scale. Large databases or those under heavy load need to be custom configured, continuously optimised and carefully nurtured. This is not the case for smaller databases, which are easy to use, self-contained and very little hassle (the definition of 'smaller' is a bit vague). If an application does not require heavy database needs, using a SQL database to do everything may be the easiest, simplest, and most cost effective solution.

Flexibility

The philosophy of modelling the business semantics accurately in the relational model, combined with the declarative nature of the SQL language, makes SQL very flexible in its support of varying requirements. Once you have defined a structure correctly, you can assume that various combinations of inserts, queries, joins and other operations can be performed on the structure without needing to know up-front what those operations will be. Because other databases are optimised for specific purposes, they are less flexible in their ability to be applied to all the data needs of an application. For example, document databases need careful thought about what constitutes a document (or collection), as it may not be applicable for another, as yet unknown purpose. Windows Azure Table Storage suffers from this problem, where the choice partition and row keys have a big impact on how the data store can be used.

Performance

For all the noise about SQL under performing in particular scenarios, it generally performs very well. Virtual Machine infrastructure available on cloud platforms is getting more memory, faster I/O (such as SSD support), and faster processors. This makes a cloud based 'commodity' machine a beast that can handle significant load. Poor database performance can also be linked to bad architecture, such as inadequate caching, or bad implementation (such as N+1 queries resulting from ORM use), or over-optimistic transaction isolation. These performance problems can be addressed in the application without throwing out SQL. Virtually any database will under-perform if it is used inappropriately or put under unnecessary and excessive load. NoSQL is still subjected to the same misuse with potentially more damaging effects.

Post-relational features

SQL database vendors have long been aware of the limitations imposed by the rational model and have, over the years, extended SQL to support 'post-relational' features. This doesn't magically turn them into solutions to every problem (the strength of alternatives is that they are optimised for specific problems), but does add useful functionality in some cases. These features should be used sparingly and with careful consideration, but are useful and powerful if used responsibly. For example, an application that needs geospatial datatype support for storing the location of retail outlets may find it better to use the geospatial functions of SQL, rather than a full-featured GIS solution.

SQL databases support some interesting and useful features, such as XML fields, semantic search, file-system binary objects, geospatial datatypes and queries, and non-SQL languages for stored procedures (Java, .NET CLR etc.). Interesting in

Windows Azure SQL Database is the support of sharding in the federations feature[48], which facilitates the automated scale-out of SQL on Windows Azure.

What data to model

Data models are simplistically thought of as static structures that can be modelled once and are applicable to the entire application. Typically models are produced that represent either the physical database using ERD (Entity Relationship Diagram) notation, or the application object model using a UML class diagram. Seldom are models produced that describe both or that describe any interaction or mapping between the two. In addition to static structures, models are required to depict the flow of data between services, but this practice has fallen out of standard practice.

The first question is what data do I need to model? Do I model the SQL database, the message structures or the data archive data store? The short answer is that everything needs to be modelled. In modern applications data exists and is persisted in so many places which all need to be carefully understood. For the purpose of ensuring that the application model doesn't stomp all over the application object or domain model, it is better to define *everything* to be all data that is persisted. So where is data persisted?

- On the client in cookies, local databases or files.
- Web server session state or cache.
- Distributed cache.
- Transactional databases such as SQL.
- Databases used for analysis and BI.
- Databases used for specific purposes, such as for search.
- Staging databases used for integration.
- Flat files (or flat database structures), such as with log files.
- Databases external to the application or organisation.

---

[48] http://msdn.microsoft.com/en-us/library/windowsazure/hh597452.aspx

Determine data schemas

Some of the architectural principles in cloud computing applications (workload model, scalability model, availability model) result in loosely coupled and independent services. In order to implement loose coupling, there should be very little shared between the applications, other than network infrastructure. The sharing of databases should be carefully considered and avoided where scalability, fault isolation, and other requirements become important. As a result, applications can have multiple database schemas.

Consider, for example, a typical e-commerce application. If we look at the stock/catalogue data, we can see that it can be separated into multiple schemas that are related to different workloads, such as:

- The 'master' catalogue that contains pricing, suppliers, distributors, seasons, and all other data needed to plan and operate the business. Administrative users would be the primary users of this data, and it is important that it is correct and accurate.
- The 'stock' schema would be a subset of the master catalogue, and contain the exact number of items for each SKU in stock. This data would result from logistics and distribution processes, and is important for order fulfilment. The load on the database may be quite low if the ratio of product views on the web to orders is high.
- The 'store catalogue' schema is the one that customers use to view products via the web. This database will be read-only and optimised for search. It will contain a subset of the master catalogue, and include links to images and related products. This schema may also contain, possibly in a separate database, all product reviews made by customers.
- The 'recommendations' schema stores browsing history of products viewed, wish lists, orders, and other data that could be used for product recommendations. The recommendations could be derived in real-time, or by a process that mines or analyses the data.

The above example illustrates that something as simple as a store catalogue can, and should, be treated as multiple schemas (and most likely multiple databases) depending on the workload and the requirement. It is easy to imagine that the master catalogue, which is frequently updated by a handful of staff members, has completely different requirements (performance, integrity, availability, etc.) to the schema that thousands of customers are using when browsing the store.

The process, when trying to determine the schemas, is to identify significant requirement variations. These will highlight suspect areas where data is either different, or needs to be handled in a different manner.

Indications of schema separation

One of the biggest architectural challenges is determining the different schemas within a single application, or collection of services. Getting the schema separation wrong can result in an application that cannot cope under certain scenarios, or is difficult to maintain or extend. The indications listed below can be used as a starting point for identifying different schemas, or as a sanity check against schemas that have already been identified:

- Business separation — In many cases, even though data may be logically contained within a single schema, there may be a clear business reason why they have to be separate. Perhaps the data 'belongs' to a different organisation or department that is responsible for the integrity of the data, or which owns the underlying asset represented by the data (e.g. accounts).
- Service separation — Decisions to separate an application into services because of different workloads (as per the workload model), clearly indicate separate schemas. Different services tend to avoid the sharing of a single database resource for availability, capacity, loose coupling, and other reasons.
- Volume — Large differences in the amount of data, either as the number of entities (rows) or the storage required, can strongly indicate the need for separate schemas. For example, in short-term insurance, there can be significantly more quotations produced than actual policies sold.
- Throughput (Velocity) — Similar to volume (after all, high throughput results in high volume), throughput defined as the number of entities/rows processed per second can indicate a separate schema. For example, the logging of products viewed by customers (used for recommendations and analysis) is going to result in orders of magnitude more writes than writes to the logging entities than the product entities.
- Variation — Data that has structural variety can indicate schema separation through the need to store the data in different databases suited to a particular structure. For example, transactional data (such as orders) can be stored within SQL, and searchable data (such as products) can be stored in a Lucene[49]-backed database.

---

[49] http://lucene.apache.org/

- Integrity — Some parts of an application may require more data integrity than others. For example, ensuring data integrity is very important for orders, but less so with product recommendations.
- Availability — When modelling availability, variation of service and feature availability becomes apparent, and this variation also applies to the availability of the underlying data. There is little point in storing data in a highly available database when the application itself neither needs, nor is capable of, high availability.
- Security and regulatory compliance — Cases where different data has different security requirements, especially when the requirements for specific data are more stringent than the rest of the data, may indicate the need for a separate schema. Increased security should be backed by a business reason. Similarly, regulatory and compliance issues may require that some data, such as customer or credit card data, is treated differently to other data.

Clearly identify shared data resources

Where data cannot be separated into different schemas and separate databases, the applications have to share the same physical resource. This can create a performance bottleneck and a single point of availability failure. There are cases (such as identity) where it is unavoidable. Shared data resources should be explicitly and clearly identified, so that they can be reviewed for absolute necessity, and dealt with as elements that require special engineering attention.

Model each schema

Once the schemas have been identified they needed to be modelled in sufficient detail.

Level of detail and format of models

It is neither practical nor necessary to model all data in absolute detail. Excessive data modelling in the absence of application design and architecture can also inhibit the design and development process. This data biased approach would effectively paint the application architecture into a corner that may be difficult to get out of.

The detail and format of the data model in each schema will largely depend on the development approaches, methodology, type of project, and make-up of the implementation teams. It will also be influenced by the technology choices that are made for both the application and the underlying database. For example, a detailed third normal form entity relationship diagram will not be applicable to a problem that is going to be solved by, say, a key-value store. The experience on the team and the maturity of traditional database modelling techniques, although logically applicable, need to be adapted to handle database requirements that go beyond traditional SQL databases.

The model detail described below extends beyond the database structure, and encourages broader questions about data and the database. The primary consideration, at least during the initial stages of design, is that a one-database-fits-all solution does not exist, so more fundamental questions need to be asked about the data. Therefore, the model detail should contain information about availability requirements, the need for data consistency, the physical location of the data, the types of queries to be run, and other aspects that are seldom asked with traditional databases. These details need to be questioned, addressed and documented.

Model Detail

Structure

The data structure would seem to be the simplest and most obvious part of the data model. This is true with applications that are underpinned by a SQL database, and are built using a bottom-up approach where the business semantic requirements are captured in the physical SQL database. This bottom-up approach is popular where applications are not greenfield developments, where architects have a strong database background and bias, and in environments where DBAs and data specialists have more power and architectural influence than their application development counterparts.

Modern applications and modern software engineering development approaches are not necessarily structured bottom-up and are more concerned with the domain model (from [Domain-Driven Design](http://domaindrivendesign.org/)[50]), which is implemented in the application layer. This application model centric approach puts physical database modelling much later during implementation. Once their classes are built and tested, developers will begin the process of developing or generating a physical database model that then gets mapped to the domain.

The reality in most enterprises is that the relationship between application developers that support a top-down approach and database professionals that support a bottom-up approach ranges from an uneasy truce to outright hostility. Both have their (valid) points of view, the debate will never be settled, and resolving it is definitely out of scope for cloud projects. For the purposes of the data model in the early stages of design, either approach is good enough, but the bottom-up approach does run the risk of making premature assumptions about the physical database technologies and implementation. Using a SQL biased model, such as an ERD (Entity Relationship Diagram) or even physical database scripts, serves as valuable input to the application design process (to help create the Domain), but should not be seen as the final structural model.

The structural model should be a logical representation, rather than a physical one, and contain metadata that represents the structure that is as close to the (logical) domain as possible. Depending on the particular development methodology it can be an ERD, Class Diagram, XSD, or similar model that uses the notations of the modelling language. It can also be a simpler and less formal diagram created in something like Visio, which uses simple shapes and a less rigorous notation. The model should at least represent the following:

- Entities/Classes
- Primary Keys/Object Identifiers
- Natural Keys
- Relationships/Foreign Key Constraints/Collection Properties
- Data types
- Naming, particularly Entities/Classes and Fields/Properties

The data structure model is expected to evolve, and become more fixed over time as the application is implemented. Some parts will end up as specific classes,

---

[50] http://domaindrivendesign.org/

with accompanying detailed SQL scripts and mapping for the database. Others may stay logical, as application developers make use of data stores where structure is less important. By the time the structure reaches those levels of detail, its influence on the overall approach to data is minimal. The initial logical structure, as part of the data models developed during design, are the most important for providing valuable input.

Unstructured data

Where data is deemed to be 'unstructured', it may be tempting to skip modelling the structure. Unstructured generally refers to data that doesn't fit well into a relational model, or has a structure that is variable at runtime. Unstructured does not mean that it has no structure at all. Depending on the type of data, the structure model should contain identifiable attributes that will be useful when processing the data, such as source, date, length and tags.

Volume

Data volume refers to the static volume of persisted data, not the number of reads/writes (dealt with as velocity/throughput). The following metrics relating to data volume need to be understood for each schema:

- The number of entities.
- The size of the data to be stored.

More volume leads to bigger databases and bigger databases require:

- More storage.
- More memory (to fit as much of the data and indexes in memory as possible).
- More load (as a lot of data needs to be processed for queries).
- More complicated operations (in order to maintain availability).

It is important to extract the number of entities that need to be stored from the business case and the lifecycle model. The primary entities are important, where some heuristics can be applied to additional entities. For example, in an e-commerce application, it is important to establish the number of products, as the primary entity, and come up with averages for the number of SKUs per product, number of reviews per product, and so on. Bearing in mind the structure model, and the application developer bias, it is easier to count the volume of classes that need to be serialised and persisted, where the collections contained within those classes are persisted with them. For architectures that tend towards a document database, counting the documents in a collection and the size of documents is also quite simple.

In order to determine volume, the size of each entity also needs to be determined. Again it may be preferable to apply some rules to determine related entities or the sizes of contained collections. The length of fields is important, including the datatype (which determines the physical size of the field). How full the variable length fields will be, by using averages, is more useful than the maximum size. Depending on the database technology used, the physical size of the index can be very important, so it may be useful to include an indication as to which fields are indexed.

Velocity/Throughput

The rate at which data needs to go in and out of the database becomes the main consideration in terms of both application and database design. It is obvious that understanding, documenting, and verifying (based on an accurate source) that data throughput becomes an important part of the data model.

However, because of application design, the database velocity is impossible to determine up-front. It can be precisely measured in a production environment, but when designing the database it is difficult to come up with definitive numbers. The application may be designed to process data asynchronously (effectively delaying and throttling write operations), or may make extensive use of a cache to reduce database load. Running applications are also subject to variations of load over time (as uncovered in the lifecycle model), and may have different (and unexpected) usage scenarios that result in a high number of (application) cache misses that affect the database load.

The data model should contain estimates on the following:

- Average and peak reads — the number of rows/entities that are read from the database. This should reflect more simple operations and not complex joins (see query needs below).

- Average and peak writes — the number of rows/entities that are inserted and updated. These will generally be fairly simple operations but may include more complex multi-table transactions.
- Average and peak inserts/appends — appending data impacts databases differently to updates (such as updating of indexes), and should be described separately. Schemas that are mostly inserting data (such as log file appending) are likely to have a different database technology to one that constantly updates an existing dataset.
- Average and peak blocking writes — While not required for all schemas, where locking can become an issue, estimating how frequently this will occur is important for application and database design.

Since exact numbers will be impossible to determine during design, it is preferable to document the velocity as part of the application velocity and allow the developers, architects and database specialists to use that information to estimate as and when it is necessary, and as the design evolves. This can be achieved as follows:

1. For each workload (from the workload model).
    2. Describe the use cases (features) that require database operations.
    3. Express each feature's database operation against the logical data structure model.
    4. Then extract the peak and average number of times the feature is used from the lifecycle model.

This would result in something like the following example:

The product search workload consists of the search and view features:

- Search is a read-only operation against the [product] only (excluding reviews, etc.).
- Searches will average 20 per second and peak at 500 per second.
- View needs to view the entire [product], including [reviews] and [personalised recommendations].
- There will be an average of 10 views per second, peaking at 200 per second.
- Each time that a search or view is performed the data about the search/view needs to be stored for analysis and recommendation.
- Authenticated users need a search/view history stored against their account.
- Authenticated users will perform 25% of active searches/views.

The above example contains critical information about data volume while not attempting to be specific. It should be a sufficient expression of volume for the data model, provided all other significant workloads and features are similarly described.

Performance

Database performance is one of the most important aspects of data in modern applications, particularly applications that need to scale and are exposed to large user bases. Perhaps database availability is on a par with performance, but other features such as data integrity, flexibility, and security (surprisingly) take a back seat to performance. Hence the rise of NoSQL databases that are performant, but only fit a narrow set of other requirements.

Requirements drive architecture and technology choices, which in turn feed back to an adjustment of the requirement based on cost effective delivery. The performance information contained in the data model needs to capture both sides; the requirements and the performance capability of the underlying technology.

Performance requirements

Application performance requirements can be lifted from existing models (availability and health models). These requirements need to be turned into database performance requirements by stripping down to the database calls.

As an example, consider a requirement for a web page that states that the page must render on the client within 2 seconds. The time taken to deliver a page to the client leaves a database time of 400ms.

Step	Time Taken
Page transmission time (200kb at 8Mbs)	.25s
Page browser render time	.5s
Web server identity and state check	.25s
Web server page generation time	.5s
Server compression and encryption	.1s

| Total (page generation, render, transmit) | 1.6s |
| Remaining time for database access | .4s |

Having a figure such as this is a good place to start. Combining it with the volume and velocity provides a requirement that can be used to make decisions about the database.

Volume/velocity/performance statements

The above example can be stated as:

- There are 100,000 products (volume).
- There are on average 20 product views per second, peaking at 200 per second.
- The product data needs to be retrieved within 400ms.

The above example statement about the volume/velocity/performance of data is detailed enough for initial architectural and design considerations (and considerably more than most projects have available). Such statements should be created for each of the primary entities, and include all of the major (or most used) features against those entities.

Format

If it is possible to model the structure of the data beyond a logical model, the model should contain the formats of the data. The amount of detail depends on the requirement, but typically more detail on the format will be required with unstructured data, data that comes in documents from external sources (such as XML documents), and data generated by applications (such as log files).

Common formats are listed below:

- SQL - Tables, rows, fields and stored procedures.
- Document serialised application object (XML, JSON).
- Binary data (audio, video).
- External documents.
- Feeds (e.g. RSS).
- Logs (files or API).

Data source

The source of the data needs to be described in the data model. This is useful for determining:

- The rate at which data can be produced. User captured data cannot be produced at the same rate as application generated data (such as a financial rates feed).
- The flexibility of the source to change how it sends data.
- The accuracy of the data.
- How much the data can be trusted (consistency, security etc.).

Data can come from many different sources. The most common classes are listed below:

- Core application data (that results from normal usage scenarios).
- Application log data.
- Operating system or platform log data.
- External transactional data (such as shipping confirmation from logistics partner).
- External analytics data (such as data from Google analytics).
- External datasets (such as a customer profiling dataset).

The identification and classification of data sources allows designers to prioritise the development of architectures for each one (core application data needs the highest priority), and feed it in to the planning and project management. Depending on the team, some data sources can be dealt with by completely different teams, such as teams that are focussed on integration work.

Query requirements

One of the biggest problems with traditional (SQL) databases is that they have become such a valuable store of business data. Because of this value, the demands for extracts and information out of them become so high that they are unable to serve their primary functions. Many of those primary functions even get forgotten, as the database becomes the source for all business critical information. The amount of data stored, and the flexibility of the query language, means that the database can serve almost any request, and these are often put in batch runs that take longer and longer. Eventually the suitability of the database is questioned as it collapses under unreasonable load.

Cloud architectures tend towards loosely coupled services that share minimal resources in order to meet availability, scalability and other requirements. This extends to the avoidance of shared database resources (see shared data below). An application should discourage the sharing of its data beyond the core requirements of the application. The first steps in modelling the query needs are:

1. Determine if the query is part of the core application functionality, or if it is a nice-to-have because of the value of the data. Too many non-core queries will bog down the database and impact the availability of the application.
2. If the query is not core functionality, consider where the data can be copied in order to satisfy the query. Look at another service that can receive data asynchronously, and store the data for future, nice-to-have, and unpredictable use.

Not all queries place the same load on the database. The queries considered core to the application and schema should be briefly described in the data model in terms of the following:

- Complexity — Single table/entity queries that make use of indexes and are forward-only (no grouping or ordering), are considerably less resource intensive than complex joins. The ability of SQL to support complex queries that can be created by people with rudimentary SQL skills (or at least no insight into the underlying impacts of the query) is the main reason for poor database performance and DBA headaches. Complex queries do not need to be avoided, it may be part of the requirement, but being clear about the level of the complexity of queries is crucial to include in the data model.
- Execution time — The time that it takes for a database to return a result is primarily dependent on the query complexity, the volume of data that needs to be queried (especially when table scans are required), and the amount of data that needs to be retrieved. The data model should explore execution times of queries and strategies to reduce them. For example, retrieving fewer rows, reducing complexity, and so on.
- Query execution environment — Traditionally the database was considered the place to do all the 'heavy lifting' with queries, but other approaches are becoming popular in order to make optimal use of database and compute resources. Where the queries actually run, which may be split between

different parts of the application, needs to be described in the data model. Options include:

- Database — the query runs on the database server (typical SQL model).
- Application - the application retrieves some data from the database and performs additional processing to get the result. The application may derive values (calculated fields), or combine one result with another from a different data source.
- ORMs and sharding are executed in the application layer and are more specific types of querying. When using an ORM, the object that is loaded into the ORM may be partially or fully loaded and the application will chose what parts of the object it is interested in, rather than building database specific queries. Manually sharded databases require some application pre and post-processing in order to obtain the required result.
- Query tools and environments — Some queries can be executed on platforms that are specifically developed to handle queries. Environments such as Hadoop and its supporting tools (Pig and Hive) are such an example.
- Dirty reads — the requirement consistency of the data returned from a query is fundamental to implementation decisions (see consistency below). Allowing for lower levels of consistency, and more dirty reads, means that queries can be tuned for faster performance and lower load directly against the database. This can be accomplished by using a 'read uncommitted' transaction isolation level, or other techniques, such as the use of cache, or materialised views. High frequency and high load queries must have their tolerance for dirty reads explicitly stated in the data model.
- Schema changes — queries that are tightly coupled to physical structures can cause problems if the underlying schema changes. For example, Windows Azure Table Storage, which requires some creativity when determining row and partition keys, will have queries tightly coupled to the keys, and they cannot be altered without having to rework queries. Any queries that are less able to handle schema changes should be explicitly noted in the data model.
- Ad-hoc queries — one of the strengths of SQL is the ability to support ad-hoc queries, whether giving the users query tools, or requesting data from support staff. Databases that have poor support for ad-hoc queries (such as Windows Azure Table Storage) may need to export data, or have code written to support ad-hoc requirements.

Geographic location

Cloud computing platforms provide the capability to store data in datacentres around the globe. Most applications will be hosted in a datacentre in the same region as the primary business and will host the data and application as close to each other as possible (via affinity groups in Windows Azure).

Sovereignty

When storing data on a cloud computing platform the data sovereignty needs to be considered. Data sovereignty encapsulates any country-specific regulatory and compliance rules that organisations must adhere to in terms of data storage. For example, there are regulations that require that data collected about European customers, must be stored in Europe. Many of these sovereignty requirements are a myth, and a project must uncover the precise regulation and interpret it according to the requirement, application and data. It may turn out, for example, that data can be stored anywhere as long as it is encrypted. Or it may be that the regulations only apply to some data, and not all. The data model will need to detail any data which is subject to regulations that limit where it can be geographically stored, including supporting analysis.

Latency

When the application and database are not co-located (for reasons such as availability), latency to the database is likely to become an issue. Because of this, it is rare to have geographically dispersed data, but if it is needed, it must be clearly described in the data model. Since latency and throughput is such a big problem, the data model should also contain some sampling and tests of what the platform is able to support.

Data gravity

Data gravity is the tendency for applications that consume data to gravitate towards the data store. This is because of the cost of data transfer, latency, available bandwidth, and ease of operations. The data model should consider data gravity and note that data that is of high importance and high volume will have a higher gravity. In enterprises, this could become an issue as there may be a resistance to running applications in the cloud just because that is where most of the data is. This might result in valuable data not being used at all.

Consistency

Monolithic SQL RDBMSs have allowed application developers to take immediate data consistency for granted. Immediate consistency is a consistency model where the result of an update is immediately visible to all observers and is common in monolithic databases because the data is in a single, shared location. Exclusive locks on resources, two-phase commits and immediate refreshes of updated data have allowed data consistency to become easy, and not worth another thought. The problem is that high database consistency is difficult to maintain at scale and with high availability; two attributes that are important in modern applications.

At some point scalable and available databases have to migrate away from a monolithic infrastructure, and move to a more distributed database. This is due to the physical or financial scale-up limitations of monolithic databases. When moving to a distributed database model, maintaining high levels of data consistency becomes a bottleneck that requires significant engineering effort, cost, or other resources, to address.

A constant questioning of the data consistency business requirement is needed. Business always seems to ask for immediate data consistency, often out of habit, or because they don't really understand the implications of what they are asking for. Questioning the need for data consistency doesn't mean making compromises on other ACID properties. Atomicity requires that a transaction must not partially succeed (through faults of part of the transaction or power failures), and a transaction that is not atomic leaves the database in an inconsistent state. It is this 'inconsistent state' that causes people to ask for immediate consistency when they are actually asking for atomicity.

The default position for any architect is that immediate consistency is unnecessary, and that eventual consistency will be the consistency model that is implemented. Once this position is created, the architect must also ensure that opportunities are created to challenge the eventual consistency position and model. This allows for flexibility in consistency options, and in turn allows for database choices that are biased towards other aspects, such as performance. This position should be clearly stated in the data model, and any exceptions should also emerge.

If eventual consistency is the default model, some situations may arise where this is problematic. These need to be discussed, and the compromises and solutions documented in the data model. For example, in an e-commerce application business may be under the assumption that an order immediately reduces the available stock, so users viewing a product will not see that there is stock when it has just been sold. Using eventual consistency there is a chance that one user (on one database node) will see stock availability that doesn't exist (on another database node). This is addressed by looking at how frequently this can occur, and what the business implications are e.g. it may be a problem for allocated seat ticket sales for a popular concert. If the business can get away with an apology (perhaps accompanied by a discount voucher), or if stock inconsistency in the warehouse is frequent in business anyway (as discussed in databases on acid), then immediate consistency may be deemed unnecessary. The architect can point out that even with immediate database consistency there is still a chance of a user assuming that stock exists due to the inconsistency of the data in the browser (which may be minutes out of date if the user is busy with something else). In this scenario, solving the consistency problem requires more than database effort, but for live updates to be sent to the browser too; something that would often seem unnecessary.

Shared data

'Shared data' can mean different things to different people, and it is important to be clear about the 'sharing' part of the term. Interconnected systems, whether as part of a single application with loosely coupled services, or as a loose assembly of different applications, need to share data. They will share product information, customer information, code tables (such as region lists), configuration, and even health information. The sharing of data is both necessary and desirable for applications. It is the ability to share the same data, and present it in different contexts for different audiences, which allows applications to be developed in order to take advantage of new opportunities. The sharing of data presents two opposing problems:

1. If the shared data is in a single place, and the applications need to share a single resource, the resource becomes a bottleneck (single point of failure and subject to excessive load).
2. If each application, or part of an application, keeps its own copy of shared data there is a tendency for divergence from the master, data to be lost, and data integrity to suffer.

When talking about 'shared data', make sure that you are explicit about whether or not it is a 'shared resource' or 'shared database' in order to avoid confusion.

The sharing of data between applications and services is an important part of the data modelling process. Places where data is shared, but not the resource, indicates a clean service boundary, and subsequently a data store or data model that could be optimised for the specific service.

The sharing of data, and database resources, is probably the single biggest problem in worldwide IT — probably with more vendors, products, technologies, methodologies, and people than any other aspect of IT. This *overview* of what needs to be considered in the sharing of data is just that, and readers are encouraged to seek out additional material and specialists, depending on their needs.

Techniques for sharing data

Data is shared in a number of different ways, clearly modelling how data is shared between services helps to define the service interface, the contract, the format, and allows the optimal data store to be chosen. Some of the logical data sharing approaches are listed below:

- Shared resource — the common approach to sharing, where a single database is used by all parts of the application.
- Replication — separate databases running the same software, such as SQL Server, and the same schema. Vendor provided replication tools ensure that data is copied between multiple databases.
- ETL (Extract Transform Load) — The most common way of sharing data in and across enterprises. ETL tools, such as SQL Server Integration Services, or custom code is run, typically in batches. These tools take data from one database (or file exported from a database), and put it in another while performing necessary transformation on it in order to fit the target schema.

- Full export/import — a database (or parts of a database, such as a single table) can be exported in full and imported into the target database. Usually this overrides all data in the target.
- Read to cache — applications can read data out of a master database, and load it into the cache. The cached item then exists in a separate physical data store from the original data.
- Messaging — applications that have a lot of asynchronous messaging contain data in the message body. TThis can be considered "Don't care" data sharing, where the sharing of data is necessary to process the transaction, rather than having to be managed in a separate database or schema.

Reconciliation of data changes

The big problem when sharing data is what to do when changes occur in the consuming database (or databases). The reconciliation of changes, and updates to the master, can become problematic. This is more frequently a problem in enterprise applications where there are so many applications that have been built up over years, with applications running in parallel after acquisitions, and everything barely held together by nightly batch runs that try and copy data back and forth. It can happen in green-field modern applications too.

Consider the example discussed in determining data schemas of a master catalogue that publishes daily to the web store catalogue. It would be fair to expect that a feature is needed to be able to update product descriptions on the web store if errors are detected, as a live update of an erroneous description would be needed, rather than waiting for the next publish. How does that update get reflected back in the master, so that the next publish doesn't stomp all over the web store catalogue again? What if the master catalogue doesn't respect changes from any consumer application, either because that is the business rule, or because it is an off-the-shelf-product that doesn't have such a feature? Is the update back to the master done directly and automatically by the web store catalogue application? Or does the user, who makes the change, have to log in to both applications and make the change twice?

Some of the approaches to reconciling data are described below:

- Expiry — shared data can be set to expire and after expiry the master can be re-fetched. Caches work based on expiry.

- Full refresh — the master is always the master and the consumer data is periodically cleared and refreshed with the master data.
- Master Data Management (MDM) tools — MDM[51] is the enterprise solution to this reconciliation problem, particularly where data is considered an asset (such as accounts data), and regulatory and compliance issues need to be addressed. MDM has tools, services, vendors, licenses, and dedicated resources to deal with the problem enterprise-wide.
- Multiple versions (irreconcilable) — it may be unnecessary to reconcile, and different databases can maintain their own versions of the data. Using the master/store catalogue example from above, the store catalogue can keep its changes to descriptions in its own database and always use those regardless of the master description.
- Manual — for low volumes, it may be possible for staff to perform updates on both systems. This is common where shared data is part of an application config file that is updated by operators.
- Custom update service endpoints — One of the most architecturally correct ways of handling reconciliation is for the master database to be exposed as a service that has service methods/endpoints that permit updates. This way, any updates can be properly applied (partial updates or resolving conflicts), be performed asynchronously, as well as being able to apply layers of authentication and authorisation. The problem is that it can be costly in terms of development and maintenance effort, for both the master service and the consuming service.
- Ignore — By far the easiest way to handle reconciliation is to ignore it and not be concerned about updating the master. In order to ignore reconciliation it is important to adapt the business processes (or at least make them aware) to be less dependent on data consistency, sharing minimal data, and making sure that explicit calls are made to the master (when data consistency is important to the process). The technical options and considerations include:
  - Expiry — Cache is the most common example where reconciliation is ignored. Caches are generally not updatable, so they never have to be reconciled with the data. Rather, items put in the cache are made to expire either explicitly or by time based rules.
  - Delete when done — Consuming applications can keep the shared data only as long as it is necessary, and then deleting it when it is no longer needed. For example, the customer details may be required by a fulfilment application, but can be deleted once the order has been successfully shipped. This reduces the

---

[51] http://msdn.microsoft.com/en-us/library/bb190163.aspx

risk of data in the consuming application being updated on the assumption that it is reconciled, or used when it is totally out of sync with the master.
- De-normalising and modelling data as temporal — Data on consumers can be modelled as being fundamentally temporal (related to time), and is often easily implemented within a de-normalised structure. For example, customer data is required to fulfil an order, but rather than creating a 'customer' structure or table, add the customer attributes to the order structure. This allows for not needing a customer entity that needs to be reconciled, as the data is only valid for the one order.

Data sharing model detail

The data model should contain the following detail on data sharing:

- Data flows — data that crosses the service boundary, either incoming or outgoing.
- Contracts that are established between the source service and the consumers of its data. The contracts are physically implemented as RESTful services, RPC calls, database APIs, and others, but should be able to be expressed logically.
- Security of the interface, authentication, and authorisation of the consumers' needs to be understood.
- Data Consumers — Even if contracts are rigid, the consumers of the data need to be listed and understood. This allows for the risks to the data (based on its usage) to be established.
- Master data approach — if the service is providing master data, how consumers reconcile back to the master (if at all) needs to be identified.

Availability

Data and database high availability is one of the most complex parts of a solution to architect. The problem with data availability is that databases generally tend to contain shared state, and the loss of a single node can take out the entire application. This makes database availability more complex than service availability.

Data and database availability needs significant attention in design, development, testing, and operations. This section deals specifically with data availability in the context of the data model, but should be read in conjunction with the availability model.

Data availability outcomes

Databases, as a bottleneck and single point of failure, are often a basis of application availability. The following availability outcomes are heavily influenced by data availability:

- Poor performance — Monolithic databases are frequently bottlenecks of the application. Databases may not be able to cope with the load they are put under. Queries will timeout, deadlocks occur, and a host of other performance related issues result from an overloaded database.
- Application availability — As a single shared resource, and often the only single shared resource of an application, the unavailability of the database can be the root cause of cascading faults.
- Loss of data — Databases can fail without recent backups or with the database in an inconsistent state. Applications can delete or corrupt data due to a bug. Rushed deployments, untested scripts, and operational panic can also cause a loss of data. Data loss can occur and not be noticed for a long time, often when it is too late to easily recover.

Data availability influencers

Before developing the approach to data availability, it is necessary to understand the availability influencers, because it is the probability of occurrence of a type of failure that largely determines the choice of technology and architecture. For example, a high traffic web application is probably more likely to have database performance issues than infrastructure failure, so an architecture that is performant would be more important (in terms of availability) than one that can recover from hardware failure. The following are primary influencers of data availability:

- Datacentre infrastructure issues — failure of something in the infrastructure hardware or software is surprisingly common. Individual disks may fail, network connectivity to particular nodes may be lost, memory leaks can cause a node to grind to a halt, or any number of problems can occur with specific hardware, networking or operating systems.
- Database performance — the most common cause of reduced data availability is the inability of the database to respond to requests. Databases

that struggle under load cause database operations to take too long, and applications to time-out and fail.
- Application errors — as the primary interfaces to databases, application defects can cause problems with databases. Applications can erroneously update data, execute too many queries (such as from misconfigured ORMs), execute sub-optimal queries, or even delete data by mistake.
- Temporary datacentre outage — outages of public cloud datacentres are well known and highlighted by technology news sites. Temporary outages will probably last for a few hours and impact availability of specific databases once every year or two.
- Platform-wide outage — similar to temporary datacentre outages, platform-wide outages do occur occasionally, but are more difficult to deal with because they are not limited to a particular region or logical fault zone.
- Datacentre destruction — the complete destruction of a datacentre, where all data in a particular datacentre is permanently lost. This has not happened to any of the major cloud providers yet but should still be catered for.
- Internet access outage — enterprise applications where users or consuming services are on the local network, and the application or data on the public cloud are susceptible to loss of Internet access.
- Data corruption — corrupt data, caused by application errors, database faults, or other problems can result in impacts on data availability due to incorrect results, or the time taken to rebuild and fix corrupt data.

Techniques for data availability

The data model should contain, for each schema, the approaches taken to ensure that the availability requirements are met. The approaches taken to data availability, particularly those that are implemented at the application level will be the same as for general availability and should be contained within the availability model. Since the data model will be developed at the level of the schema and will reference particular database technology choices, the detail should be more specific than is contained within the availability model.

The base principles for highly available data (for systems that never fail) are the same whether it is for a communications satellite in space or a large web application. These principles can be summarised as:

Parallel storage and parallel retrieval with isolated stores.

This means that when data is written it is to more than one place (parallel storage). A process needing data should retrieve it from more than one place, in case one source has failed (parallel retrieval). Data stores should be shared as little as possible, so that there is less likelihood of a rogue process reducing the availability of a data store (isolated stores). These simple principles are not easy to achieve because of the nature of shared state, the volume of data, and the development costs. Practical compromises have to be made; after all, not all applications have a requirement for such high availability (where the system never fails). Some of the approaches to increasing data availability are detailed below:

- Data isolation — a service should have its own data source that is not accessed by any other services. This reduces the likelihood of unexpected load, data corruption, or other problems caused by other services that are not immediately controllable. Isolated data also improves the recoverability of the service. If other services require data, it should be shared by giving them copies, rather than sharing a single resource.
- Reduced dependency on a particular data source — a dataset that only exists in one place is effectively a single point of failure. The dependency on a single data source should be reduced by storing data in an alternative store (even a cache can be considered an alternative), and having an alternative access path to that data store. Applications can, for example, be developed to retrieve data from both the underlying SQL database, and the document contained within the search index.
- Eventual consistency — not aggressively pursuing immediate consistency opens up architectural options that increase availability. Eventually consistent data reduces the demand on single nodes, thereby removing performance bottlenecks and failure points.
- Distributed databases — distributed databases allow for load to be spread across multiple nodes, i.e. the same data to be stored in a multiple places (including multiple datacentres), which decreases the impact of failure of a single node. Distributed databases require eventual consistency, and should be considered a single store, as a software defect in the database software itself can bring down all nodes.
- Database snapshots — taking database snapshots so that point-in-time restores can be made is a common technique for restoring the database to a good, known state after data corruption.
- Data replication — where databases have the same technology and schema, data can be replicated from one node to another. Replication is frequently used for geographically dispersed applications, or as a technique for sharing data. When applied to availability, replication can be used to synchronise data

to a passive standby node, and is particularly useful when applied between geographically separated datacentres as part of a geographic disaster recovery strategy.
- Fail-over — because SQL databases are not distributed, the most common technique for availability is to use a database that supports fail-over. Fail-over can occur through automated replication or shared storage. The big problem with fail-over for application developers is that the switch-over to a new node can take a few minutes and requires retries or other fault handling.
- Application fault tolerance — Applications need to be able to handle data availability problems. This could include retries for transient faults, switching to alternative data sources, delayed processing and, at the very least, graceful failure that communicates the problems clearly.
- Platform reliance — one of the advantages of cloud based data and storage services is the high degree of availability, durability, and fault tolerance built-in. This means that nothing needs to be specifically implemented, as the platform will take care of some of the most serious issues. For example, Windows Azure Storage has built-in support for redundantly copying data to multiple locations, so durability is of little concern to application architects and designers.

Windows Azure specific data availability features

Windows Azure has been engineered with availability in mind and has built-in support for availability, as outlined below:

- Windows Azure SQL Database has a default configuration where data is stored in three replicated databases, and if the primary node fails, the connection will fail-over to one of the other two, and a third database will be instantiated. Other operator accessible features[52] include database copies, backup to Windows Azure Storage, and data synchronisation.
- Windows Azure Storage is designed as a highly available redundant storage service that underpins many features of Windows Azure, including drives for virtual machines. Apart from service availability, data is stored in multiple locations, using either locally redundant storage[53] or geo-redundant storage.

---

[52] http://msdn.microsoft.com/en-us/library/windowsazure/hh852669.aspx

[53] http://blogs.msdn.com/b/windowsazurestorage/archive/2012/06/08/introducing-locally-redundant-storage-for-windows-azure-storage.aspx

- Virtual Machines do not have any built-in support for high availability when used as hosts for databases, and it is up to the database software to satisfy availability needs.

Data model availability detail

In terms of availability, the data model should initially contain the availability requirements for each schema. This should be fairly easy to lift out of the availability model, and review specifically for data.

As the architecture and design progresses, more can be added to the data model, particularly the approaches to availability. There will be some overlap with approaches documented in the availability model, and care should be taken to deal specifically with data and databases. As architectural decisions are made and database technology choices are finalised, the availability will be dependent on the solution chosen, and further detail may be unnecessary. Also, different schemas will share the same approaches, architecture and technology, so repetition per schema is unnecessary.

Ultimately, the detail described in the data model is to elicit discussion, reduce risk and find solutions, so sufficient detail is required to be able to make the decisions. For some applications and schemas it may be quite simple, but for a high throughput web application that serves millions of users, a significant amount of detail is necessary.

Security

The data model should not attempt to address all security issues relating to data. Data security should be dealt with more holistically within the security model, rather than independently within the data model. Only covering security in the data model exposes the database to the risks and threats of an unsecure application.

The data model can be used to highlight specific, known security requirements of the schema. These requirements can then be fed into the security assurance process in the security model. Such requirements include:

- Statements about privileged access to raw data, including physical datacentre access.
- The need for encryption of data when it is stored (either at application or database level).
- Security of backups.
- Security requirements of transport protocols used for data access.
- Level of database exposure to data access endpoints. For example, does a RESTful API really need full table access, or should some authorisation be applied?
- The requirements for different database access credentials across multiple services.

Health monitoring

The health model needs metrics for data and database operations. The data model should list available and useful metrics to be tracked for health monitoring. This allows engineers to determine the best source of metrics, such as the application, database environment, or platform API. Ensure that the metrics are made available for the following:

- Performance — including execution times of queries, I/O performance (if available), and network latency.
- Volumes — including number of transactions (total and per second), amount of data transferred and number of rows/objects
- Storage — database size, and storage space used.
- Data sharing — health of replication, and similar data sharing methods, and rate of messages sent or processed.
- Failures — query timeouts, deadlocks, and update/insert exceptions.

Monitoring data in Windows Azure

Data in Windows Azure is usually stored in Windows Azure Storage, in Windows Azure SQL Database, or in self-hosted databases in virtual machines. Virtual machines are easy to monitor as they support all of the profiling and performance monitoring that is accessible to the deployed operating system or database.

Windows Azure Storage offers health monitoring metrics that are accessible via the management portal, and can be viewed on the Azure monitoring dashboard.

Storage accounts can be configured to monitor data via varying levels of verbosity, and the data retention period can also be set. For more information, see How To Monitor a Storage Account[54] in the Windows Azure documentation.

Because it runs on a multi-tenant environment, Windows Azure SQL Database does not have the same monitoring options that are familiar to DBAs monitoring SQL Server. There is a distinct lack of OS level metrics which are usually viewed in Perfmon. Windows Azure SQL Database has dynamic management views[55] that can be queried for information on blocked or long-running queries, resource bottlenecks, poor query plans, and other database specific information that excludes lower level metrics, such as disk I/O.

Operations

Considerations need to be made in the data model for the operational requirements and effort, as they can vary greatly depending on the technology choices. SQL databases tend to have higher operational demands than non SQL services (such as Windows Azure Table Storage). NoSQL databases that are hosted within Windows Azure (such as MongoDB) may require lower operational effort, depending on how they are used. Knowledge and skills for monitoring SQL databases are also more widely available and better understood than NoSQL databases. This means that although SQL databases require more operational support, the learning curve will be shallower, and the likelihood of mistakes lower.

As with health monitoring, the operational detail should be contained within the operational model, and care should be taken not to include such information in the data model. The data model should only document specific aspects of the data, and the schema in particular, that are relevant to operations. The following operational tasks should be documented within the data model:

---

[54] https://www.windowsazure.com/en-us/manage/services/storage/how-to-monitor-a-storage-account/

[55] http://msdn.microsoft.com/en-us/library/windowsazure/ff394114.aspx

- Health monitoring — how health metrics collected about databases, and database operations, are monitored, and how operators respond to diminished health.
- Scaling — one of the responses to diminished health may be to scale the database. This needs to be thought through carefully, as it is potentially one of the most complex tasks to be performed by operations. The ease at which operators can scale the database, against the realistic requirements, has a significant input on database design. Depending on the technology, it may be as simple as adding extra nodes, or more complicated such as re-sharding a database, or even having significant downtime, as a monolithic database is moved to a larger infrastructure.
- Backup and restore — requirements and processes for backing up data, securing backups, testing backups, and restoring backups.
- Deployments — how changes are made to the database when application deployments are made. This influences the database design, as services may be independently deployed, and database changes should be limited to a single service and/or schema. Data deployments may include schema changes or the updating of data.
- Data corruption resolution — Operators are frequently called in to fix a database after it has been corrupted due to application errors, partial data imports, mistakes, or even database software issues. The data model should at least try and identify the probability of corrupt data and the impacts of it, in order to determine the need for explicit operational processes to repair data.

Assess data storage options

Once the detail has been documented for each schema, a set of technologies should begin to emerge. This will be additionally influenced by non-technical factors such as:

- Available database skills.
- Organisational bias towards a particular technology.
- Existing licensing or support agreements.
- Maturity of the technology.
- Suitability of the technology vendor (e.g. open source may not be seen as enterprise friendly).
- Experiences from other teams.

This book does not attempt to cover the database decision process. The answer to such big decisions is always 'it depends…', and the detail is contained within the data model. An architect that has such a good level of detail in the data model is in a good position to make the correct decisions about the database. There are some points that are worth highlighting which are discussed below.

Cover all data

Take care not focus only on transactional data (e.g. SQL), or the technology choices are likely to lean towards a one-size-fits-all technology that may be unsuitable in some cases. Make sure that time is spent on other data stores such as:

- Cache.
- Persistent messaging.
- BLOB and rich media.
- Unstructured data, such as log files.
- Data storage for analysis and BI.
- Feature optimised databases, such as search data.

Rationalise technology choices

The data model encourages modelling for each schema. This places a focus on the database needs for particular services, rather than trying to share a single database resource between multiple services. When choosing specific technologies it makes sense not to choose different databases for each schema and/or services. Confronted with, say, MongoDB being best suited for one service and CouchDB for another, it would be better to choose one for both. Even if the databases are separate instances, which they probably should be, the benefits of shared knowledge, operational procedures, known performance characteristics, and simplicity, favour making compromises to fit a particular technology across multiple services and schemas.

Assess candidate technologies

Once technology choices are narrowed down, they need to be assessed in order to make a decision on the best database choices. Assessment of candidate technologies need not be arduous, and the cloud computing platform provides a mechanism to test and deploy on a production quality infrastructure without having to wait for test hardware to be procured and installed.

Research

The first step to assessment is to perform the necessary research on the candidate technologies. Since most of the choices will either be from well-established vendors (such as Microsoft), or well-known open-source projects, the research is fairly easy to do. The following steps are necessary when researching the technologies:

- Find the experts — experts seem to congregate on specific websites and forums. Microsoft technologies have a number of experts that frequent the Microsoft forums. Open source technologies have experts that frequent product specific forums, but views (to varying degrees of being balanced) can be found in the (Hacker News)[http://news.ycombinator.com/] threads. Paid-for expertise can also be found through consulting services, or the packagers of open source distribution.
- Establish the current state — whilst not too relevant to SQL databases, the opinion, suitability, and features of other databases change more frequently. Be careful not to use information that is too old and make sure that both sides of the argument are understood. For example, blog posts are often titled "Don't use <some product>", relating a specific scenario where the product let them down, only to be lambasted by some really smart people on a Hacker News thread.
- Establish support available — a selection of an unfamiliar product is going to create a steep learning curve and support is important. Find out what support exists from the vendor, from specialised fee-based consultants, and from the community. Be careful about putting too much faith in vendor support on a per issue basis. Also, look for training resources such as presentation recordings.
- Find out the known issues — most technologies have well-known issues. This is less of a problem with well-established platforms, such as SQL databases, but does exist with other products. Some of the issues may be by design, but still require compromises or additional effort to work around (such as the lack of indexes on Windows Azure Table Storage).
- Ask friends and colleagues — many developers work on side projects, or have recently joined from projects that may have used one of the candidate technologies. Many of the technologies that are considered 'new' have been used on smaller projects for years.

Technical Assessment

Assessment cannot be performed without writing code, doing a deployment, and pushing around some data. Opinions gleaned from the Internet are not necessarily applicable to the application that needs to be developed. Again, the technical assessment need not be arduous, and a detailed assessment cannot be performed on every possible angle or edge case. Enough technical assessment needs to be performed in order to gain sufficient confidence that the specific technology will satisfy the requirement. These steps can be followed:

- Establish what is being assessed — Are you assessing the eventual consistency between nodes? Or the performance under heavy read load? Or the availability when an instance fails? Or the ability to handle unstructured data? Be specific as assessing the entire product will take too long.
- Technical spikes — Spin up an instance, create a database, write code and run it to perform the assessment. This gives valuable input into the development environment and operational processes too.
- Performance — Specifically test performance. Performance can vary greatly between your particular deployment environment and other reference sites. Performance is impacted by network latency, disk I/O, and other parts of the infrastructure, and the behaviour of the product on the production infrastructure absolutely has to be assessed.
- Data access API — New technologies require the mastery of a new data access API. Developer productivity has to be assessed. Some of the technologies have APIs that are very easy for developers to master (such as document databases), and others may be more complicated. How the application will behave at scale, with the new API needs to be understood. ORMs, for example, may seem easy to develop against, but become problematic when performance is crucial.
- Operations — Keep an eye on how easy the database will be for operators to use when doing the assessment. Assess how easy it is to perform backups, deployments, monitor health, and so on.

Approach to abstraction

The ability to swap out one data store for another once an application has been delivered is an unachievable holy grail. Applications architectures that intend to engineer database portability, will cost too much in development, or make many compromises where the strengths of individual products are not taken advantage of. But with new technologies there is significant, and valid, concern about the risk of choosing a technology that may turn out to be unsuitable.

When assessing a specific product, pay attention to how the data access can be abstracted. Look at how it implements standard data access patterns, and whether or not it takes specific advantage of features that need to be written in the application code. From this, formulate a practical approach as to how much data access abstraction to put into the application architecture.

Select a technology per database class

A typical cloud computing application will have more than one database. The semantics of the definition of 'database' can be argued one way or the other, so as a looser definition it could be better argued that there will be more than one data store where data is persisted. Part of the assessment of storage options is to understand that there are different classes of database (or data stores that persist data), and it is unlikely that one database will fit all purposes. In terms of rationalisation of the technology choices, there should generally only be one choice per class. If there are multiple technology choices in a class, there has to be a very good architectural reason.

The table below lists classes that will be common to most modern applications:

Database Class	Examples
Cache	Windows Azure Caching, Memcached
Persistent messaging	Windows Azure Queues, Service Bus Queues
NoSQL (Non-ACID database)	Windows Azure Tables (key-value), MongoDB (document)
SQL database	Windows Azure SQL Database, mySQL
Blob (and files)	Windows Azure Blob Storage Service, Windows Azure Drive
Business Analytics	SQL Server Analysis Services, Hadoop
Feature specific	SOLR (search)

Problematic Data

Some types of data present special challenges and need added attention in the data model. These become particularly problematic at scale due to the bandwidth, processing cost, or bottlenecks created by shared resources. Although not a definitive list, pay attention to the following:

- Blobs — Blobs (binary large objects) are used to store unstructured data in a binary format, such as images or video. Blobs can create storage issues, deletion problems (if a user wants all of their data removed), security issues (they should generally be browser accessible), and others. Due to their size, Blobs may also need to be distributed to CDN (Content Delivery Network) edge nodes to improve performance.
- Identity — Storing identity natively in an application should be avoided if possible. Apart from the hassles of resetting passwords, security needs to be based on solid identity to work properly, and if identity is broken, security is compromised. Use should be made of third-party identity providers where possible (as encapsulated in Windows Azure Active Directory).
- Network and graph structures — It is tempting to include functionality that relates many things for the benefit of the user experience. This has been encouraged by the more 'social' nature of applications, where activity of friends and other circles is expected to be visible and current. Databases that need to store and navigate a social graph (or any other graph, such as related products) in real-time are hard to get right at scale. Take care when promising functionality based on graph data.
- High volume, low value — A lot of data has a very low 'per row' value. For example, tracking the geospatial co-ordinate from a mobile device when a request was made may be useless as a single data point. Such data only becomes valuable when combined with other datasets, aggregated, analysed and, most importantly, actioned for some clear benefit. Such data can have an insignificant cost to record and store and can become really expensive to extract value from. By all means record as much data as possible, but be careful of the load this data places on the application, and about overstating its value in its native format.

Big data

When 'cloud' and 'data' are mentioned together, it is quickly followed by 'big data'. Big data is currently a hot topic. Much of the interest is reasonable as the amount of data being generated by consumer-oriented applications, with millions of users, is both phenomenal and valuable. It is modern applications providing the functionality to users that enable data to be collected. Much of this data is behavioural or generated as a side effect of user interactions, rather than users explicitly capturing data. Those same applications are running on cloud platforms, or distributed commodity-hardware environments that underpin the ethos of big data; namely the use of distributed data and processing (in a map-reduce style) to get answers quickly and cheaply. The dark side of big data is the hyping of the technology by vendors desperate to cash in on the 'next big thing'. Big data, almost by definition, requires a lot of storage, processing and network infrastructure. This is bound to attract vendors that need to retain (or grow) market share in a rapidly changing, on-premise datacentre environment.

The truth of big data is somewhere between hype and reality. Applications do indeed generate a lot of data, but the generation of data, and the need to analyse it, doesn't make it a big data problem. Sometimes the big data tools, such as Hadoop, are the best tools to extract value from the data, and sometimes more simple data access is good enough, especially when the questions are both known and simple. Indeed the initial principles of big data, started as the '3 Vs' of big data (Douglas, Laney. Gartner "3D Data Management: Controlling Data Volume, Velocity and Variety"[56]),are recognisable as part of the data problem of modern applications. They are:

- Volume — the amount of data exceeds physical limits of vertical scalability.
- Velocity — the speed at which data moves in and out of the system, whereby the decision window is small compared to data change rate.
- Variety — the range of data types and sources.

These are echoed in the model detail that needs to be generated for each schema, namely Volume, Velocity/Throughput, Format, and Data source.

Since these initial principles, another 'V' was added (variability, the variations in interpretations of the same data) to make '4 Vs'. The madness of adding Vs has not stopped and there is now validity, volatility, viscosity (resistance to flow), value, and possibly many more.

---

[56] http://blogs.gartner.com/doug-laney/files/2012/01/ad949-3D-Data-Management-Controlling-Data-Volume-Velocity-and-Variety.pdf

While big data should be on the table when looking at the data requirements of an application, it should be treated with caution. Big data solutions should be used appropriately and not promise to magically solve all data problems.

Summary

Choosing approaches to data and specific underlying database technologies is one of the most important steps in developing an architecture for cloud-based applications. The breadth of the problem, the compromises that need to be made, the complexity of the underlying technologies, and the risks can be daunting to any implementation team. Glossing over the data model only delays (and increases) the risk, so early and focussed attention on it is imperative. To make sure that the data model doesn't become overwhelming, focus on the requirements and match them to approaches; inevitably a technical fit will emerge.

To simplify the effort:

- Focus on schemas that are derived from the workload model. Small chunks of data will be easier to understand.
- Make sure that the business requirements are clear, and make sure that there is an underlying reason for the requirement. Specific areas include the need for real-time consistency, availability, and the need for data flexibility in terms of multiple uses and queries.
- Make sure that the development team is actively involved — many of the solutions to data come from development practices and approaches, as much as it comes from DBAs.
- When choosing 'new' technologies, build a small technical spike, and deploy it on the cloud. This tests assumptions and gives developers a feel for what it takes to implement.
- Don't be tempted to use every tool and technology available. Stick with those familiar to the implementation team (such as SQL), and minimise the number of other technologies used.
- Don't wait until the data model is 'finished' before development, but use it to make quick decisions to get the development going. Continually add to the data model during development.

Steps

1. Determine data schemas.
2. Model each schema.
3. Assess data storage options.

Capacity Model

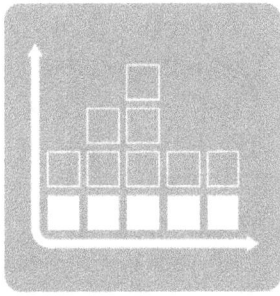

One of the most widely understood aspects of cloud computing is the concept of 'infinite capacity', where capacity can be acquired on demand, used as needed, and disposed of when no longer in use. The idea is that consumed capacity runs optimally, without straining available resources or having expensive servers sitting around idle.

The concept of on-demand capacity only works when applications have been specifically architected to take advantage of the available capacity. This is covered extensively in all CALM models. Taking advantage of available capacity requires more than just spinning up a machine; some capacity planning needs to be done. The capacity model addresses this need for planning and architecture related to capacity, in order to be able to make use of this very important feature of the cloud.

Capacity planning on the cloud

Traditional on-premise application development requires capacity planning to ensure that the physical infrastructure is available when the application goes live. Of course, since the capacity has to be determined early in the development cycle, it is often a best guess, based on experience and generally overestimated, rather than being an accurate analysis. Traditional applications, where capacity takes a long time to provision, also need to plan for a peak load at some time in the future (6–12 months out, depending on procurement processes and budget cycles). The style of capacity planning needed for traditional applications is completely different to that of cloud applications, and very few of the practices found in on-premise datacentres are transferrable.

Cloud computing applications have the advantage that capacity can be provisioned on demand. This means that estimating medium-term physical infrastructure needs of an application is unnecessary. Indeed, the provisioning of capacity becomes more of an operating cost issue (as covered in the cost model), and an operational problem (as a response to diminished health, covered in the health and operational models).

Capacity planning on the cloud then becomes more of a modelling exercise, where it is not the availability of capacity that needs to be planned, but rather:

- The architectural approaches to consuming that capacity.
- The configuration of services to make optimal use of consumed capacity.
- Determining when capacity is needed.
- The operational triggers and processes required to provision the capacity.
- The de-provisioning of capacity when it is no longer needed.

Just because capacity can be provisioned on demand, it doesn't mean that an application can use it easily. You can spin up as many instances as you like, but if you are stuck with a struggling, single shared database, no extra capacity will help. On-demand capacity doesn't automatically translate to on-demand availability or scalability. This can be an issue in the following instances:

- Unavailable capacity — while infrequent, there may be times when capacity is simply unavailable. Despite cloud providers' promises of infinite capacity, it is obviously not infinite. Maybe the specific datacentre is running out of capacity itself, or there is a partial outage that prevents the spinning up of new instances. Also, your demand for capacity will frequently be placed on a single datacentre, and whilst there may be capacity elsewhere on the network, it may not be available where you need it.
- Bottlenecks — The provisioning of new compute or virtual machines is relatively easy and not prone to failure. The provisioning of storage, network, database, and other throughput is more problematic. Windows Azure Storage, for example, has limits on the number of transactions that can be processed per second. Yes, you can provision more storage, but how is the application going to work across multiple storage accounts? What if hundreds of storage accounts are provisioned? Compute has the advantage that capacity is provisioned behind a load balancer, but with storage it is not so simple. There is no such thing as a load balancer for SQL databases. The provisioning of capacity needs to take these bottlenecks into consideration.
- Health monitoring — When there are hundreds of instances running, it can be difficult to keep track of what is running well and what isn't. Some

instances will be running hot, while others are barely ticking over. Some databases may be timing out frequently, while others are snappy. Where do you start with adding or removing capacity when so much is running, and there are so many interdependencies?
- Costs — The decision to add capacity may be easy in the moment when customers are flooding the site, and the argument for low costs during the 'difficult period' is easy to swallow. It becomes surprisingly difficult to remove capacity, and make the decision to actively slow the application down. There may be so much interdependency between services that removing some capacity has a drastic effect on the availability of some services. Those initial, easy decisions on costs become monthly bills that keep mounting.

Influence of capacity planning on application development

Because of the promise of on-demand capacity, implementation teams are tempted to leave capacity planning until late in the development cycle, if they get around to it at all. Attention should be placed on capacity planning early on in the development process in order for it to exert the right kind of influence on the architecture and application design.

Capacity planning early in the development lifecycle influences:

- Application architecture — the inability of a component to handle the expected load needs to be identified early. The answer to the question *"Will the addition of capacity solve this performance problem?"*, will influence the architecture. If the answer is "No", then the approach needs to be reworked until the answer is "Yes". This is an important role of the capacity model. In order to solve scaling issues, capacity should be added without additional rework required. For example, with an implementation that uses Windows Azure Queues, if all messages are sent to one queue, then the addition of capacity may not solve scaling problems, because the queue becomes the bottleneck. In this case, the application needs to be able to handle multiple queues, where additional capacity contains a new queue in the scale unit.
- Cost model — the predicted operational costs of the application are related to the capacity provisioned. The outputs from the cost model may be fed back into the architecture when the cost exceeds the value provided by the component. Perhaps the component needs to be optimised for cost, as opposed to throughput or performance.

- Scalability — it may be impossible to determine an application's ability to handle target loads, as simulation may be impossible. The capacity model provides units of capacity that are used to predict the behaviour (performance, cost, etc.) of the application under peak load.
- Workload scheduling and optimisation — the capacity model combines the capacity requirements across all relevant workloads and lifecycles, providing an insight to which workloads should run when, and with how much capacity, in order to optimise cost, operations, or cross-workload contagion.

Developing the capacity model

The capacity model provides a bridge between application design and application operations. This is what makes development of the model difficult, as application developers are seldom concerned with the operation of applications. Most of the time developers hand over source code and an indication of the target configuration, leaving the operators to figure out the rest. The capacity model brings the operational needs to development, and requires that developers consider how their applications will run and respond to load.

Isolation of services and workloads

Cloud computing architectural approaches encourage the use of discrete, independent, decoupled and isolated services. This principle is especially relevant in the availability model, where isolated services improve availability because they allow for fault isolation, feature shaping, asynchronous processing, and other architectural approaches for availability. One of those approaches is the ability to scale by adding capacity, which is where it touches the capacity model.

Although the use of isolated services is encouraged, it doesn't always work out that way. The most common example is where worker roles are used to process messages from a queue. The number of messages on a queue for particular workloads may be very low. It doesn't make sense to have a worker role (with at least two instances for availability) running constantly in order to process ten messages a day. Application designers then decide to combine a number of workloads into a single worker role, and end up with a 'back-end' worker role, or something similar. This doesn't make sense in the context of isolated services, because a poison message from one workload can bring down another. But it does make sense from a cost optimisation point of view. Things get more complicated where the same code is run on a number of roles, and the messages to be processed are set in the configuration. Similar examples exist with other types of services, such as combining an occasionally used web API (e.g. WCF) with an MVC web application.

This approach of combining workloads and services for practical reasons can complicate the capacity model. Capacity cannot be easily planned where differing workloads, with differing load, scale and availability requirements are combined in the same executable. Unfortunately the situation is largely unavoidable. Even good architecture that allows code to be easily moved around, such as by deploy-time dependency injection, creates planning problems because there is no clearly defined relationship between functions and Windows Azure roles (or virtual machines).

The process of capacity modelling can draw attention to these issues and force architectural decisions about service isolation to be made early in the development process.

Understanding the role of a scale unit

As per the analysis undertaken in the lifecycle model, we understand that the demand placed on a workload is going to vary over time. At its most basic, we also understand that in order to handle additional demand we need to scale. The preference, particularly in the context of cloud computing, is to scale out rather than up, as attempting to scale up introduces limits as to how far we can scale. We are also generally familiar with scaling out certain parts of the application, particularly web servers, and it is common practice to add a number of web servers behind a load balancer. The big question is, once we have scaled out one component (say the web server) what else needs to be scaled out? What about cache, storage, access control, or any other components that are assembled to handle the workload?

The role of the scale unit is important in being able to group a set of components that, in response to demand, can be treated as a group and scaled together. This allows for improved planning, provisioning and releasing of the resources required to handle the demand.

The example below shows two workloads with distinct, and different, components (Windows Azure services or features). These components are grouped together to form a 'scale unit'.

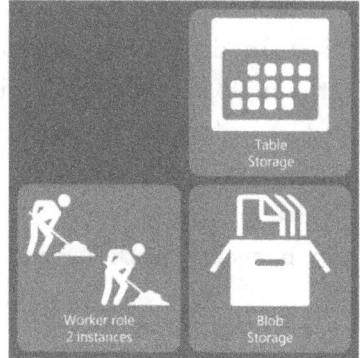

Workload 'A'   Workload 'B'

Based on output from the lifecycle model, you should be able to determine how many of each of the scale units are required for each workload. In this example, 'Workload B' is not very spiky, or under much load, and remains constant at a single unit throughout the day. 'Workload A', on the other hand, is subject to daily load fluctuations and additional scale units are required to handle the load. Those workloads can then be summed, in terms of capacity, for a particular lifecycle. Bear in mind that this example shows only one lifecycle, and there are others which need to be considered, such as the monthly lifecycle.

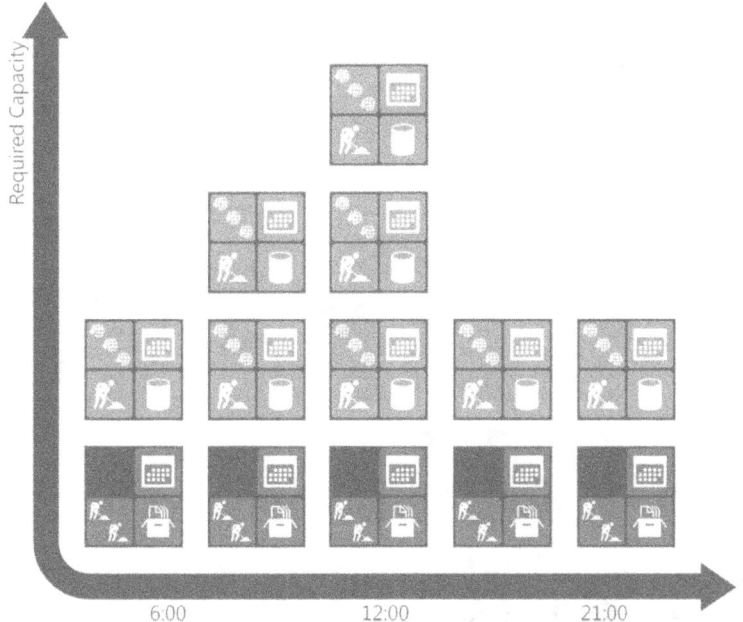

Once all workload capacities are overlaid, a clear picture of overall capacity requirements can be painted for all lifecycles. In the example below, further workloads (in grey), are depicted on the same lifecycle graph, giving a total view of consumed capacity.

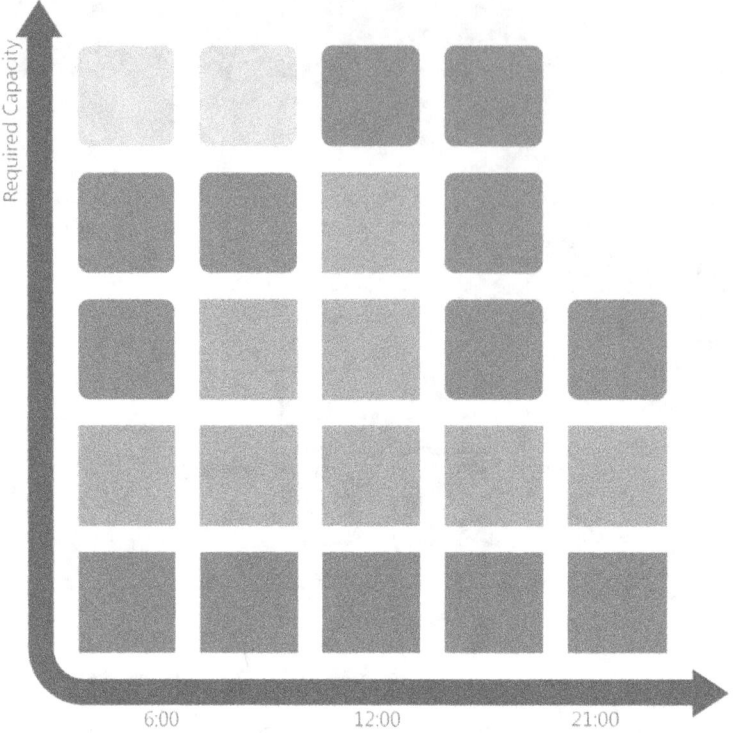

Determine the load and spikiness of the workload

Extensive capacity modelling is only required on workloads that are subject to high loads and/or spiky traffic. For example, an application that has an administrative website accessed occasionally by a handful of people should probably be skipped in the capacity model. Such a workload, that is satisfied by a single web role running at low utilisation, with no chance of needing to scale, can be left as is.

Workloads that are very spiky need careful capacity modelling. A workload that is subject to massive load over regular cycles needs attention, as the ability to add and remove capacity to match the load is important. For example, an application that is for millions of consumers in a single region will need a lot capacity during the day, and virtually none at night. This requires special attention as the application availability is important, but so is the optimisation of costs.

Determine the platform requirements for each workload

In order to determine the scale unit, the platform requirements for each workload need to be determined. These include the components, resources, consumption, and anything else that is needed in order to be more specific about workload requirements. These requirements should be directly translatable into consumable features on Windows Azure. For example, the instance size needs to be determined as accurately as possible, as it has a direct impact on the cost model and the deployment in terms of configuration (in terms of the configuration of what needs to be deployed).

Identify platform components

An initial design needs to be completed on each workload to determine the platform components required to implement the workload. These components will include roles (web, worker, VM etc.), storage, queues, cache, and service bus endpoints; any underlying component on the Windows Azure platform. At this stage, the individual components do not have to be named, designed or described in much detail. Some components may be shared by different workloads, so be careful not to double-count (see Isolation of services and workloads above).

Estimate the consumption of resources

The size of the components required to satisfy the demand of the workload must be estimated.

Instance size

Whilst we endeavour to scale out as much as possible, there is a minimum component size to be considered. For example, whilst a simple web application may be able to run on an 'Extra Small' instance, if there is a need for resource intensive image processing, then a larger instance with more memory may be required.

In the context of Windows Azure, it is the compute instance size that needs to be estimated. Most other Windows Azure components do not have an instance size, and are only sized in terms of consumption. Windows Azure SQL Database has an instance size, but should be considered in the data model, not in the capacity model. See [Considering shared state in the capacity model](#) below.

Metered consumption

The consumption of most resources in Windows Azure is on a per unit basis. These can be general, such as bandwidth, or specific to the component, such as Windows Azure Storage transactions. It is important to understand the constituents of metered consumption otherwise there is the risk that consumption will be undercounted. This can be in the context of:

- Side effects — for example, processing a message from the queue will probably read from a queue and then write to another place (say storage) after completion, so there is more than one storage transaction
- Counting all the underlying transactions — On Windows Azure, every single rest call is counted as a transaction, and it may not be clear from the API how many underlying rest calls are being made. For example, reading a message from a queue may result in two transactions (one to read the message and another to delete it).

In many cases, more than one consumption item needs to be considered. For example, writing to table storage will have a storage transaction, and a persistence cost. These can also vary depending on whether or not the data is being consumed inside the Windows Azure datacentre. For example, reading from table storage from a web role will have no cost, but reading the same data from an on-premise application will have an outbound data cost.

Counting redundancy

The extra capacity required for redundancy (in order to achieve some fault tolerance) needs to be considered when planning the capacity. Windows Azure roles, for example, may have an instance count of two or higher (required as part of Windows Azure SLA) in order to satisfy availability objectives, even if they both only run at 50% of capacity. In more complex redundancy scenarios, additional components may be added, such as would be required for geographic or off-site redundancy. Depending on the workload, redundancy may not be required at all e.g. a queue reader that has a high latency tolerance and low availability requirements, where a single instance will satisfy the requirements.

Component specific consumption

Some components may require that we estimate consumption specific to the component. These should be chosen carefully and only considered if they are seen as architecturally significant. Examples include:

- Cache hits and misses — the number of cache misses may be relevant in estimating the size of a cache.
- Storage partitions — the number of partitions may need to be estimated as they can affect performance.

Considering shared state in the capacity model

Shared state components should be included in the scale unit for a workload if there is little performance, data consistency or other impacts on, or by, other workloads. Something like messages on a queue should be added to the capacity model or table storage used exclusively for the workload.

A monolithic shared Windows Azure SQL Database should not be included in the scale units of the capacity model, as it does not fit into any particular workload, and the capacity model is workload oriented. Even in the case where a SQL database is for a single workload, it can't scale out and cannot be included in a scale unit.

A distributed, eventually consistent database, such as Cassandra, on the other hand, may be included in the capacity model. When using a distributed database, the database nodes are able to handle a specific load and can simply be added as demand increases. For example, if one database node is required for every ten web roles, both the web roles and the database node can be contained in the scale unit.

The scalability of databases is covered in more detail in the data model.

Rationalise to the minimum scale unit for the workload

Scale units should be as small as possible, and should only be able to handle the absolute minimum load. Only by having small enough scale units can the capacity be provisioned and decommissioned depending on the demand.

This rationalisation should consider components that can be scaled out, as well as those that will be single (larger) instances.

Determine the demand capacity of the scale unit

Once you have small enough scale units, we need to estimate the demand that they can handle, as well as the consumption of resources when they are under load.

The primary input should be a single event that is specific to the workload and make sense in a business context. Examples include:

- For web role, a user performing a general set of tasks (pages).
- For worker role, a message being read from a queue.
- For a service web role, processing particular incoming data.

This single event should then be counted in terms of the number of times it occurs within a given period, preferably the shortest possible period (an hour is the smallest billing period offered by Windows Azure). The period chosen should not be based on expected load during any particular hour, but the load that can be handled by the scale unit.

The load that can be handled by a single scale unit can only be determined by quantitative performance testing, as covered in the test model. It may take a few cycles of development and testing to accurately estimate the capability of a scale unit.

When to develop the capacity model

The capacity model should be started in the early stages of design. As the design evolves, architectural variations, the accompanying estimates of capacity needs and the components that make up a scale unit will be assessed and documented in the capacity model. Towards the end of development, when more features are complete and performance testing gets underway, the detail in the capacity model will increase and be more accurate.

Summary

The result of capacity planning is a set of small, well described and understood units for planning, provisioning and decommissioning capacity. They play an important role in determining the application architecture, and become useful when used within other models, such as the cost model and the deployment model.

The ability to efficiently operate the application is highly dependent on the quality of the capacity model. An incomplete capacity model will make deployment and scaling of the application by operators in a production environment very difficult.

Steps

1. Determine the load and spikiness of the workload.
2. Determine the platform requirements for each workload.
    1. Identify platform components.
    2. Estimate the consumption of resources.
3. Rationalise to the minimum scale unit for the workload.
4. Determine the demand capacity of the scale unit.

Deployment Model

It seems odd that deployment needs to be considered so early in the design stage. We are used to building applications with a vague idea of how it will be physically deployed and, as the release date approaches, throwing it over the wall to IT for deployment (assuming the hardware is available).

With cloud computing applications, the deployment needs to be considered much earlier in the development cycle. Not only does the unfamiliarity of cloud deployments require that more time is spent understanding it, but also the deployment has an impact on the overall application architecture. Early consideration and planning of deployment is an important aspect of cloud computing that should not be glossed over.

Differences with cloud deployments

Arguably every deployment is different and, particularly with high load systems, the deployment is non-trivial, requiring highly skilled hardware, networking and other engineering expertise. Cloud application deployment is, at least in some ways, far easier (there is, for example, no great big specialised database cluster with complex underlying storage), but it is significantly different. This difference is reflected in both the physical deployment and the impact it has on how the application is built. It is that departure from what is known, understood, and for which there are skills, that makes cloud deployments more difficult.

Some of the differences between cloud deployments and traditional application deployments are described below.

Unfamiliarity

Windows Azure deployments are unfamiliar to most people. There are no physical servers, power, networking equipment, or other traditional reference points. Even for teams that are accustomed to managing virtual infrastructure, things look different. There are no servers hosting virtual machines, no SANs or virtual network cards. The management tools are unfamiliar, with a web based management portal as the interface to the deployment with hosted services, storage accounts, affinity groups, and other unfamiliar services and terminology. That unfamiliarity also extends to the development team. Some developers may have been on an Azure project, or played with it in their spare time, but for others, even if they understand what a web role is, they are unfamiliar with how the applications are to be deployed.

The architectural approach may also be unfamiliar, with loosely coupled services, multiple instances, asynchronous processing, and a data model that extends beyond SQL Server. There are no clear lines to draw between *this* server and *that* server when services are only tenuously coupled with messages in a queue. There are also no existing mental models on how things should work, so developers struggle to depict (and even keep track of in their minds) the complex flows of data between services, when all failure and edge cases are considered.

Testers, who are accustomed to running a specific test and checking that the data is indeed over *there* and in the correct format, find themselves struggling to write test harnesses that make allowances that the result will get *there* eventually.

Even project managers, already sufficiently distanced from the technology, can find grey areas of deployment difficult to come to terms with. Determining completeness can become tricky when an application is deployed to test and production on the same platform, at the same time, with different services stopped for one reason or another.

Deployment of services versus hardware and software

The concept of deployment of services to the cloud versus hardware and software in a traditional datacentre is one of the most unfamiliar elements. The traditional process of installing hardware, then operating systems, then third party software, then the application, with configuration steps along the way is no longer the practice. Applications are deployed as services that run on top of existing services (the 'S' in PaaS) that are already available, configured, running and just need to be consumed. The custom application itself is not even 'installed' or 'configured' but rather has its source and configuration deployed to the service, ready to be automatically installed on an instance as and when it is needed. This conceptual difference is fundamental in the day-to-day design, development and operation of cloud based applications.

Influence of deployment on availability

Modern applications that take advantage of cloud computing platforms generally have higher availability requirements. There may be little or no downtime window that allows for major releases, and application features may, by design, go through rapid release cycles in response to customer demand. This requires a different view on deployment, where parts of the application can be deployed and tested in a production environment without negatively affecting the overall availability of the application. This is accomplished using a combination of application design (asynchronous processing, feature shaping etc.), features built into the Windows Azure platform (staging, virtual IP address swaps, etc.), and product development (Test In Production). Deployment becomes more of an operational extension of the implementation team than something that happens in the early hours of Sunday morning.

Cost model

Although we try not to prematurely optimise the cost during design, the deployment model and the cost model do work hand-in-hand during design. For example, the size of Windows Azure SQL Database databases chosen, and approaches to partitioning based on the cost of the databases, can influence design choices. Logically separate workloads may be combined because the workload on one is so low that it doesn't cost justify a deployment that mirrors the separation. For example, a single worker role processing messages from multiple queues, or a web application and WCF interface being in the same web role.

Rapid provisioning

If one of the benefits of choosing a cloud platform is the ability to bring an application to market quickly, then the ability to deploy quickly should match the expectation. Leaving deployment considerations too late in the application lifecycle could mean that when it comes to launch, a host of poor assumptions and unfamiliarity with the process come to light. Since the 'production' platform is available, deployment to 'production' whether it is publicly accessible or not, should be part of the POC (Proof of Concept) and development processes.

Billing

Billing is a difficult point throughout development and into production. One of the first problems that cloud implementations encounter is the question about whose credit card is used to buy the service during the POC. Pay-per-use services such as Windows Azure don't lend themselves to normal business accounts payable and procurement processes, and the financial impact of deployments, particularly for development and testing, often create problems. The person responsible for deployment is often the first person to run into questions about billing.

Internal IT

Enterprises with good perimeter security and other IT practices may create problems for cloud deployments. Firewalls often limit access to outgoing SQL ports, have bandwidth restrictions, or other rules that get in the way of delivering cloud applications. Considering deployment during design, and involving internal IT, helps to create an understanding of what needs to happen on the internal infrastructure in order to support the implementation and delivery of the application.

Principles of the deployment model

First Principle - Provide an early view of deployment

Due to the differences in deployment on the cloud versus traditional deployment, it is important to publish a view on your approach as early as possible. This is why we encourage the development of a deployment model during the design stage. In publishing a view of the deployment early:

- Developers unfamiliar with Windows Azure begin to understand where their code fits into the overall architecture.
- Testers have a reference for developing the complex test scripts that are required in asynchronous environments.
- Testers have a view on what can be scaled up early on in the project for performance testing.
- Operators (or devops during development) have a document that they can take to internal networking, or existing operations, in order to facilitate the required cooperation.
- The cost model is dependent on the deployment model, and there is an obvious need to have an idea of platform costs early in the project.
- Project managers have a reference that has many uses, such as completeness, costs, and dependencies

Second Principle - Let the deployment process influence the application architecture

The ability of all or part of an application to be deployed (which includes scaling) in a production environment, without negatively affecting performance and availability, is a primary architectural goal of cloud applications. It is important that when design choices are made that they are checked against deployment considerations and reworked if necessary. Constantly questioning the ability to deploy, and the deployment processes that surround a particular design decision, influences service decoupling, asynchronous processing, and the adoption across the application of similar design patterns.

Developing the deployment model

The deployment model consists of two distinct parts. The layout view describes, in as much detail as is available and necessary, what the services and related configurations are. The process view describes what is deployed, how and at what stages, in an operational context, in order to maintain adherence to the application SLAs.

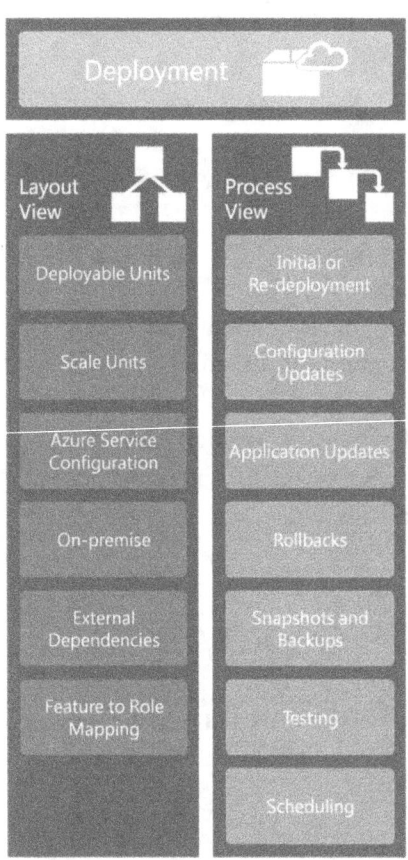

Develop the Layout View

The layout view contains as much detail as is known about what will be deployed, where it will be deployed, and configuration specifics. Although some diagrams may be useful or required, the goal of the layout view is to provide as much detail as possible to various interested parties.

Documentation and depiction of the layout view

Views of deployment of hardware and software in a datacentre have traditionally been diagram biased with representations of servers, network connections and even user workstations on a single diagram. Cloud applications tend to be more difficult to depict diagrammatically due to their dynamic nature and loose coupling between services. How do you draw a line representing data flow or dependency between two services when there may be hundreds of geographically dispersed instances, eventually consistent data flow and a tenuous, dynamic coupling between the services?

While there may be pressure to create a single, representative diagram of an application deployment, don't let it divert attention from the content. It may turn out that the deployment is too complex to represent in a diagram, and trying to visualise it will either over simplify the deployment model, or reduce the likelihood that the diagram will ever be delivered or understood. Focus on providing the content over pretty pictures.

Deployable units

A Windows Azure application will have many deployments; from the initial deployment during development, to the final go-live deployment and frequent (perhaps daily) deployments as defects are fixed, configuration updated, and features added.

The deployment layout view has to be aware of the deployment process and the impact of deployments on the availability of the running application. This means that deployable units need to be grouped together in a way that makes both architectural and operational sense. For example, it does not make sense to package a service's database scripts together with the application, as the database will be deployed once and the service frequently. The first consideration when grouping together artefacts into deployable units is:

- Frequency of deployment — Some parts of the application will need to be deployed frequently. This will mostly be application code that is packaged for a service. When critical defects are found and changes made, it should be possible to deploy the unit to production (via test) within a matter of hours.
- Impact of deployment — Parts of the application on which there is a high dependency can have a significant impact on the application availability when they are deployed. Shared databases are the obvious example, but databases are seldom deployed from scratch anyway because ALTER scripts are deployed to live databases. Services on which there is a high dependency, and little consideration for availability built in to the consuming application, can have a significant impact. Shared identity services are an example of a service that can have a significant impact when it is (re)deployed.

When determining the deployable units, and considering the frequency and impact, the following deployable units will tend to emerge:

- Infrastructure — Usually a one-off deployment that includes virtual networking, storage, and subscriptions.
- Shared data — Shared database resources, such as a Windows Azure SQL Database that is shared by many services, also tend to be one-off deployments and, in this respect, behave a lot like infrastructure. Database changes (either DDL or DML) need to be carefully scripted and tested in order to reduce the impact of the deployment.
- Services — Services are the most common deployment unit, where everything for a particular service is packaged together. This could include the application code, as well as other services, such as a cache and database services, and configuration that comprise the unit.
- Configuration — Configuration can be deployed as individual units, particularly when used to store infrequently changing configurations, such as integration endpoints.

Scale Units

The capacity model defines the scale units for a service. These scale units specify all of the infrastructure services with their sizes (compute, database, cache, etc.), as is needed for application scalability. Because scalability should largely be automated, a scale unit should be configured as an individual deployment unit and managed accordingly. Changes to the size of services within a scale unit (such as instance size) would be part of the configuration and should deploy fairly easily.

Azure service configuration

When describing the configuration required for Windows Azure, step through the available options in the Windows Azure management portal, and document the relevant configuration. It doesn't matter if some detail is not available, but it is important to use it as a reference to ask questions. There is a lot to cover in the service configuration, and it depends on the Windows Azure features that are used.

The deployment model should detail all of the service configurations that need to be kept track of. This includes subscriptions, storage account keys, affinity groups, virtual networks, certificates, and many more.

On-premise infrastructure, services and integration

Enterprises are understandably nervous about allowing public access into their perimeter, and Windows Azure is, at least from a networking perspective, indistinct from any other public IP address (hence the 'cloud' notation of networking diagrams). If the application deployed on Windows Azure has a dependency on on-premise infrastructure, then it is imperative that this is described up front. This allows the necessary design decisions to be made, and the all-important interaction with enterprise IT to take place (particularly perimeter security).

Discussion about the deployment may influence either the architecture, or the existing on-premise network. For example, say the application needs access to an on-premise SQL database it is unlikely to be accessible over port 1433. The solution is either to move the SQL database outside the perimeter (which may be a bad idea), to synchronise data up to Windows Azure SQL Database (which may be unworkable due to data volumes), or to develop an on-premise service that resides outside the perimeter and exposes the necessary data. All of these are significantly different technical and architectural solutions to a problem that may seem, at first, to be relatively simple. Finding out which solution works for everybody, and finding it out as soon as possible, is facilitated by ensuring that on-premise infrastructure requirements are detailed in the deployment model.

The deployment model should cover:

- Networking — any assumptions about ports that need to be opened for incoming traffic (from Windows Azure to on-premise).
- Active Directory — that may be used for federated identity.
- SQL Databases — for database integration that may be required, either to read from or post data to, and involves the sharing of logins (and perhaps certificates). It may also involve punching a hole in the firewall when SQL Data Sync is not used.
- Other internal services may also be used, such as web services, email infrastructure, or even file shares.

Much of the detail of the infrastructure used will be contained within the Integration Model, but this should not be skimmed over in the deployment model, as the deployment (or the inability to deploy) influences the integration architecture and model.

External service and integration dependencies

External services on which the application depends tend to be more publicly accessible than on-premise infrastructure, but still require documentation in the deployment model. External services may require specialised identity mechanisms, or even machine based licensing that must be addressed and dealt with. The detail of these services will help to determine the location of configuration information to be administered by operations.

As with on-premise integration, the consumption of external services, as far as the actual implementation and use, is covered in detail within the Integration Model.

Mapping of features and components to roles and virtual machines

The traditional developer view on application deployments is both quite simple and, from the developer perspective, somebody else's problem. It used to be that a web application or IIS hosted WCF service would map to a virtual directory on IIS. The administration of the virtual directory would be left to IT/operations, or simply created on an existing server.

With Windows Azure, different components can be scattered across multiple roles, or combined into a single role if individual usage is low. Consider the example of a web application that is accompanied by a service API. Within Visual Studio, these would be built as separate projects in a single solution and deployed independently (either to the same or separate physical services). In an Azure project, these components may be deployed within the same role, requiring some manual configuration of endpoints[57] which, at the very least, creates developer confusion when developing and debugging; as the developer tools only support one application within a role.

This gets more complicated when working with worker roles that read messages off queues. In a traditional environment, queue readers could be implemented as Windows Services, and deployed on the same machine or multiple machines as required. The combination of multiple readers of queue messages within a single worker role is a design-time decision that cannot be easily undone. If, for some reason, one queue needs to be moved off to a separate role, it may require a significant code change (new project, moving of libraries).

The deployment model should attempt to map these individual applications/components/websites into specific named roles. While the *Single Responsibility Principle* (that good developers embrace) would favour the separation of functionality into roles, the costs of having a multi-instance role hanging around to perform some occasional low load function may be too high. Since the deployment model is one of the primary inputs into the cost model, these costs will only become clear if the individual roles are teased out. Try and create (and

---

[57] http://msdn.microsoft.com/en-us/library/windowsazure/gg433110.aspx

maintain) a table that maps between Visual Studio projects and roles, the example below (which uses fictional project and role names) will help during discussions with the development team.

Role/VM	Application/Project
WebAppRole	WebAppMVC, WebAppAPI, AdminWebAppMVC
SmallTasksWorkerRole	BackgroundQueueReader (inject emailProcessor, lostPasswordProcessor, startImportProcessor)
OrderfulfilmentWorkerRole	Orderfulfilment
IntegrationWebRole	IntegrationWCF
IntegrationServer	SSIS Packages

Develop the Process View

The deployment layout view facilitates the architectural and project management processes, but represents a 'to be' static representation of how the application is deployed. The process view of the deployment model represents how deployments are undertaken and getting this sorted out is crucial. "How to deploy an application" is likely to fall through the cracks if not specifically addressed. Developers don't care much, and operators are more concerned with post-live maintenance, so there is generally nobody concerned enough about the bit in the middle.

This middle space is starting to be filled by 'devops', which is a role that emerged out of the continuous integration and continuous build environments. In a nutshell, devops within the development team perform functions that seem operational in nature. Devops don't work on application features, but rather with infrastructure and deployment features. Defining the devops role and ensuring you have someone in that role, is part of the process view of the deployment model.

The architectural influence of the deployment process

When an application needs to be highly available, scalable, fault tolerant, and other attributes common to cloud computing applications, the deployment process influences the architecture. There would be no way, for example, to meet high availability targets if the application required downtime for an hour every time a new version was deployed. Applications can indeed be architected to handle frequent deployments and the process needs to be understood in order to accommodate this within the design.

Questions that might be asked with respect to the deployment process include:

- How can we deploy updates to the application without impacting availability?
- How can failed deployments be quickly identified and rolled back?

Typical cloud deployment activities

The following activities illustrate the differences in cloud deployments and what they mean to the deployment process or application design.

Redeployment of the entire application

The physical Windows Azure deployment of services, and the configuration of various services (as detailed in the deployment layout view), is often performed during development as requirements become clear, detail of interfaces becomes available, and finished components are deployed for testing. This *organic* deployment is common in traditional datacentres where it is assumed that the infrastructure will exist until it is decommissioned. It is tempting (or overlooked) to follow a similar approach on Windows Azure and not to script out the ability to rapidly redeploy the entire application, with all of its configuration. What if the subscription was cancelled for some reasonable administrative reason? What if the entire application needed to be deployed to a different datacentre in the event of an extended outage or insufficient capacity in the current datacentre? To manually redeploy the entire application and its configuration, with no documentation of the configuration and the sequence, would be a time consuming and risky task.

The correct approach is to script out the deployment (using the Windows Azure Management API[58]) as a development activity. Ensure that the scripts are

---

[58] http://msdn.microsoft.com/en-us/library/windowsazure/ee460799.aspx

checked into source control, and are subject to the same disciplines and rigour of application code. These scripts should include scripts (or clear documentation for manual configuration) of external dependencies (such as on-premise firewall configuration).

Configuration updates

Configuration data can be stored in many different places, and the handling of updates by the application needs to be understood and considered. Some places where configuration data is stored include:

- Service definition — changes to the service configuration generally require a restart of the roles that are impacted by the configuration.
- Service configuration — the service configuration file is a good way to get the Azure fabric controller to ensure that configuration changes are deployed to running roles. However, in order to prevent unwanted restarts, the RoleEnvironmentChanging event is triggered and code needs to be written in order to determine if the configuration update requires a restart.
- web.config — the traditional place for configuration data is the web.config file. This should not be used for configuration information in Windows Azure, and the service configuration should be used instead.
- SQL — configuration data is frequently stored in the database. If it is frequently accessed, it also means that it is probably cached, and the invalidation of the cache (or recycling of the roles) is needed when the configuration is updated.
- Cache — storing data in a distributed cache is a good technique to ensure that data is both available and up-to-date.

Deployment of updates to Windows Azure hosted services and roles

Windows Azure provides extensive support of updates to services and roles. Upgrade domains, virtual IP address swaps, and production versus staging environments provide many options to deploy updates without impacting availability. Which of these features are used, and in what cases, needs to be properly understood and assessed by deployment teams. The features enable:

- A 'rolling thunder' update of roles where not all instances are updated at once, allowing running roles (whether on the old or new version) to handle the load while others are being updated.
- The ability to deploy to a staging environment and swap the staging and production environments quickly without having to start up new instances.

While these features provide critical functionality that ease deployment, some resulting issues need to be dealt with, such as multiple versions of a single role running at the same time and the ability to 'point' services to staging addresses if necessary.

Deployment rollbacks

Updates to applications can, and do, go wrong for any number of reasons. Whenever an application is deployed, the question always needs to be asked "What if this doesn't work?", and plans put in place 'just in case'. This may require careful consideration in the application, particularly if contracts (message schemas or other fixed schemas) change. A worker role, for example, may need to be able to handle message payloads from previous versions just in case the message originator has to rollback to an earlier version.

Database snapshots

Performing database snapshots (database copies in Windows Azure SQL Database) is frequently used as a technique in deployments where bulk database updates or schema changes are implemented in order to have a database (or data) to rollback to. When using database snapshots the deployers need to be considerate of inconsistent data. The application may need to support the temporary suspension of database operations while a snapshot is taken and the deployment rolled out, or allow for updates to multiple databases at once (almost like having an equivalent of a deployment 'staging' database). This becomes more difficult, and even impractical, at a scale where there are many databases.

Design considerations for deployment process view

Techniques that need to be built into the application to handle deployments are similar to the techniques used for availability (as covered in more detail in the Availability Model) — after all, the ability of an application to handle the failure of a component due to unplanned failure is indistinguishable from a component that is unavailable because it is being deployed. Indeed, the ability to handle deployments gracefully can come about as a side effect of good design and architecture to accommodate any type of failure. In this way, the 'design for failure' mantra becomes 'design for deployment' as deployments are more frequent than failures.

Availability techniques that are particularly relevant for deployments include:

- Stateless services — when services (particularly websites) are stateless, the updating of a service will be transparent to the user. Before a role is shutdown, the current request will be properly processed, and the next request will pass to an updated instance. This can cause problems if there are significant changes that prevent a single session being served by different service versions. In such cases, the session may need to be abruptly terminated and the user redirected 'home'.
- Stable interfaces and contracts — if services are loosely coupled and not dependent on a particular contract or schema, the calling service simply interacts with the available service, and doesn't care whether or not it has been updated. This requires that the contracts do not change, otherwise the services have to handle multiple versions.
- Asynchronous processing — if extensive use is made of asynchronous processing using a persistent message store (such as Windows Azure Queues), the updating of the worker role that processes messages is completely independent of the application that puts messages on the queue. Provided that there is enough storage (at 100TB for a Windows Azure Queue and 5GB for a service bus queue) and that the worker role can be updated quickly enough in order for the processing to proceed, there will be no impact on availability during the deployment.
- Retries — while not the best fall-back position for deployments, retry logic that can handle a brief unavailability of a service could be applied for some updates that result in a brief downtime (such as changing the number or type of endpoints for a service).

- Alternative data store — applications that can cope with the failure of a database can handle deployments where the database is taken offline. This may involve insertion of data into another database (or other storage), or the reading of data from an alternative, possibly out of date, data store.

Development approaches that influence deployment

Deploying an application to production is only one part of building and operating applications, and other processes influence the overall deployment process. The deployment process of a well-tested application will obviously differ from one that is quickly patched and moved to production with insufficient testing.

Testing

By far the biggest influence on the confidence of deploying an application update is the confidence in how well the fix has been tested. Where testing is weak, deployments are delayed or batched, as nobody wants to take responsibility for pulling the trigger (and rightly so). The testing extends beyond simple button pushing UI testing, and should include performance and load testing. Unfortunately, not every tiny little update can demand a full set of regressive UI, performance and load tests, which leads to the need for other quality processes, to avoid a reliance on testing alone.

Test driven development and continuous integration

TDD, software craftsmanship and other practices and processes are concerned with ensuring that the maintainability of software is high. With these processes, a change can confidently be made to a class knowing full well that it will be contained with a set of unit tests to ensure that the change behaves as expected. This is very important with deployments, as it ensures that developers can confidently make changes without having to attempt to understand the ramifications of their change. That confidence is transferred to deployers who have to make the call on quality before deploying.

Continuous delivery

An extension to continuous integration is the concept of continuous delivery. Continuous delivery extends continuous build by being able to automate the build, test and deployment on a continuous basis, even to production if necessary. While a high level of maturity (and a limited type of application) is required for continuous delivery, many of the practices can be individually applied. Some of those include:

- Automating deployment by selecting a candidate build from the build server (as used in continuous integration).
- Creating and running integration tests using unit test frameworks.
- Automating performance tests, including the automated instantiation of test agents.
- Continuously running tests on a production using test frameworks and feeding this in to health monitoring

Test in production (TiP)

TiP is the idea that at scale not all errors can be picked up in testing due to unpredictable load and edge cases. In TiP, the application may be deployed with updates that are only available to certain users, such as employees or beta testers. In such cases, the application may need to be developed to connect to services at different addresses based on a user profile or originating IP address.

Scheduling deployments

While small, urgent deployments could be made at any time, deployments generally need to be planned to take place at specific times or intervals. Cloud computing deployments need to be considerate of platform/SDK updates and the lifecycle model.

Lifecycle model

The Lifecycle Model heavily influences many aspects of the design, and its value in the deployment model is high. Deployments need to be planned (or at least scheduled) for when there is going to be minimal impact on user satisfaction, this is because:

- Deployments often result in reduced capacity (as roles are taken offline).

- The time taken for a deployment may cause a backlog that needs to be cleared (such as a backlog of messages on a queue).
- The deployment may need to be rolled back or result in extensive downtime, in which case it would be preferable if as few users as possible are trying to use the application.

The lifecycle model should provide all of the data necessary in order to determine the optimal time for deployments. Things to look for include:

- Daily peak load times — deployments should be scheduled when load is off-peak, and when sufficient capacity is available. Remember to consider availability of developer, test and operational resources for deployment. Even though 2am may seem to be the best time for a deployment, if anything goes wrong there is nobody available to fix it.
- Planned high load events — the lifecycle model should contain data that represents when an increase in load is expected due to marketing or a release of new features. Scheduling a deployment to occur far enough in advance, or after the event, is advisable (in order to iron out bugs).

Platform and SDK updates

Although Windows Azure allows applications to run different host OS versions and different versions of the SDK, running an application on an outdated version immediately incurs technical debt. Delaying deployments because the application is lagging the platform can cause problems. The schedule of updates to the Windows Azure platform needs to be understood, communicated to the development team, and allowed for in the deployments.

In addition to well-publicised platform updates, occasional tweaks are made to the platform (particularly incremental updates to Windows Azure SQL Database), which need to be considered in the deployment model. Also, CTP services, for which there is no official support, and the expected release date of official versions need to be described within the deployment model.

Summary

An application developed without consideration for deployment will not run optimally on the cloud. The deployment processes whereby live services are updated, tested, or even rolled back, without affecting application availability, are not simple. It requires an application architecture that supports partial availability, multiple versions, and live updates. It requires developers, testers, operators, and even the business to work well together, according to a clear view of the layout and the processes. The deployment model creates these layout and process views, making it invaluable for a running application and providing useful input into application design and development.

Steps

1. Develop the layout view.
2. Develop the process view.

Integration Model

Applications do not exist in a vacuum, and almost every application needs to communicate at some point with another. This communication between completely separate applications is more complicated than starting a conversation and requires integration; protocols need to be established, languages, agreed formats, schedules and even what to do when the other party doesn't respond. Integration is absolutely critical for any application but, as people who have worked in IT environments will know, can be very difficult, time consuming and expensive.

In developing a model for the integration of applications, it is important to frame what we are referencing. Integration is a huge business, with specialist tools, vendors, patterns, frameworks and just about every technology that has ever been used in IT. To produce an integration model that encompasses every type, variation, load, and complexity of integration is virtually impossible. After all, integration is about the complex interdependencies between systems with all of their nuances, edge cases, defects, failures, and oddities exposed. This is why integration is a specialist area with wildly varying approaches depending on the market, need, technologies and budgets. Within CALM, we have no intention of solving every integration problem you may encounter, and if your integration environment is complex then we recommend that you build your approach based on a model capable of handling your particular needs.

Anecdotal evidence suggests that while cloud computing applications have some integration, it is seen as a secondary feature. This is probably because:

- Integration-heavy, core enterprise systems are not being moved to the cloud due to risk aversion.

- ERP and other large vendors are still shaping their cloud services. These applications are heavy consumers of integration and their absence on the cloud is reflected in an absence of extensive integration in the cloud.
- Enterprise middleware (MQ Series, Oracle Fusion, TIBCO, etc.) is taking time to be established on public cloud platforms, probably as a result of customers not asking for it yet.
- Integration tools, such as SQL Server Integration Services, that run millions of daily integration jobs worldwide are not yet built for cloud environments.
- Traditional tried-and-tested methods for integrating, such as using text files on FTP, are not seen as cloud friendly, due to their vulnerabilities and difficulties running in a load-balanced environment.

As a result, the integration that a cloud application will contain is likely to be fairly simple, is not a core feature and does not take much effort or consume much of the overall project budget. This basic integration requirement is a result of the type of applications that run in the cloud, combined with the immaturity, or at least lack of coverage, of established integration technologies.

The aversion to integration-biased projects in the cloud might suggest that the tools and technologies available are fairly basic. This may be valid when assessing tools across the board, but Windows Azure does have specific integration solutions that are advanced and solve particular integration problems very well (such as Windows Azure Active Directory and Windows Azure Service Bus). Cloud platforms, specifically Windows Azure, may not have a breadth of integration technologies, but do have depth where it is required. For example, while most applications won't need the support of a mainframe based TP monitor, they may need to integrate authentication using Facebook as an identity provider[59], which is surprisingly simple to do on Windows Azure.

When researching integration options for your application be aware that cloud applications generally have a low integration requirement and cloud platforms, that are PaaS biased including Windows Azure, are not architecturally aligned to traditional integration. This influences the extent of the integration in the project and the choice of technologies, and this in turn, is reflected in the integration model.

---

[59] http://msdn.microsoft.com/en-us/library/windowsazure/gg185919.aspx

Challenges of integration in the cloud

Before examining how integration is tackled in the cloud, it is useful to highlight why integration is difficult in the cloud. This should help clarify why there is tool immaturity, few implementations, and provide clues as to possible problems that may be encountered when integrating applications with an application being developed for the cloud.

Integration is already difficult and risky

Integration is always harder than expected, despite vendor promises or project delivery pressures. Cloud projects are under scrutiny as they chart new waters, and there is little point in making them harder than necessary by adding complex integration work. While the cloud specific part of the project may be running well, the integration part can drag the project down and if it fails it will go on record as a failed cloud project, not a failed integration project. This alone should initially qualify out integration-heavy applications and create a preference for lower hanging fruit that is better suited to the cloud.

Lack of control

The compute/role PaaS model specifically limits what can be run on Windows Azure, and these limits can be a problem for integration approaches. Even in the IaaS model with the existence of persistent VMs on cloud platforms, some control is surrendered; be it networking, disk I/O, OS versions and even physical controls. This lack of control may be problematic, but it may not be immediately obvious. For example, a service that needs integration may want communication over a specific port or protocol (say UDP) that is just not possible with the available networking infrastructure. Another example is email, which is a shockingly common protocol for integration. Sending and receiving of emails is not straightforward on Windows Azure or any other cloud platform, due to the risk of clouds being blacklisted as sources of spam.

Custom configuration

Integration often requires custom configuration of the server that hosts the technologies or acts as an integration endpoint. Whilst persistent VMs make it easier to have a hand-configured virtual server, this goes against cloud architectural principles, and the configuration should at least be scripted so that it can be recovered in a different location if a failure occurs. This scripting may simply not be possible with the particular integration tool in use, which may require an operator to step through installation while setting up the server.

Authentication

There are many different authentication mechanisms used in integration, some powerful and sophisticated, and others less so. While Windows Azure supports complex federated identity mechanisms, processes running in Windows Azure won't have things that may normally be taken for granted, such as being on a domain, fixed IP addresses, hardware dongles (yes, they are still used), and other parts of a physical infrastructure that may not normally be a problem.

Licensing

Many integration tools and services have licensing conditions that don't translate well into a cloud computing environment. Even if they can contractually accommodate the deployment of the client service across multiple machines, they can fall flat during implementation because they require that a key be generated for each specific machine. Generating keys for specific virtual machines, which may not exist if they are rebooted, is not easy to do or even desired in cloud architectures.

Data providers (systems that need to be integrated with) and tool vendors (of the tools and libraries necessary for integration) aggressively protect their domain. They are likely to have a combination of licensing terms or technologies that mean that they either cannot be used in a cloud environment, or are very expensive to license.

Long-running batches

One of the fundamental architectural principles of cloud applications is the concept of 'design for failure' on the back of a commodity infrastructure. This is where the availability of the service, not an individual machine, is of concern. This means that applications are built to expect failure at any point in time and generally have very simple stateless processes that, if unexpectedly terminated, have little impact because they start again somewhere else (either explicitly developed for, or because the user has clicked again). This is in contrast to integration applications that frequently have long running processes with transactions containing multiple operations that cannot handle the fallout, if they terminate unexpectedly. Consider, for example, running SQL Server Integration Services on a VM in Windows Azure. The Windows Azure SLA and operating environment means that, at any time, the Fabric Controller can bounce your VM for any reason it sees as valid. So, if you have an SSIS task that runs for four hours you will need to build in recoverability for cases where the underlying VM is shut down. At the time of writing the SLAs for Windows Azure Virtual Machines have not been announced, but it is likely to be lower than a high-end, on-premise database cluster.

Many integration approaches require that a single process runs either as a listener, polling for changes, or taking a long time to run jobs. These are not particularly suitable in a cloud environment because single-instance processes are difficult to build in dynamic environments.

Scheduling

Scheduling of (cron) jobs is surprisingly difficult on Windows Azure. This is not necessarily a platform limitation, but the result of the fault-tolerant environment; where any number of processes need to be able to kick-off a task at a particular time, and then need to discuss it amongst themselves to make sure that only one of them is executing it. This is in contrast to environments where stable machines wait patiently for a particular time of day to kick-off a job. Integration often requires scheduling, be that specific times of day (often after hours), or according to a predetermined frequency. Sophisticated job scheduling tools are an important aspect of integration that simply does not exist on cloud computing platforms.

Orchestration

Orchestration creates a layer of abstraction over services that need to be integrated. It separates the process logic from back-end services and provides an environment to redefine business processes on the fly, without needing to alter any of the services. In many ways, it shares some of the cloud computing application architectural principles of loose coupling, asynchronous processing, and fault tolerance. It would seem, at least in theory, that orchestration should be relatively easy on the cloud. Unfortunately, the technologies and products to do orchestration are complex, expensive, resource intensive, and difficult to use. Orchestration never comes packaged as something simple and is included as part of ESB (Enterprise Service Bus) technologies, such as IBM's WebSphere and Oracle's ESB (as part of Oracle SOA Suite). Products of this scope and pedigree require infrastructure that, in most cases, will not be satisfied by the commodity infrastructure offered by public cloud providers. Even Microsoft's own product for orchestration, BizTalk Server, has struggled to be ported to Windows Azure and only went to CTP (preview) on a VM in August 2012, illustrating how complex it is to get orchestration technologies running in the cloud.

Implementing fully-fledged orchestration can be done using tools from major vendors and run on Windows Azure VMs, but the cost, effort, and energy required is not conducive to a simple integration task. An application that requires such extensive integration should be qualified out as an unsuitable candidate for Windows Azure.

Outdated integration approaches

As much as sophisticated EAI (Enterprise Application Integration) tools and platforms exist, a lot of integration is implemented using outdated approaches. Integrating complex applications is frequently undertaken with CSV files that are shared using an FTP server, or emailed back and forth. These approaches result in integration that is unmanaged, brittle, error-prone, and accomplished in so many different ways across the organisation that it is difficult to keep track of what is going on, or whether or not it is working.

The problem with these outdated approaches is that they are difficult to get working within a cloud environment. They require too much manual configuration, operator input, and their reliability can be a problem for applications with a high availability requirement. As there is little standardisation across the enterprise, it is neither easy nor worthwhile to try and convert them to modern approaches.

Since many of these approaches were developed before security became a major concern, they are fairly unsophisticated in this respect. In the case of protocols such as FTP, simple username/password keys are sent in plain text, making them vulnerable to hacking. Many other outdated integration approaches create vulnerable, insecure endpoints. As a result, network security is used to enhance integration security by limiting access to machines with fixed IP addresses.

Data gravity

Large enterprises with large databases tend to keep integration close to their centralised data. Applications in need of data have a tendency to stay in the same datacentres as the source data. They share the same infrastructure (including database, networking, and backup), and are safe, from a networking point of view, behind the same perimeter security. Integration that requires large volumes of data to move from the primary datacentre and out of the control of the organisation will be questioned, and may even be impractical from a bandwidth, encryption, or other points of view.

Cloud based applications, where a lot of data is moved from centralised control, have to escape the data gravity well. This may include technical solutions, as well as the need for significant executive-level support.

Networking

Although cloud based applications can be configured to be more private and static, by their very nature they are dynamic and publicly addressable. A cloud service should be referenced by a DNS name, not a static IP address. Many enterprise integration approaches demand the opposite, and expect services to have static IP addresses in order to create a firewall rule that allows a single machine to have specific access. Although cloud applications can be configured to use static IP addresses and VPNs, it is too close to having the architecture dictated by infrastructure. While this kind of configuration may be possible with

IaaS, the further an application moves from the infrastructure, to PaaS and SaaS, the more difficult it becomes to configure the application to work with enterprise security practices.

Opportunities of cloud-based integration

The infrastructure available in the cloud allows for interesting possibilities for the provision of datasets that need to be integrated with, and the availability of compute resources to process data at a rate that would be impossible or impractical in on-premise datacentres. As larger workloads and applications are moved to the cloud, the need for integration increases. People who develop cloud applications are aware that their applications do not run in an isolated environment, and extensively integrate with other services, such as third party identity providers. Applications architected for the cloud have accessible, well-described endpoints, can scale to handle load, communicate securely, use message based asynchronous protocols, and are generally open to necessary integration.

Unfortunately, approaches to integration are different to existing on-premise integration approaches and in many cases, such as the use of network perimeter security, are in conflict. The solution sits somewhere in the middle, where cloud based architectures adjust to conform to on-premise practices (such as the use of VPNs), and on-premise integration approaches adopt more of the cloud-oriented approaches (such as SAML authentication tokens).

Enterprise focus

The enterprise is a big market that public cloud vendors are trying to penetrate, whether that is Amazon on the back of its public cloud brand, or Microsoft leveraging existing enterprise relationships. Due to the amount of integration in enterprise applications, cloud vendors need to add more extensive integration-specific features and services. This can be seen with Microsoft's addition of IaaS features that allow the use of enterprise integration approaches, and include:

- Persistent IP addresses (through infinite DHCP leases) — Allow firewalls to allow access from cloud based services.

- Persistent VMs — Allow the installation of specialised integration technologies that have not been engineered for the cloud.
- Virtual Networking — Allow cloud based virtual machines to connect to the enterprise network via a VPN.

Over time, more and more features will be added to Windows Azure that facilitate integration with enterprise applications.

Cloud specific integration technologies

As market demands better technologies on the cloud to integrate applications, more will become available. Technologies that are cloud specific and deal primarily with integration are still emerging, and are in the early phases of the adoption cycle. Cloud specific integration will be split into the following areas:

- PaaS message-oriented platforms — Most cloud providers offer some sort of message-oriented infrastructure that, while useful within the application, is also useful for integration. Some features, such as the Service Bus Relay in Windows Azure Service Bus, are important for enterprise integration because of their ability to work around network security issues.
- SaaS integration platforms — Integration should be offered as a service, where the familiar approaches to integration using integration-specific tools are adopted for the cloud. Examples include Bableway[60] and Boomi[61], and many more are sure to emerge in the future. Microsoft does not offer any such integration platform.
- On-premise tools — It is possible to run an integration tool on-premise to the cloud (such as using SQL Server Integration Services), but problems still exist because of the assumptions that these products make about infrastructure. Vendors will need to adapt these on-premise tools to become more cloud-aware, even though they remain firmly rooted on-premise. An example of this approach is IBM's WebSphere Cast Iron[62].

---

[60] http://www.babelway.com/

[61] http://www.boomi.com/

[62] http://www-01.ibm.com/software/integration/cast-iron-cloud-integration/

Increasing use of standards

Applications that make use of standards improve interoperability and the ease at which they can integrate. These standards are not specific to cloud applications, and are shared by modern applications built on the web to web standards. Examples include:

- Web services — Applications that expose web endpoints and allow communication over http (and https). This has been enhanced by a wider adoption of SSL for encryption and REST patterns.
- Data interchange — Modern applications are getting better at sharing data in agreeable and understandable formats. The use of browser-based JavaScript has increased the use of JSON for data exchange. ATOM and RSS are still good standards for exchanging data, but are falling out of practice. OData[63] is Microsoft's open protocol for querying and updating data but hasn't gained sufficient traction amongst non-Microsoft developers.
- Identity — Web applications have a great need for identity services to authenticate and authorise the use of resources. Standards include OpenID[64], SAML (Security Assertion Markup Language), and OAuth.

Increasing use of services

Cloud architectural patterns promote the use of discrete, loosely coupled services with publicly addressable endpoints (generally over http). Decomposing application functionality as services, and adding authentication and authorisation to access those services, creates an environment that can make integration easier. For example, if a service exposes some JSON data to the web browser as part of normal functionality, it is not too difficult to expose further data via the same endpoint and protocol. After all, to a web server, the authenticated browser consumer is indistinguishable from another authenticated application, accessing the data over http.

This allows many integration problems to be solved using existing approaches, where an application simply consumes data from another service, without having

---

[63] http://www.odata.org/

[64] http://openid.net/

to worry about formats, location of files, schedules, and networking problems. Likewise, an application that is a source of data for integration simply needs to expose the data, and have little concern for how it is consumed. This does not solve all integration problems and more sophisticated protocols may be needed that require, for example, confirmation that data has been correctly received.

Virtual Machines and Virtual Networking

The IaaS cloud features of Virtual Machines and Virtual Networking ease integration on the cloud by allowing cloud applications to behave more like their on-premise counterparts. The primary uses of Virtual Machines and Virtual Networking are:

- Installation of specialised tools — In some cases, there may be a specific need to integrate using a tool that is not able to run on a PaaS platform. These tools might offer a specific set of features that may be required, or there could already be a significant investment in integration scripts or models and in-house skills. In these cases, installing the tools on a virtual machine may be the only way to integrate the application.
- Integration with on-premise networks — Networking specialists on existing datacentres are nervous about exposing endpoints to services outside the datacentre network perimeter. In the context of some of the methods of integration, such as the use of FTP, these concerns are valid. Virtual networking provides a relatively simple method to get around security concerns, by making the cloud-based application part of the on-premise network through the use of VPNs. Most hybrid cloud solutions have some sort of virtual networking as their architectural base.

Developing the integration model

Against the backdrop of the complexity of integrating applications, developing the integration model is difficult particularly when at least one of the integration points is within enterprise datacentre. Readers with extensive experience and existing organisational processes for integration are encouraged to make use of them where possible. As expressed in the beginning of the chapter, this book does not attempt to provide a complete solution to the highly specialised integration business. Readers may look at other integration methodologies and guidance, and use that as a basis for their own version of the integration model, using this as a checklist to ensure that all areas are covered.

Regardless of the coverage of integration in CALM, the need for sufficient and clear documentation of the tools, technologies and approaches to integration, are required for the application. The use of the CALM integration model should drive sufficient questions about integration in the application, and highlight solutions to satisfy those needs.

Understand the applicable scenarios

The first step to understanding integration within the application is to understand how complex the integration is going to be, and potentially how much effort is required. Integration can be simple or highly complex, and it is the complex integration scenarios that should be carefully considered or avoided altogether.

Consider each type of integration against the following scenarios:

- Client or server — Simple integration where a client requires some data. This can be a JSON document that has some data that needs to be used on the client.
- Services Integration — A service endpoint provides an interface for integration using a well-described contract, and communicates over a standard protocol (such as http). The service may allow for pagination, updates and other more complex data operations.
- Application Integration — Integration between entire application stacks, rather than simple client/server or services. This may involve large datasets that are integrated using ETL techniques (Extract, Transform, Load). It can often involve scheduled integration, where jobs are started at particular times of day.
- Workload Integration — Where small data is transferred, using messages, from one service or application to another, in order to continue the logical workflow of data. Workload integration can be performed intra-application (as is a common cloud pattern) or between different applications on different networks (such as order placement integrating with order fulfilment).
- Orchestration Integration — Where business rules are implemented on the fly and data is routed to the correct destination based on the executing rule, specific data within the message, and reference data that may only be relevant at the time. For example, routing of financial transactions based on the time of day, order size, and the spot price of a financial instrument.

The scenarios can be fed back to project management to assess the risk of the integration work to the project, and the effort involved. If the application absolutely requires orchestration, or has a significant number of application integration scenarios, then it may be better to qualify out the application as an unsuitable candidate for the cloud.

Determine the scope of integration

Since integration is not a strength of cloud-based applications, it's logical that an application that is primarily about integration is going to be difficult to execute and won't show off the best features of the cloud. On the other hand, all applications require integration. The amount of integration, counted in both the number of integration points and the integration scenarios, needs to be carefully considered and weighed up in terms of viability.

As illustrated in the diagram above, using the cloud as part of a broader enterprise application, where most of the application is hosted on-premise, is a viable solution. Certain features can run on the cloud, and if those features are consumer facing, possibly free, and subject to variable demands, the cloud can be the best option. In such cases, the integration between the on-premise application and the cloud is one of the most important features. Without integration, the on-premise application is not publicly exposed, and the cloud application will have so little data that it will be worthless. Yet the integration points need not be complex. The cloud application has a subset of requirements many of which require less data consistency, can cope with slight data inaccuracies, may not send all data back to the on-premise application, and similar aspects that mean that the integration can be simplified.

Detail each integration point

Across all projects, not only cloud projects, integration detail is left very late. This may not be much of a problem for traditional applications hosted on-premise, where skills exist, and tried-and-tested approaches can simply be rolled out. On a cloud project, failing to consider integration early can derail the project. For example, an assumption can be made about how integration is going to work, only to find when everything is tested on production, that on-premise networking requires a fixed IP address on a purely PaaS based solution. This would require some rework of the architecture, and possibly some cobbling together of solutions such as Virtual Machines and Virtual Networks.

The integration model requires that integration be documented in sufficient detail to make necessary adjustments to the architecture, so that specific integration issues can be accommodated.

Cover all the integration points

Make sure that **all** of the integration points are covered in sufficient detail. Don't just cherry-pick the easy and obvious ones. It may be that the apparently simple requirement of 'FTP us a CSV file', is the one that is the most difficult to deal with. Often it is the smaller integration points that create problems because the project cannot influence any change in the 'corporate standard' of how applications integrate with that specific application.

Determine the integration class

The integration class encapsulates the technologies used, approaches, people involved and the complexity of the application. Capturing the class of each integration point is a good way to get a high level view of what is involved. The integration classes are detailed below:

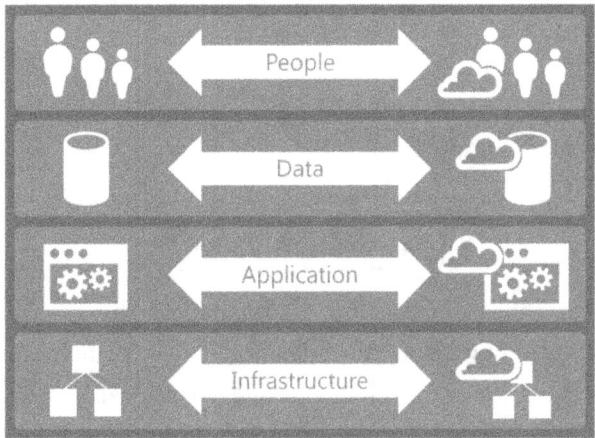

Identity

Used for making use of an identity service that is not part of the application itself. The identity service will provide authentication and authorisation at a minimum. Some may provide additional identity attributes, tokens, delegation and other features.

Technologies used in identity integration include:

- Windows Azure Active Directory.
- Integration with Azure hosted identities.
- Federation with other identity providers, such as Windows Live ID and Facebook.
- Federated identity with on-premise Active Directory.

Data

Data integration is the most common integration in enterprises, where large datasets are exchanged, or databases are synchronised. Data integration is complex because the differences between the source and target schemas, representing differing business semantics, need to be resolved. At a basic level, field mapping needs to be completed but other complexities, as a result of (mostly) undocumented business rules, can take a long time to resolve. Data integration is covered in further detail within the data model under Shared data.

Technologies used in application integration include:

- ETL using staging databases or flat files.
- Replication.
- Master Data Management.
- Data synchronisation (SQL Data Sync).

Application

Application integration requires that contracts be established at the interfaces between applications. Application integration can take many forms, including a type of data integration, but is mostly associated with single service calls that pass a relatively small piece of processed data. Where possible, and especially within cloud architectures, applications should integrate asynchronously using persisted messaging technologies. Application integration can become difficult because both parties in the integration may have to write custom code to perform the necessary actions on the data, and there may be a lot of variations of data and many methods needing to be developed.

- RPC style service calls.
- RESTful service calls over http(s).
- POX (Plain Old XML) over http(s).
- SOAP.
- WCF (Windows Communication Foundation).
- Messaging (Windows Azure Queues, Windows Azure Service Bus).

Infrastructure

Most infrastructure integration with cloud applications comes down to the configuration of VPNs so that the cloud application is part of the on-premise network topology. Other infrastructure issues, such as punching holes in firewalls, become part of the specific integration being dealt with.

- VPN (Virtual Private Network).
- IPSec tunnels.
- Shared storage.
- Cron job scheduling.
- Programmable load balancers (ADC - Application Delivery Controller).
- Operations integration (System Center).

Understand the other party

Integration, by definition, involves disparate systems. These systems have different technologies and different approaches. Most importantly, they have different teams or organisations that the project team needs to work with. Many problems exist when working across technical teams. Perhaps the other party has integration options that are not in the available documentation. Almost certainly, the other party has different pressures and project schedules, so will probably not be able to bend to the will of your project.

Make sure that the integration model includes as much information about the other party as possible, including:

- Technical information — As much information as possible should be collected about the other system. Include all available documentation such as formats, protocols, schedules, and integration workflow.
- Project team — Document as much as possible about the other party's team. Include project managers, technical contact points, developers, testers, operations, and anyone else that may be an asset when trying to bring the integration to a conclusion.

Networking in the middle

Despite the desire of primary integrating parties to work well together, the third party is always networking and security operations. Networking, for valid reasons, has a tendency to lock things down to such an extent that the planned integration will simply not be possible within the deployed environment. When working with other parties make sure that networking and security operations are included in the review of each integration point. Getting guidance, approval, and signoff by networking and security operations as early as possible in the development process is a large risk that is easily managed.

Detail the integration requirement

The integration model needs to contain the detail of the requirement for each integration point. As the integration model, like all CALM models, is intended to evolve over time, the degree of detail up-front is low. Describing the full requirement to implement the integration can be a time-consuming exercise, with participation from many stakeholders, as all of the integration business rules and edge cases are hammered out.

The simpler and quicker requirements to document include:

- A basic description of the data.
- A sample of existing data (either in the documentation, or an example used for another application).
- A list of preferred protocols for integration (web, FTP, etc.).
- The data format that will be used (JSON, XML, CSV, etc.).
- Approaches to authentication and authorisation (username/password, active directory, etc.).
- The general networking requirements (ports, static IP address requirements, etc.).
- The schedule or trigger for integration (daily schedule, on-demand, per transaction, etc.).

Further requirements that take longer to document include:

- Fields and field mappings.
- Validation of incoming data (datatypes, required fields, domain lookup, etc.).
- Business rules for transformation from source to target schemas.
- Handling of errors and failed integration (halt import, rollback, compensating transactions).
- SLAs (Service Level Agreements) between the parties.
- Health monitoring and operational procedures.
- Testing of the integration (test data, test platforms, etc.).
- Detailed network requirements (specific ports, logins, IP addresses, firewall rules, etc.).
- Detail of security risks and how they are addressed (authentication, authorisation, encryption, non-repudiation, etc.).

Proposition of alternatives

The reason why we have such a proliferation of outdated integration approaches in our systems is because we let it happen. When an architect or application designer is told that data will be provided, for example, by placing a CSV file on an FTP server, it is accepted as being feasible and, to a degree, trivial. Because some integration problems are simple to solve, and we are under pressure to deliver features quickly, the de facto integration approach is accepted as 'good enough'.

Once some detail of the requirement and the other party is known, see if you can push the technical solution to something that is more cloud-friendly. Perhaps the other party will welcome the opportunity to integrate 'the right way' instead of persisting with an approach that is outdated. For example, if the stated requirement is to send data using a daily CSV file, enquire whether or not sending the data per transaction is better (this is easier to implement in your application). If this is acceptable, see if it is feasible to put the data on a message queue (such as a Windows Azure Queue) that the receiving application can pick up.

You may find that suggestions of alternative approaches are welcomed, and an integration point that initially seemed clunky, prone to failure, and tricky to implement, all of a sudden becomes message based, loosely coupled, and well aligned to your own application architecture.

Schedule the integration effort

Each integration point needs to be worked into the project schedule. The integration model is not a substitute for project management but should be used as a source for the project schedule. Integration takes a lot longer than expected, not just because of increased effort, but also because of the elapsed time waiting for other parties to do what they need to. Milestones include:

- Date specification complete. This will depend on the integration point, as some interfaces will be product-based and be better described at the beginning. Others may take longer as both sides need to be developed.
- Date development starts.
- Date that the other party is ready for testing.
- Date of initial test data and test runs.
- Date of full integration test start.

Assess integration technologies

Integration is assisted by various technologies. The technologies range from simplistic FTP servers, to Windows Azure services, to sophisticated integration tools. The integration technologies chosen are going to be part of the application architecture for a long time, as changing them requires another organisation to make changes too. Because of their architectural longevity, the technologies should be chosen very carefully and, in addition to their technical suitability, must be considered against:

- Their suitability for cloud oriented architectures. This needs to consider the use of non-persistent virtual machines, as used by web and worker roles, load balancers, and other concerns.
- Cost considerations as per the cost model, which tends to be based on consumption, rather than licensed per node.
- The effort for the other party to make use of a particular technology. For example, some parties may not be able or willing to read a message off Windows Azure Service Bus.
- Development effort to implement the technology. Minor integration points may not be worth the effort to implement on top of sophisticated tools.

Technologies considered can be from third parties or Windows Azure. Third party software can be of the following types:

- Virtual Machine installed tools — A specific tool, technology, or service can be licensed and installed on a VM. For example, SQL Server Integration Services (SSIS) can be installed on a VM and integrate with many databases (including SQL Azure).
- On-premise tools — Tools can be used on the on-premise network, and used to integrate with the application through the firewall or across a VPN. Again, SSIS would fit this model, as will any number of tools that IT has skills and licenses for.
- Hosted or cloud integration services — Something as simple as a managed FTP service, or more sophisticated integration services that are cloud-based or more traditional.

Windows Azure also offers many technologies useful in integration, and these need to be understood and considered.

Windows Azure integration technologies

Windows Azure offers many features that are applicable to integration, both with on-premise applications as well as other cloud-based applications. There is a lot of material available from Microsoft and third parties on how these technologies can be used for integration, and it is not covered in detail in this book. Architects and application designers are encouraged to investigate them in sufficient detail to determine their fit.

Windows Azure Service Bus

Windows Azure Service Bus[65] is a powerful set of services that has been specifically developed for application integration. The approaches of Windows Azure Service Bus are more cloud-centric than on-premise, but do offer very useful features for enterprise integration, such as the Windows Azure Service Bus relay[66] that allows services to be exposed without the need to open up firewall connections, or changing of enterprise network infrastructure.

The Windows Azure Service bus team is continuously evolving the product to deal specifically with integration issues. The TechEd 2012 presentation, Achieving Enterprise Integration Patterns with Windows Azure Service Bus[67], by Clemens Vasters and Abhishek Lal, specifically works through examples that reference Gregor Hohpe's Enterprise Integration Patterns[68]. The Windows Azure Service Bus team is also beginning to add more orchestration-like features to their product (although these are not yet production-ready) using the Windows Azure Service Bus EAI & EDI - April 2012 Release[69].

Virtual Machines

Windows Azure Virtual Machines[70] are important for integration as they allow existing technologies that have not been developed for the cloud to be used within a cloud environment. This is demonstrated by Microsoft's addition of pre-

---

[65] https://www.windowsazure.com/en-us/home/features/messaging/

[66] https://www.windowsazure.com/en-us/develop/net/how-to-guides/service-bus-relay/

[67] http://channel9.msdn.com/Events/TechEd/NorthAmerica/2012/AZR317

[68] http://www.eaipatterns.com/

[69] http://msdn.microsoft.com/en-us/library/windowsazure/hh689864.aspx

[70] https://www.windowsazure.com/en-us/home/features/virtual-machines/

built VM images for SQL Server 2012[71] and BizTalk Server 2010 R2[72] to the Virtual Machine gallery.

Windows Azure networking

Windows Azure offers two features to help with integration, namely Virtual Network and Windows Azure Connect[73]. Virtual Network allows the creation of VPNs (Virtual Private Networks) in Windows Azure that extend the on-premise network using DNS configuration and IP address ranges. Windows Azure Connect is agent-based and works by being installed on an on-premise server, and setting up an IPSec tunnel between the on-premise server and Windows Azure.

SQL Data Sync

Data can be synchronised between on-premise SQL Server and Windows Azure SQL Database using SQL Data Sync[74]. SQL Data Sync differs from SQL Server integration techniques (using replication, SQL Server Integration Services, or custom tools), by being entirely service-based, negating the need to setup an additional server. SQL Data Sync is also simpler, both in features and user interface, and does not require custom code to be written.

Windows Azure Active Directory

Windows Azure Active Directory[75] provides identity management and access control features that integrate with other identity providers. Where this plays a

---

[71] https://www.windowsazure.com/en-us/manage/windows/common-tasks/install-sql-server/

[72] http://blogs.msdn.com/b/biztalk_server_team_blog/archive/2012/08/29/getting-started-with-biztalk-server-2010-r2-ctp-in-windows-azure-virtual-machines.aspx

[73] https://www.windowsazure.com/en-us/home/features/networking/

[74] http://msdn.microsoft.com/en-us/library/windowsazure/hh456371.aspx

[75] https://www.windowsazure.com/en-us/home/features/identity/

role in identity is two-fold. Firstly, having an existing identity platform that has support for so many identity providers is a type of integration service itself. Secondly, the ability to use on-premise Active Directory is useful for integration with on-premise applications or user credentials.

Foundations

Integration is often seen as something that is tacked-on to an existing application and is subject to lower levels of quality. Treat integration points as first-class features that require the same development and architectural rigour as any other parts of the application.

Ensure that standards are followed

Make sure that the integration isn't hacked together with little concern for standards. Follow the established standards within the project environment, enterprise, and broader industry.

- Engineering standards that are developed by the team should be followed, including technical standards, such as unit testing, and process standards, such as peer review.
- Follow standard approaches for sharing data across the cloud, web, and enterprise. This may include web data interchange standards (such as JSON) and security standards.
- Treat incoming data as if it were your own, by making sure that it is stored properly and responsibly. This includes correct data models, encryption, backup procedures and controlling data access.
- Test integration points as thoroughly as any other parts of the application, or even with more attention.

Develop the security model for integration

Many of the fears and concerns about the cloud surround security, and integration requires additional attention to allay security fears. Because your application is hosted on the cloud, it may be perceived as being insecure, and any data stored in it considered at risk. For each integration point, for each party, security needs to be adequately addressed. The security of the integration falls within the scope of the security model, but also needs to be highlighted within the integration model. Aspects of security that should be addressed include:

- Perimeter security — Where the system that needs to be integrated with is inside the enterprise network, open ports, permitted source machines and other firewall rules need to be carefully considered. There may also be similar firewalls used in public cloud endpoints too.
- Authentication and authorisation — Ensuring that the identity of the calling service is confirmed, and permitted to perform the operation. This includes the expiry of identities and permissions.
- Channel encryption — Making sure that the data cannot be read (sniffed or man-in-the-middle attacked) while in transit by using SSL or another encryption mechanism.
- Data security — Where data is moved from an on-premise application to a cloud based application, how the data is stored, where it is stored, and how it can be accessed needs to be addressed. This may require the involvement of compliance experts and auditors.
- Data retention — To reduce the risk of data being compromised, try to keep only as much data as is needed for the current operation and discard the rest, either immediately, or over time. The data should be owned, controlled and managed by the source system where possible.
- Operational security — Address the security of data that is stored in database backups, as well as the access that operators have to any data received via integration.

Develop an approach to availability

Points of integration are a problem when building available applications. Integration points are prone to failure due to the complexity of handling all edge cases, network issues and availability of the other service. There is little that can be done to increase the availability of services on which the application depends, as it is owned and operated by an organisation that is outside your control.

The integration model needs to be aware of the approaches defined in the availability model and each integration point should have a strategy for dealing with the failure or diminished health of the other service. This may mean implementing approaches such as asynchronous message orientation, feature shaping (service degradation), retries, alternative data stores, and so on. The integration model should be specific about how availability is going to be dealt with for each integration point, so that developers can estimate and plan accordingly.

Estimate the integration effort

Integration effort is generally severely underestimated. This is due to:

- Business understanding of integration — Non-technical people involved with projects have a good idea of specific data that is required for integration. They are involved with understanding what data they need, and what is available, so believe that they understand how the data is integrated. They have little understanding of the complexities involved as there is a big difference between a sample spread sheet of data and fully integrated, reliable applications. This misunderstanding results in estimates that are either set or influenced by the business, and not technical members of the team.
- Involvement of many people — Integration of applications requires the integration of people across teams. Developers of one application do not know the detail of the other, so must work together. Business representatives need to get involved, from both parties, to describe the rules for data, field mappings, and edge cases. Testers need to run tests across multiple systems. Operators and network security staff exist within both parties, and need to be involved. The participation of so many people, across many teams and organisations, is a big project management task, and the time taken from start to finish of integration can be very long indeed.
- Implementation of business rules — Whether it is in workflow, or data transformation, integration requires the translation and mapping of business rules and semantics from one system to another. This can be quite difficult, as the systems satisfy different needs and customers with differing data schemas and processes. There are always edge cases, odd hard-coded rules, default and required data issues, cardinality differences, and even seemingly simple data such as times can cause problems if the source and target systems are in different time zones. Failure to consider the complex business rules can make estimates far lower than they should be.
- Painstaking development processes — There is no easy way to write integration code. Unit testing adds minimal value and development is done largely by trial and error, where undocumented behaviour of source systems has to be slowly and methodically picked through. Developers with little integration experience have a tendency to greatly underestimate the effort involved.
- Testing is difficult — When testing a fully integrated system, it would be useful if a fully representative test platform were available. This may be

difficult to achieve, particularly if a full test requires that all of the integration points are available in a test mode, but running at production capacity. Finding errors using 'live' data and production systems is often the only way to fully test the application, and this happens very late in the project. Failure to estimate and consider how much effort remains once the integration is considered 'code complete', can severely impact delivery very late in the project.

The integration model requires enough (realistic) estimation to cover the effort required to implement all integration points. It is important that all integration is considered, as the points that may seem small and insignificant can often be the ones that create the most problems.

Remove unnecessary integration points

If integration does not show the best of a cloud application and exposes the application to significant risk, it makes sense to minimise the number of integration points. Go through each integration point and classify it in terms of the adopted project classification of features ('Critical', 'Nice to have', etc.). Together with the estimate of effort and the technical complexity, use this classification to prioritise and aggressively remove unnecessary integration points. This may require that an entire feature be cut from the application and moved to a later phase. You can also consider the interim use of manual integration, such as the ad-hoc, manual importing of data into the database.

The integration model should clearly reflect the team's choices on which are the priority integration points and the motivation for including them. The amount of development effort spent on integration should be minimal, say less than 5% of the total effort for the application.

Review the project qualification

If an application has too many integration points, the effort to implement integration is too high, or the application functionality suffers greatly from the removal of integration features, consider the viability of the application as a good candidate for the cloud. Feed this back into the qualify process, and consider selecting a better suited candidate project that requires less integration. If the project absolutely has to proceed, make sure that the delivery of features is staged in such a way as to defer the implementation of integration features into later phases (post-live). Allow the application to mature and demonstrate its viability on the cloud before allowing it to get bogged down by integration effort and brittleness.

Summary

Few applications exist in isolation, and the ability of an application to integrate with others is an important part of being able to deliver value. Indeed, much of the web is built on applications that have little of their own core functionality, but are able to present data in innovative and useful ways. Even Google search is built on integration with millions of web servers around the world. Cloud applications are well positioned to integrate successfully with other applications by being on the public internet with few firewall or bandwidth problems to deal with, and are good candidates to show the value of integration done well.

However integration is difficult, requiring significant effort to get right and often more effort than is initially estimated. Integration has to deal with a variety of source systems, from those that are architecturally similar and based on the same standards, to those that use outdated protocols and proprietary interfaces. Some source systems sit on similar, publicly accessible platforms while others hide deep behind enterprise firewalls. Some source systems are fast and reliable, while others slow and prone to failure. Some source systems have well matched schemas and implement similar business rules, while others require significant effort to transform data from their unfamiliar models. The breadth and variety of applications is what makes integration difficult, time-consuming and full of surprises and also introduces significant risk to the project.

The integration model encourages the collection of detail about all of the interfaces and the devising of technical, business and project managed solutions. Effort put into the integration model at the right time during the development process, will pay dividends by aggressively managing risk early in the application lifecycle.

Steps

1. Understand the applicable scenarios.
2. Determine the scope of integration.
3. Detail each integration point.
4. Develop the security model for integration.
5. Develop an approach to availability.
6. Estimate the integration effort.
7. Remove unnecessary integration points.
8. Review the project qualification.

Integration Model **317**

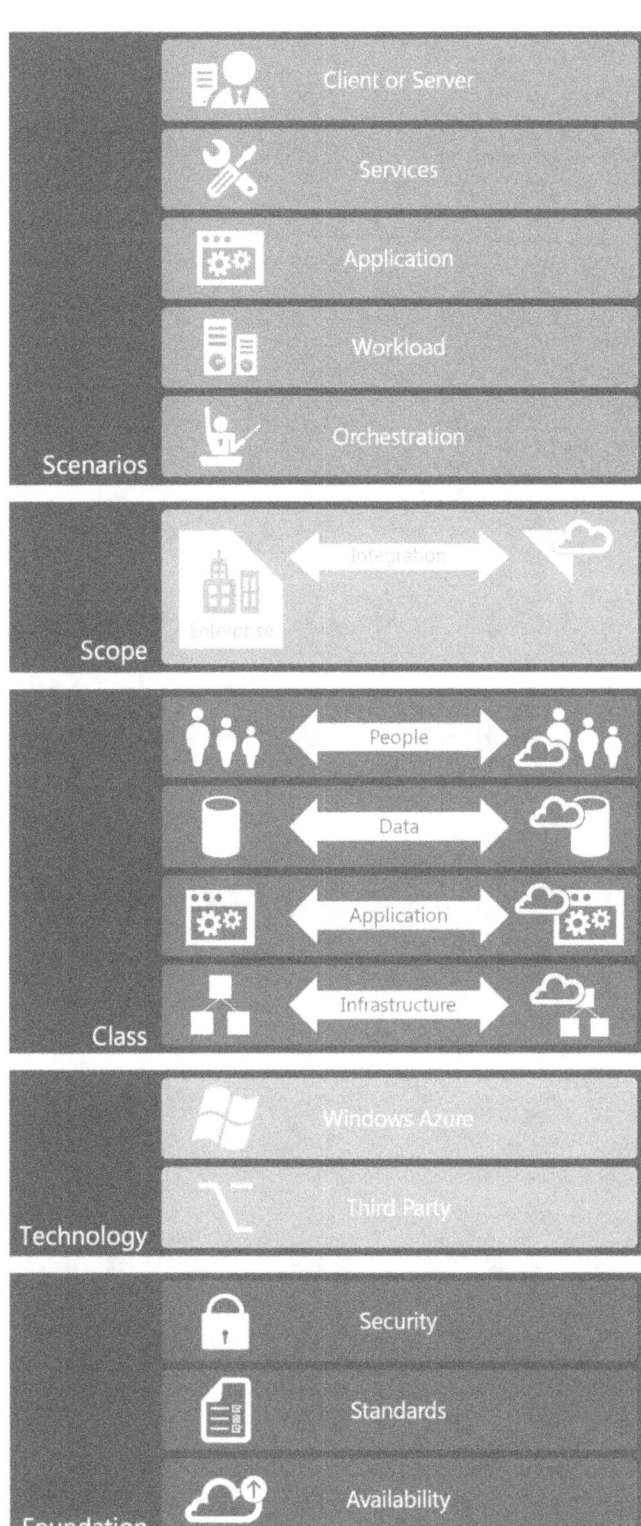

Operational Model

Applications designed specifically for a cloud computing environment are different from traditional designs, and have familiar attributes to modern application design and architectural approaches. The common theme is the demand for high scalability and availability, on top of commodity infrastructure, for a low operating cost. Traditional data centres with specialised high-end servers struggle to come to terms with this new approach, which has changed how IT infrastructure is owned, procured and managed. Similar changes are being felt by those who are expected to support and operate the applications deployed in cloud environments.

In many ways, cloud computing applications are quite complex:

- Applications are composed of various, loosely coupled and isolated services that require an understanding of how they fit together.
- Data is stored in many different places, not in a single SQL database, and is not quite consistent or easy to backup, manage and control.
- Some parts of the applications will work when one part has failed or is failing.
- Applications are updated constantly and out of sequence, meaning that a deployment downtime window is a thing of the past.
- Applications run on a publicly accessible, multi-tenant infrastructure that creates security risks and odd performance characteristics.

These complexities mean that the operation of the applications changes. Operators need to be able to understand more about how an application hangs together and what to do when things go wrong, or how to prevent them from going wrong in the first place.

Marketing hype would have us believe that applications in the cloud magically run by themselves, with availability and scalability built into the platform and little need for skilled operators to ensure smooth operation. While that may be true in some cases, the demand on operators in the cloud is arguably higher than ever. Operators no longer have roles where they monitor infrastructure, back up the database, reboot suspect servers and call the developers in all other cases. Operators now need more familiarity with the application because the developers don't (and shouldn't) understand the nuances of running the application on a public cloud. The rise of the 'Devops' movement is an indicator of a general demand, including in non-cloud environments, for operators with skills that span both development and traditional operations. Only with these skills can operators develop the automated environments, handle deployments on live applications, determine application bottlenecks and make the necessary changes to the cloud platform in order to resolve issues.

Principles for cloud enabled operations

In order to facilitate the operation of cloud applications, there are some basic principles that should be top of mind.

First principle - Build the application for operations

Just as security is difficult to retrofit into applications, so too is the serviceability of the application. It is important to develop the application in such a way as to:

- Collect the necessary data and metrics for health monitoring.
- Eliminate dependency on manually installed or configured components (as many legacy applications require).
- Implement retry and failover within the application, in order to handle failure or diminished health in services on which the application depends.
- Build services that can be independently tested, deployed and rolled back.
- Provide administrative service APIs so that operators can build scripts to automate operation.

These application features need to be planned, designed and budgeted for implementation as part of the initial application development. Serviceability aspects of the application need to be considered first class features, just like end user functionality, otherwise it will be difficult to operate and many of the benefits of cloud computing will be lost.

Second principle - Eliminate reactive manual operations

Applications taking advantage of cloud computing tend to exhibit unpredictable behaviour. They no longer have flat 9–5 lifecycles but rather have to respond to high load spikes, huge amounts of data storage and processing, and rapid releases of fixes and new features based on user demand.

When applications need to scale and updates are being released daily, things can break. The platform may not perform as it did in testing, multiple versions may be running at once and operational teams (and their supporting development and test teams) may have immature processes or simply crack under the pressure. Using a skilled operator to sit and manually fix problems in a production environment where things are falling to pieces, users are frustrated, and the business is prowling for scapegoats, is not an ideal situation for any operational team.

Therefore operations must mature to a state where most of the work that they do is either:

- Proactive — where tasks are undertaken before things become a problem, or
- Automated — where diminished health requires none or little human intervention.

Evolve operational maturity

Blowing half of the development budget on an awesome operational dashboard is going to be a difficult sell. Part of the problem with the unpredictability is you may not know up front the hot points that need extra instrumentation or automation. Ensure that the basics are in place and add operational functionality over time. This evolution needs to be planned and considered up front, and there are things that can be done in order to ensure that it receives focus.

- Add operational 'features' as first class features to the product backlog in an agile environment.
- Encourage that operational features are implemented properly, preferably with APIs, so that they can be automated.
- Communicate and provide feedback between operations, testing and development teams in order to ensure that the right features are implemented.

Developing the operational model

The first step in developing the operational model is to consider what aspects of the application and infrastructure the operations team should focus on. This is achieved by understanding the architectural models of the application, being familiar with the actual deployment of the application, and working with any available health monitoring.

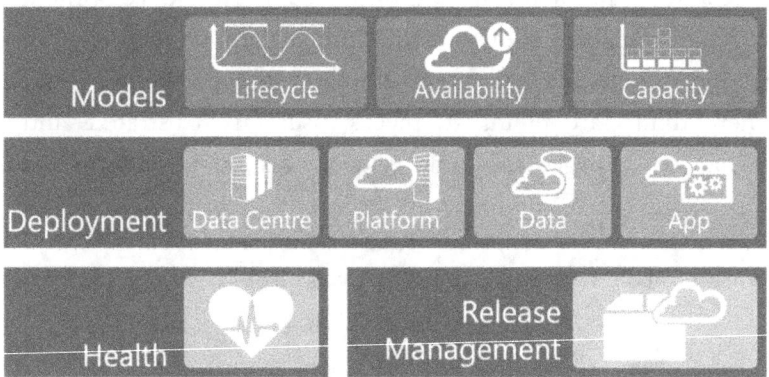

Architectural Models

Most of the architectural models are relevant to operations as they influence how the application is built for, and deployed in, a cloud environment. Some models require extra attention and understanding within an operational environment. The following models are pivotal when developing the operational model.

Workloads

Operations need to understand the workloads defined within the application. It is likely that what would have traditionally been a single workload would be split into separate workloads with queue based messaging in-between. So operations would need to understand the decomposed workloads, the messaging subsystem and how the diminished health of one affects the other.

Lifecycle Model

The most important model for operations to understand is the lifecycle model. This provides the information to be able to plan capacity and respond to increased or decreased load. For example, the lifecycle model would indicate, in a retail 'Black Friday' lifecycle, the events (catalogue update, sale begins) and the phases (initial sale rush, order fulfilment, stock availability updates) that require attention from operations. The Black Friday example may seem obvious, but business reality and diversity means that there are many lifecycles that may be obvious to business insiders but unknown to operational staff. The lifecycle model provides information about what is expected to happen to a running application which is absolutely vital to operations.

Availability Model

Operations are measured on the availability of an application and this is not simple to define or achieve. The availability model, which describes differing availability requirements, is important for operations to be able to perform proactive tasks and respond to any events that affect availability.

Data Model

The data model needs to be singled out for operations, mainly because in a cloud environment the data model is more complex than a traditional single SQL database. When the application is under load or when health is diminishing, operations need a clear understanding of where data is, and where it is supposed to be, in order to react.

Capacity Model

The capacity model is operations' blueprint on how to plan capacity and scale accordingly in order to respond to load. By being familiar with the scale units defined in the capacity model, operations can easily ensure that availability SLAs are met and automate the rapid provisioning of extra capacity as needed.

Deployment

When an application first goes live, the deployment of the application will be familiar to everyone on the team, including developers and testers. As time progresses the application stabilises, growth becomes more constant, the initial deployment plan and the actual deployment in production diverge. It is the responsibility of operations to own the deployment as it is operations that made the decisions to change the deployment, add additional capacity, and make the necessary tweaks to get things working properly.

The additional complexity of cloud based applications means they may be built with loosely coupled services, heterogeneous data stores, varying configurations handling different workloads, and multiple versions that may be in production at once. Keeping a handle on the deployed application is an important and difficult task. While the deployment may match an understood and documented pattern, the details are relevant and will differ. Deployments will be in specific accounts (possibly more than one), multiple databases, have different instance counts for different roles, have specific certificates for different roles, different storage endpoints and any number of important specific aspects. Operations need to maintain an accurate picture of these details.

The tools for obtaining the data on the current landscape will vary from one implementation to the next and will be based on a combination of different tools. Tools that come as part of the platform are useful, as are self-assembled dashboards that use the platform APIs (although there will be a development cost). Health monitoring data may also be used to keep track of the underlying deployment, but some of the metrics may be missing and not all will be applicable.

While the application and its data are the most important parts of the deployment for operations to understand, the lower levels of the stack require special attention. It would seem counterintuitive that a PaaS platform such as Windows Azure would require lower level operational knowledge. After all, Windows Azure is supposed to abstract the underlying platform and remove the need to understand or control it. While this may be true for application developers, there is still a need for operations to understand the Windows Azure platform in some detail, including:

- How the Fabric Controller works and how it automatically allocates resource.
- The role statuses and how they relate to an application being deployed.
- The Guest OS and how applications that target a specific OS behave.
- How Windows Azure fault and upgrade domains work.
- How load balancing works and the capabilities of the load balancer and traffic manager.

Health Monitoring

As per the health model, all data from the application and Windows Azure platform needs to be collected and presented to operations. This data is used for:

- Real time monitoring of key metrics, particularly during the beginning of a phase (as expected by the lifecycle model) that results in extra load. Real time monitoring should be on minimal data points that can be presented on a single screen, as too much data can be difficult to action.
- Historical analysis of health data in order to determine the health trend of the application and to establish whether the application behaved as expected after changes were applied (particularly those by operations).

It is important to note that health monitoring forms the interface between operational activities to be actioned (either proactively or reactively) and the deployed application.

More detail on the health monitoring aspects of the operational model can be found in the Health Model.

Release management

As part of the application lifecycle, release management comes well after design. It is not expected that the operational model, which is developed early on in the design phase, will have much detail on exactly how releases will work.

It is worth asking questions about releases during design so that everyone on the team is considerate of the role of operations in releases. Some aspects that should be highlighted at this stage are:

Out-of-band and frequent releases

Because cloud applications are composed of a set of loosely coupled services, it is easier to make changes to one part of the application without affecting the other. For example, a worker role that processes messages from a queue can be updated without having to update the web role. Indeed, because of the queues, there will be no need to stop the web role while the worker role is updated.

This means that there is no single version of the application running and no batching of updates for a single release of the entire application, during a planned release window. Small parts of the application will be released and even during a peak period if necessary. This reflects the increasing adoption of 'continuous integration' where there are sufficient, automated tests of the application to maintain high quality. It also ensures that quality control is part of the development and continuous build process, rather than being addressed after development is complete.

Availability of infrastructure for testing

Because cloud computing platforms provide infrastructure on demand, it is possible to spin-up a massive deployment just to test an application. When preparing for a release it may be desirable to deploy to a test environment that may represent a peak capacity deployment, and is therefore larger than the current production deployment. Additionally, the cloud can be used to run simulations from instances deployed all over the world and possibly on a completely different cloud platform. In such cases, the management and operation of the test platform may be more complex than most operational teams are used to — and all of that effort to run some tests for an hour or two before it is all dismantled and reassembled for a release the next day.

Ability to roll back releases

Windows Azure has a staging environment where deployed applications have virtual IP addresses and can be swapped between production and staging. This allows applications to be tested in staging, moved to production and, if problems are detected in production, quickly swapped back. The virtual IP address swap enables this to happen quickly as no roles need to be started or shut down so there are effectively two versions of the application running at once.

This adds to the ability of operations to deploy releases but it can become confusing, particularly when releases are out-of-band and services are kept in staging for long periods 'just in case'.

Multiple versions in production

One of the problems with out-of-band releases is that changes to services can have breaking changes, where there is a dependency on a specific version of the output or interface. Because of the loose coupling of services it is perfectly reasonable to have multiple versions running in production, where the dependency between versions is set in the configuration of a particular part of an application.

For example, a web application may have an endpoint defined for a search service. When something changes, multiple versions of the web application may exist with multiple versions of the search service running at once. Only after the eventual shutdown of all instances of the old version of the web application can the old version of the search service be shut down.

This is also seen with asynchronous processing using queues. A worker role processing messages off a queue may be version specific. When something changes, the queue name changes as an endpoint configured in the application, and the new version of the worker role processes messages off the new queue. Only when the old queue is empty can the old worker role be shutdown. This requires operations to be familiar with how things hang together and the ability to monitor queues to recognise if they are empty or not.

Operational Activities

The operational model needs to have a view on the activities that operations will perform.

- Focus attention on proactive automated support. Trying to detail all reactive support activities goes against this principle and may be futile as events,

triggers and responses will be less fixed. If they were fixed, they would be automated.
- Remember to evolve the operational maturity. Use the process of identifying activities, to build the operational model as an opportunity to create a list of operational features for the product backlog.

Proactive Activities

Proactive operational activities are defined as those which:

- Occur during normal working hours (operational working hours may differ from user working hours e.g. it may be performed by a night shift).
- Are performed in a consistent and calm manner.
- Are planned to take place.
- Are well documented.
- Provide feedback of their success or failure.

Typical proactive operational activities

Proactive operational activities are generally those that either attempt to maintain a stable state of the application, or prepare for an upcoming event. General areas of proactive operational management are:

- Risk management — activities are not required if all goes well, but since things seldom do, should be done anyway. Examples include making database backups, changing or expiring authentication tokens, and testing availability and recoverability.

- Preventative maintenance — ensures that parts of the system are well oiled and in a state where they will function normally when the application is under load. Examples include ensuring that sufficient storage is available, clearing out unnecessary log files/data and may even extend to a 'rolling thunder' style of restarting of application pools or roles.
- Preparation for load (capacity provisioning) — while we should be able to scale up applications immediately, or even automatically, in some cases it may not be the safest option. Prior to an event (from the lifecycle model) occurring, operations can pre-provision, and even test, additional capacity so that when the rush starts, sufficient capacity is immediately available. Other load preparation activities may include warming up the cache and rebuilding indexes.
- Preparation for release — releases can cause major disruption if things go wrong and planning for a release helps manage the risk. Include proactive operational activities that can be performed before release in order to reduce the risk of the release failing and make it easier to roll back a release if necessary. Activities include backup of databases, termination of excess capacity and the graceful termination of non-critical processes.

When to perform proactive activities

Proactive operational activities are, by their nature, activities that can be planned and scheduled in advance.

- Scheduled activities — these activities run on a specific day at a specific time. For example, database backups may run daily, weekly and monthly.
- Time triggered activities — are a special case of activity where the time that they run is of importance. For example, activities may be timed to run before a data export is due to kick off, or immediately after the market closes.
- On demand activities — will make up most of the activities that result from the lifecycle model and health monitoring. They are the result of an event but are not reactive; they are not trying to restore health, but rather proactively prevent diminished health from occurring. For example, capacity may be provisioned based on the lifecycle model, caches may be flushed or reconfigured based on the number of cache misses, and additional database shards may be added as data volumes grow.

During the process of defining the operational model, a table of scheduled and time triggered activities can be drawn up as per the example below.

What	When	How
Full database backup	Weekly, Sun 02h00	Automated database backup
Differential database backup	Daily 02h00	Automated database backup
Rebuild full text indexes	Weekly, Sat 02h00	Run rebuild_index.ps
Purge old Perfmon data	Monthly, 1st, 04h00	Run purge_perfmon.ps
Close stale connections	Daily, market close	Run stale_con.ps

Reactive Activities

Reactive operational activities span from simple task changing, the instance count for a role, to an all-hands panic with lots of meetings and finger pointing when a major outing occurs. Reactive activities are always needed, but it is the level of skill, preparation and maturity that makes the difference between a quickly restored application health and those that go into a spiral of failure, bad decisions and problematic fixes.

It is beyond the scope of the operational model to describe all of the practices, procedures and management of an operational centre, as reactive operational activities vary greatly depending on the environment and team.

What the operational model should begin to define is listing out possible events and triggers, with responses for those events. In many cases, health monitoring will pick up a problem and the defined responses make up a subset of the overall reactive operational responses i.e. recovery from a diminished health to good health. See the table in the Health Model for an example.

- Triggers — are things that happen, usually faults, which set off a chain of failures. Although there is a tendency to brush off many triggers as unlikely (such as an aeroplane crashing into the data centre) variations of the big ones need to be listed. What if there is a complete Windows Azure outage, can you redirect to another address? What if the database becomes corrupt, can you restore the database and keep some functionality working? When working through the triggers, it is probably better to start off big and unrealistic to set

the mood and get them out of the way, before going into detail on smaller, more likely triggers.
- Events — are things that happen, generally an external influence, that cause diminished health to occur and require reaction in order to restore the application health. Examples include increased load due to a marketing campaign, increased size of data that needs to be processed and the addition of a feature that requires increased capacity. While events can be prepped by proactive activities (such as knowing that the sale is going to start), in many cases it may be appropriate to wait until a health indicator shows diminished health before responding.
- Responses — to the events and triggers and where the interesting stuff happens in reactive operations. The operational model needs to identity some of the actions and the detail should be filled in over time by the operational team. The responses can include standard fault detection workflows, escalation procedures, responsibility assignment, case management, diagnosis and prepared planned responses. Responses are also the result of diminished health and are covered within the Health Model.

Operational maturity levels

As per the principles for cloud enabled operations, reactive, manual operational activities should be avoided. Reactive operations happen too late and manual operations are error prone. It may be preferable to have everything automated, but generally that will not be the case. Operations should still strive to increase their level of maturity, across the entire application, to a point where reactive, manual activities are rare.

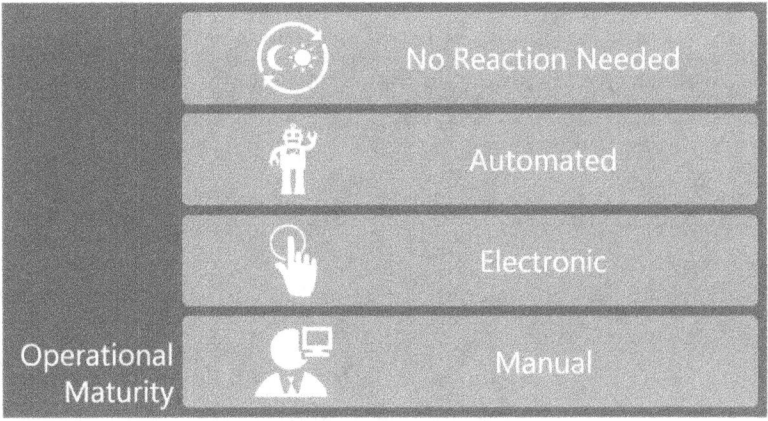

Level 3 - No reaction needed

The holy grail of cloud operations is that there is no need to do anything; the system takes care of things by itself. From the perspective of a Windows Azure consumer, a lot of this is done for you. If a Windows Azure SQL Database falls over, it is taken out of commission and another takes its place without the application even noticing. Likewise with roles that are always kept at the same instance count by the Fabric Controller.

The application needs to do a few things in order to take care of things by itself. The easiest is to ensure that retries are properly implemented, in which case a minor timeout or throttling will not result in an error, and may not be noticed. Others may be more complex, such as taking data from an alternative source, or temporarily and automatically shaping features while load is high.

Level 2 - Automated

In an automated operational environment, an operational system (or more than one) monitors the health of the application and automatically takes corrective action. The most common is services (possibly third party services) that monitor load on web servers and increase (or decrease) the instance count in order to take the load. Applications can also manage a degree of automated response by, for example, increasing the number of threads for processing messages in a queue by monitoring the length of the queue.

Automated operations can be built up from electronic operations by taking scripts that are produced over time and hardening them for an automated environment.

Level 1 - Electronic

Electronic maturity refers to an operator performing an operational activity (either proactive or reactive) and using a script (such as a PowerShell script). These scripts may take input parameters and perform complex tasks but require that an operator explicitly executes them while monitoring for errors. There is a degree of risk associated with running scripts in this manner. The incorrect script may be run, the parameters may be wrong and errors may not be detected.

Level 0 - Manual

Manual maturity is the lowest level and often results in operational environments where there is continuous panic and lack of predictability in response to diminished health. In this environment the operator, on detecting a problem, starts manually 'pulling levers' to try and get the application working again. Manual operations are error prone and rely on a skilled operator that may not always be available.

The existence of a manual operational environment can be tolerated when the application first goes live, as the operational team may not yet be familiar with the application.

Over time, manual tasks must move to a higher maturity level. The table below summarises the maturity levels and shows the only benefit of lower levels of maturity is the reduced initial cost.

	Cost to develop	Speed of recovery	Risk of mistakes	Headcount required
No reaction	High	n/a - no failure	None	None
Automated	High	Quick	Low	Low
Electronic	Low	Medium	High	High
Manual	None	Slow	High	High - may include dev team

Summary

The cloud computing benefits of elastic resources, scalability, automatic recovery, and the associated cost reductions can only be realised with a mature operating environment. Not only is the operations of cloud computing applications different from traditional applications, but applications need to be engineered with operations in mind.

Developing the operational model brings operational concerns to the fore early enough in the application lifecycle for them to be actioned. Operators need to familiarise themselves with how to keep cloud computing applications running long before the application goes live. Architects and application designers need to ensure that features are implemented with a view to being operable. The importance of operations in cloud computing applications and the general disregard of operational issues by developers makes the operational model one of the most important CALM models.

Summary of steps

1. Discuss the principles of enabling cloud operations and create an initial list of features that operations require.
2. Extract elements from other architectural models that are of relevance to operations.
3. Develop the initial view of the application deployment, including details such as accounts, that are important to operations.
4. Identify the health monitoring data and instrumentation needed.
5. Develop an approach for involvement of operations in release management.
6. List proactive operational activities.
7. List possible events, triggers and reactive responses.
8. Create a plan for migrating to a higher level of operational maturity.

Operational Model **335**

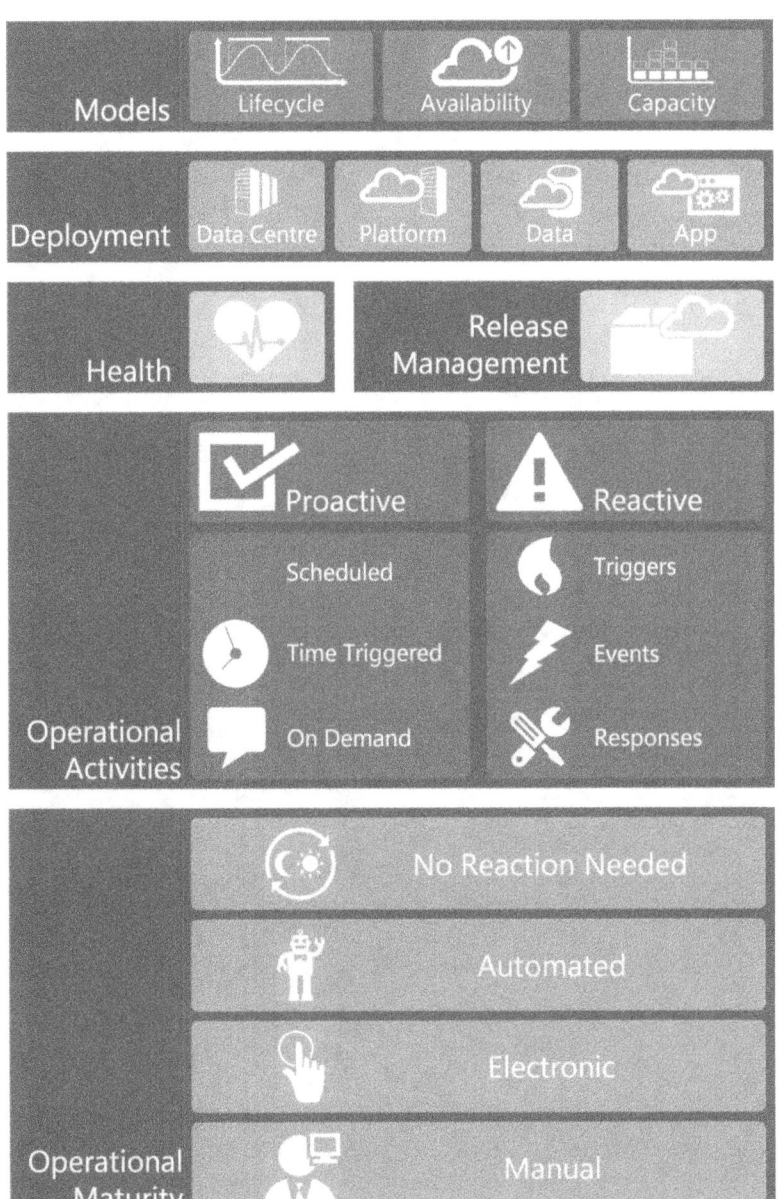

Test Model

In traditional applications, testing has become a secondary activity that attracts little attention, budgets and skills. This has a lot to do with the maturity of current stacks, where defects are mostly relegated to the web front-end, and caught by 'button pushing testing' rather than rigorous test strategies, plans and execution. Applications have, over time, become more robust as frameworks take care of problem areas and developers embrace test driven development, where quality becomes a developer focus rather than something addressed later in the process. Testing skills reflect this reactive and distanced role, so testers tend to be less technically capable. Many testers are only able to use testing tools, are unable to write code or scripts, and have a tenuous grasp of the technical detail of the applications being tested.

The new approaches, architectures, and implementation of cloud applications create a demand for high quality testing. The blasé approach to testing has no place in a cloud computing project, and of all the teams involved in building the application the testing team may be the one that needs the most attention. Not only does testing have an important role to play in ensuring the quality of the application is high enough, but should also become a core part of the development and operations. Testers will cement their role by finding defects specific to the differences of the cloud, and providing input and data about application behaviour that cannot otherwise be collected.

The process of testing highlights cloud application problems that need to be addressed, as well as presenting opportunities to add value to the application lifecycle that are not apparent in traditional environments. These are discussed below.

Testing Opportunities

Testing Early

In traditional environments, there is an intention to test as early as possible on a production environment, but the reality is that simulating production loads on a production platform often gets left too late to be of much value. Testers are left with a development or test platform that is not configured as it would be in production. This creates problems with configuration management, and the platform is not up to the required specification, making some of the tests pointless. The cloud provides the opportunity to turn this around, and enable testing early in the project. The ability to test early can benefit the quality, simply because it enables defects to be detected much earlier. The cloud also offers specific benefits related to having production capacity and configuration in order to simulate exactly how the application is supposed to run.

Platform configuration

Since the platform is not configured by hand and needs to be automated (as Windows Azure does for every instance with the Fabric Controller), so the configuration used for test environments will (mostly) be exactly what is intended for production. The OS version will be the same, the database version will be the same, and all libraries that are used in development and testing are the same as would be used in production. Each instance is configured as would be expected, as are the network, storage and other infrastructure components. The network is the same public network as production, so there will be no nasty firewall surprises. Storage and databases will also perform the same way as they would in production, allowing realistic benchmarking to take place.

Availability of production resources

A simulated production platform can be spun up as if it were live, immediately, and for very little cost. An application that will have a peak load on launch of, say, a million page views per day, can easily be tested for two million per day without the need to go and buy resources that will sit around idle after the test. Indeed, the platform can be provisioned for as little as an hour, allowing potentially thousands of instances to be spun up, tested and shut down for minimal cost. This is important for testing functionality, scalability, availability, and other aspects of testing that require production platforms.

Confirmation of architectural assumptions

Because cloud computing is new, a lot of assumptions about how the platform will behave are made during design. In many cases, these assumptions are not even identified or made explicit, but rather the result of an understanding of traditional infrastructure and transferring that knowledge to the cloud. For example, the throughput and latency between an application and its database is seldom considered (provided it is on the local network), and those assumptions about throughput and latency are brought into a Windows Azure environment. Unfortunately, the behaviour of the application in response to database latency and throughput may not be as expected, and this only comes out when doing load tests on a production platform.

Stating the 'confirmation of assumptions' is the positive spin on the function, but the important aspect is the ability to reduce the risk on the project by uncovering unexpected bottlenecks as a result of the platform not behaving as expected, marketed, or documented.

The importance and value of this cannot be understated, as unlike traditional on-premise applications there is little that can be done to improve performance without a lot of rework. On-premise, for example, an underperforming database can have its hardware upgraded (processor, memory, disk I/O, or network) fairly late in the process without having to rework the application. On the cloud it is simply not possible. If an application has a dependency on, say, database throughput being higher than is provided by the underlying platform, there is nothing that can be done to the infrastructure to change it. In which case, the application itself will have to be reworked, sometimes at great cost. Testing and the ability to test on a 'production' platform on the cloud early in the development process help to uncover these potential problems before the cost to rework the application becomes prohibitive.

Capacity and cost planning

As discussed in the cost model, costs are estimated up-front, but need to be continuously reassessed during the application lifecycle, both as part of development and post-live operational procedures. Testing plays an important role, as it allows the application to be simulated in a production environment so that the costs can be better understood. This includes:

- Choosing correct instance size — One of the biggest negative influences on costs is developers choosing instance sizes that are bigger than they need to be. Testers can simulate different configurations of instance sizes and the number of instances. These simulations can be run under varying loads (as described in the lifecycle model) to determine the optimal configuration. Bear in mind that the effort to perform the simulation may be more than the cost savings, so be careful not to over-test for optimal instance sizes.
- Understanding data costs — Windows Azure can throw up nasty cost surprises for the data egress from the data centre, a number of transactions performed against Azure storage, and other areas that are not traditionally considered. Tests accompanied by the billing details for the subscription over the test period, will go a long way to feeding data and insight into the cost model. This is also a hint to be able to run tests in separate subscriptions so that the costs are better understood and not cluttered by other activities.
- Extrapolation for capacity planning — Tests should be conducted on a scale unit (as defined in the capacity model), so that it can handle can be determined. This can then be fed into the capacity model to determine how many 'scale units' will be required to handle the loads expected by the lifecycle model.

Testing problems

While testing on the cloud does provide opportunities for greater participation and value in the application lifecycle, there are also complexities for testers to deal with that are specifically found in cloud applications. The reasons are similar to those for architects, developers and operators, where different patterns, architectures, development approaches and hosting platforms require that testing approaches need to be adapted to reflect the new way that the applications work.

New technologies

Any new technology implementation introduces the need to learn, not only how to use the technology, but also how it needs to be tested. Cloud applications throw a bunch of new technologies at testers that they will need to understand in terms of:

- How the technology fits into the overall application architecture.
- The tools required to use the technology, such as different tools to view the output.
- The expected behaviours and possible failure points of the technology.
- The deployment of the technology into various environments.

While the development team will generally assert that the applications developed for Windows Azure are familiar .NET applications, the platform requires that some new technologies and frameworks will be introduced. Specific examples within Windows Azure include:

- Different storage locations for configuration data — no longer in web.config, but at least in the service configuration.
- Different logging frameworks — application logging data is fundamental to understanding the behaviour of applications, and Windows Azure has a specific approach to logging that will be unfamiliar to testers.
- Different data models — where testers may have been used to just looking in SQL Server for data, Windows Azure applications make use of other data storage technologies (in addition to Windows Azure SQL Database) such as table and blob storage. The tools to access these data stores are not as familiar, or user friendly, as SQL. For example, writing queries may be more difficult.

Complexity

Well-architected cloud applications are more complicated to test. The adoption of asynchronous processing, using message queues, the loose coupling of services, the stateless nature of services, and other architectural principles make things more difficult for testers to understand.

For example, in traditional applications a tester can fill in some data in the UI, and check the database directly after pressing the button. But, asynchronous applications make this more complicated. Data, in this example, *eventually* gets stored correctly and when this happens is subject to many external influences.

Just looking at asynchronous processes, testers now need to understand:

- The flows of data between services.
- The delay in processing that it is subject to (perhaps even days).
- The confirmations and changes in state of long-running transactions.
- Where data is stored before it is committed (such as in the queue).
- What happens if there is resource contention? What happens if data is processed multiple times (idempotence)?
- Whether or not the feature can tolerate dirty reads (as can happen with eventual consistency).
- How errors are handled and communicated back to the user.

The above list is just for one aspect of the increased complexity of cloud applications, and there are many more. Testers were traditionally able to get away with a much simpler understanding of how the application works, but this is not the case for cloud applications. While architects and developers can, and should, be able to describe how the various bits work, and what to look for, it is only with a clear understanding that testers are able to do their job properly. This heightened understanding is particularly required if they are expected to spot potential problems that the developers have not thought of, or catered for, in their code.

Multiple concurrent versions

Because cloud applications don't run on dedicated hardware, the opportunity exists to run multiple versions of the application in production concurrently. Perhaps they share the same underlying database and route requests to different services depending on the type of user? Maybe the traffic manager is used to route to different regions depending on the source of the request? At the very least, some parts of the application will be deployed in a staging environment, where they can be thoroughly tested, even by end users, before being 'swapped' to production. This can last for minutes or days, depending on the risks involved.

The traditional model of deploying from dev, to test, to UAT, and finally to production (after much paperwork), should not exist in a cloud environment. It may do, at least initially, but as the application, and the operation of the application matures, it will tend to result in a more continuous delivery model. This trend towards rapid release cycles does not mean that testers are able to do less work; after all, the quality still needs to be maintained. Testers are left with more to do; more automation of testing, including spinning up of test platforms, more understanding of deployment processes, including feature shaping (where parts of the application are shut down while a deployment is in progress), and more understanding of the Windows Azure deployment model, including how upgrade domains work.

Out-of-band releases

Related to the running of multiple concurrent versions, is the idea that when building applications with loosely coupled services any service can be changed at any time (provided the contract remains the same). Windows Azure applications will typically be built out of many different services, and these services will need to be updated and deployed, as demand requires (bug fixing and enhancements). They will typically be deployed in a cycle that is out-of-band with any other services or parts of the application. This means that, at a point in time, multiple services can be in various states of development, deployment and testing. While this is primarily the concern of operators that need to deploy the bits and pieces, testers need to participate in the process. A typical test team may be performing a number of different tests, on different parts of the application, in different environments, all at the same time. There is no consistency in the test cycles, where all testers are performing similar tasks for a set duration where they can report definitively on the overall quality of a release.

Availability testing

Part of the attraction of cloud platforms is the cost-effective availability. Applications that would normally not be concerned with availability are now considered to have an availability requirement, and where previously an application would not be undertaken due to availability constraints, it can now be developed. This means that many implementation teams will be exposed to availability development and testing for the first time. Two primary questions need to be asked by testers:

How do you develop for availability?

It is important for testers to understand what they are looking for when things go wrong, or cases that developers haven't taken care of.

For example, if a worker role that is processing messages fails, the message is returned to the queue (with Windows Azure queues; other queues may differ slightly) and is processed again. What happens if a message was partially processed? Was the data committed to the database, or rolled back? If the message gets processed again, will the data be duplicated?

Other examples relate to the timeout or unavailability of services. Using the 'design for failure' approach, if a dependent service is unavailable, the application should not fail and should gracefully continue. But this will vary on a case by case basis and, in some instances, the service may be so important and reliable that if it doesn't respond the application collapses in a heap, thereby breaking the 'design for failure rule'. So, if a service does not respond, does the application retry immediately, retry after a delay (if possible), try an alternate address, attempt an alternate service, or store the data somewhere so that it can be sorted out later? These are the sorts of questions that testers need to ask developers so that they can develop their test plans.

Testers should not have to do all of this work themselves and must be involved in the development of the availability model, using it as a reference for the test model and test plans.

How do you test for availability?

Availability is more than just outright failure of services and includes the responsiveness of the application — which is generally related to its ability to scale (see availability outcomes and influencers in the availability model). So the primary ways to test for availability are to shut down or disconnect services, and to put the application under extreme load to see if it scales well.

Chaos monkey

The shutting down of services is often referred to using the term 'Chaos Monkey', which refers to a technique developed by Netflix[76] to test availability. They developed 'Chaos Monkey' scripts that will **randomly** and indiscriminately **disable production** instances. While haphazardly disabling production instances should not be at the forefront of any test plan, the principle remains valid. One of the best ways to test availability is to shut things down and see what happens. This may be easier said than done as it's not that easy to shut down external services (but may be possible to change the password), but it should be relatively easy to find a way to break something on purpose.

Testing response to increasing load

Windows Azure applications should be designed to scale, but not necessarily to auto-scale. Testing the application under load should uncover when capacity negatively influences availability (load is too high for current capacity and the responsiveness suffers) as well as the triggers necessary for operations to respond to degraded health (refer to the operational maturity levels in the operational model). As most experienced testers will be aware, testing under high load uncovers bottlenecks in unexpected places. With cloud platforms, those unexpected places are even more remote or obscure.

Testing at scale

As with availability, cloud platforms also offer implementation teams the ability to handle massive scale that would previously have been ignored. Adding social media and free options to applications suddenly exposes the application to an unprecedented load. How do you test an application that is intended to handle hundreds of thousands of page impressions *per second*? Well understood testing tools cannot cope with these volumes, as they are not able to scale themselves, and the reporting of test results becomes a problem at scale as the amount of data generated becomes a bottleneck itself.

---

[76] http://techblog.netflix.com/2011/07/netflix-simian-army.html

As much as we would like to think that the solution to testing at scale is to use the cloud to perform the testing, by throwing unlimited capacity at it, it is simply not possible to test at scale without the tools, experience and methodologies. In most cases, the solution is to test *scale units* as a basis for understanding the behaviour with fixed capacities, and outsource a large part of the testing to organisations with the capabilities. This is discussed in more detail in scale test below.

Multi-tenant variability

When an application runs on the cloud, it is not alone. It sits on shared servers and communicates across a network shared by thousands of other applications. While Windows Azure does its best to ensure that the multiple tenants running on its platform play nicely together, occasionally there may be 'noisy neighbours'. It could happen that one of the physical machines on which an application is running is subject to degraded performance because other applications on the particular physical machine happen to be under load simultaneously. While this shouldn't affect available memory, and may not affect the processor (as there is a dedicated core), it could degrade the network throughput if all of the roles are trying to communicate at the same time. The Fabric Controller will do its best to ensure that this doesn't happen, by letting noisy neighbours run on their own, but it can, and does, occur. It is particularly common with Windows Azure SQL Database, where performance can vary wildly depending on what other databases on the same machine are up to.

While this is an architectural problem that needs to be catered for, the problem presented to testers is variations of performance with no apparent pattern. Having a successful performance test may not be good enough, because it just happens to be done at a time where other tenants on Windows Azure are not under load. Tests need to be conducted at different times in order to allow for variation and particularly when all other applications may be under load, such as during month ends or early mornings.

Guest OS Upgrades

Windows Azure roles, which run on top of Windows Server, are upgraded from time to time (at least monthly) and, if so configured, automatically. Although it can be limited, it is good practice to ensure that the applications are always running on the latest version of the guest OS. It is more of a concern to operations when upgrades are due (or occur), but can become something that testers become involved in if the application behaves erratically after a guest OS upgrade. If operators are risk averse and choose to manually upgrade the guest OS, they will probably want testers to perform tests before the upgrade takes place. See Managing Upgrades to the Windows Azure Guest OS[77] for more information.

Lack of developer skills

As can be expected with cloud development being different, developers may not have much experience with the tools, approaches, and patterns that they are using. While it is the responsibility of team leads and senior developers to ensure that a lack of skills doesn't mean an increase in mistakes, there will be examples that either senior people themselves are not aware of, or cases that simply fall through peer review cracks. It then becomes the responsibility of testers to pick up any poor implementation due to lack of skills on behalf of developers.

In many cases, the problems will occur in places that testers have previously glossed over because they are in areas they are not used to seeing faults in. It then becomes difficult to create tests for application areas that, traditionally, have been considered unnecessary to test. For example, saving data to a SQL database may be something that is so familiar to developers that they never make mistakes and as a result over time testers pay less and less attention because faults are never found. If the developers are introduced to new data storage technology, such as Windows Azure Table Storage, new problems could start to appear in previously reliable operations. Testers need to have enough tests to handle this apparently regressive behaviour.

Testers should work with senior developers and architects to identify any new technology being used, and in areas that developers may be unfamiliar with, so that sufficient test coverage can be implemented.

---

[77] http://msdn.microsoft.com/en-us/library/windowsazure/ff729422.aspx

Tester skills

In many cases, testers lack the basic skills to be able to test cloud applications fully. Traditional testing approaches have focussed on 'button pushing' testing using automated browser-oriented test tools, and possibly some SQL querying. The nature of cloud platforms is that they are fundamentally self-service, and this extends to testers who need to provision capacity, configure and deploy for testing purposes. It is no longer good enough to wait for a physical test platform to be setup by the datacentre operations team, as testers need to be able to provision and deploy themselves. In order to do this, as well as analyse logs and data (which may not be conveniently in a SQL database), testers need to develop some basic script programming skills.

Scripts are required to automate provisioning, deployment, configuration, and possibly analysis. It virtually doesn't matter which language is used. While PowerShell may be dominant in a Windows Azure environment, the SDKs and REST interfaces can be developed against using PHP or even Ruby. Testers without some script writing skills will struggle in a cloud environment.

Test plan content

Cloud computing obviously does not negate the need for proper testing, and while there are differences tester should take their existing skills, approaches and experiences, and adjust them for a cloud application.

The points discussed below as content for the test plan should not be taken as the complete and final list for what is a specialised and complex discipline. They are simply to highlight areas that are of specific relevance to cloud applications.

Tests should continue as per their normal processes to ensure application quality and produce familiar documentation. This includes test plans, test strategies, test cases, test script or any other relevant artefacts. They then need to consider the adaptation of existing approaches with items highlighted below, in order to enhance their processes to make them cloud capable.

Role of testing and testers

As discussed above, the role of testers within the application lifecycle can, and should, change. Testers can add value much earlier during the design process, and are crucial for effective operations once an application is in production. The first step in extracting value from testers is to discuss and understand their role within the team and how it relates to the cloud application.

Items for discussion and inclusion include:

- Will testers help architects and application designers test the platform by running extensive tests on technical spikes?
- Will the testers run full batches of performance and load tests on the application at the end of every sprint?
- Are testers expected to deploy to Windows Azure themselves, out of the build environment, or are they expected to develop their own deployment scripts?
- How much will testers be included in senior developer design discussions, so that they can understand the complexities of what is being implemented?
- How involved will testers be in developing the health monitoring metrics destined for use by operations?
- How are testers involved in feeding data back to the cost model?

Test schedule

Fundamental to every test plan is the test schedule which should reflect existing approaches that the test team is familiar with, particularly for functional tests. In addition, the schedule should highlight tests that are either unique to cloud applications, or are scheduled differently with cloud applications, such as:

- Performance and load tests on the 'production' platform early in the development cycle.
- Tests on staging platform, when in-place upgrade deployments are done.
- Tests that need to be conducted at varying times, in order to remove the influences of multi-tenancy.
- Automated tests that run for long periods (to pick up memory leaks or similar) due to the availability of capacity.

Functional Tests

Applications that run in the cloud are no different in terms of functionality to traditional applications. There may be opportunities for different functionality as advantages are eked out of the platform, and there may be subtle differences that suit the architecture, such as feature shaping (the turning off of features subject to load). But functionality is determined by the requirements and the need, not the cloud platform. So functional tests developed for cloud applications are no different to functional tests for a traditional application.

Qualitative Performance Test

Before subjecting an application to a high load test, it is necessary to determine if the performance of features is adequate when isolated from performance degradation caused by contention for resources.

The qualitative performance test ensures that individual features perform adequately on the target platform when the application is not under load. Qualitative tests are, therefore, run in a single user mode.

Objectives of the qualitative performance test

Identify initial bottlenecks

Provided sufficient logging exists, or a detailed logging framework that is able to extract interfaces is in place, the qualitative performance test will be able to pick up performance bottlenecks. Testers should have a view on all of the operations in the workload, particularly those that are subject to network latency, network throughput and (virtual) disk I/O. This will allow them to understand if the underperformance is infrastructure related, in which case it may need to be worked around, or is a more fundamental defect in the application that is causing the bottleneck.

Diagnose issues

By knowing the detail of the tests, the precise deployment and configuration used, and the initial dataset, testers are in the position to diagnose the root cause of performance issues. They can also change configurations quickly on the 'production' environment, to confirm or rule out suspicions.

Identify performance related defects

Some performance issues are clear defects that need to be addressed. For example, testing may uncover that for a particular operation a cache is not used and that the database is put under unnecessary high load (a frequent culprit). Testers should use the qualitative performance test to identify such defects, and are in the position to correlate expected load against underperforming processes, in order to focus on those areas where the defects have the most significant impact.

Provide input for optimisation

The optimisation of performance issues can only be planned if sufficient data exists on the gains that will be achieved, against the cost of coding the optimisations. Data gathered by testers during the qualitative performance tests forms the basis for planning of performance optimisations. Developers may be keen to cherry pick and optimise a particular part of the application that interests them, but it needs to be supported by test data as being relevant.

Performing qualitative tests on Windows Azure

Some points to bear in mind when performing the qualitative performance test on Windows Azure are detailed below.

Deployment

No dedicated test platform exists in cloud projects, and testers can deploy however much capacity they need, whenever they want to. With this power comes the responsibility to make efficient use of the platform, and the responsibility to take care of things by themselves. Testers should not rely on operations or developers, and perform tasks on their own, such as:

- Testers need to be familiar with the Azure management portal, configuration and deployment of roles, and possibly be able to deploy out of the build environment.
- Testers may need to create their own deployment scripts.
- Testing may need to run in a separate subscription (account), so that billing data can be meaningfully extracted.
- Testers need to make sure that roles are shut down, databases and other objects deleted once the tests are complete; otherwise the costs may be significant.

Multiple workloads as part of a single feature

Architects of cloud applications will endeavour to decompose workloads as much as possible (see Workload Model), and the result is that a feature may be split across multiple workloads. For example, the 'Submit' of a form may not save data to a database straight away, but will add the data to a queue, and have a separate workload that saves it to the database. This means that a functional test that describes, for example, 'Save data to database on submit', spans multiple workloads, and is virtually impossible to reliably test as a single test case. It is particularly difficult to understand the performance issues and bottlenecks when multiple workloads are used, as the application, by design, introduces a processing delay, which is not necessarily a performance problem. On the other hand, the testers should be familiar with the requirement and test in the context of the requirement. Just because developers have chosen to split functionality across workloads, it doesn't mean that it is adequate to satisfy the requirements, and the processing delay may turn out to be unacceptable.

Logging

Logging is very important in a cloud application, and forms the basis for health monitoring (see the Health Model, so should be included by default for testers to use. Particularly when performing the qualitative performance tests, testers need to make use of the logging infrastructure, as direct access to the underlying infrastructure doesn't really exist and logs need to be used. Some aspects to consider include:

- Turning on logging — Logging can be very resource intensive, and full diagnostic trace logging will almost surely be turned off for production use. Testers need to understand the difference, and use of, perpetual logs versus diagnostic logging. Diagnostic logging can be used in cases where the root cause of defects needs to be determined.
- What to log - Logging for health monitoring and other operational needs may differ from logging that is useful in testing. Testers need to be clear on what they need to log, such as latency for service calls, and influence developers to put logging in at the correct places in the code to facilitate testing.
- Viewing logs - Logs are not stored on individual instances (as the machines may cease to exist, taking their logs with them), but rather in Azure Table storage, or some other data store (depending on the logging framework). Tools that testers may be familiar with for viewing logs will probably not work, and they will have to pick up or develop alternatives.

Quantitative Performance Test

The idea of the quantitative performance test is to quantify the load that can be handled by a specific scale unit (as defined in the Capacity Model). When building scalable architectures, it is necessary to define a scale unit that describes the roles, instance sizes, data storage, and other aspects that and the demand that a scale unit can handle.

For example, say the architect has initially defined a scale unit to consist of web roles to handle web traffic, worker roles to process the data, and queues to handle the data between the two. There will be an optimal ratio of web roles to worker roles in order to handle the demand, and also at some point the queue is going to be throttled as the amount of data processed increases. Testers need to assist in establishing the load that can be handled by this scale unit (in terms of page impressions, number of concurrent users, or some other metric), the number of web and worker roles, as well as the instance sizes.

Testers may think it unnecessary to spend time establishing the capacity of scale unit in such detail, after all, with unlimited capacity, it makes sense you would just throw what you need at it. But this becomes critical as part of the overall test strategy, particularly when performance and scale tests are conducted. Testers need to be able to communicate using a base metric, otherwise there will always be arguments about the particular deployment and configurations used to render particular test results.

Testers should:

1. Assist in baselining the scale units for particular workloads or features.
2. Develop deployment scripts that deploy the exact scale unit for testing.
3. Perform a load test against the scale unit to baseline the capacity that a scale unit can handle.
4. Tweak configurations, ratios of roles, and instance sizes to help find the optimal configurations of scale units.
5. Report **all** test results in the context of the scale unit used for the test.

Scale Test

How do you test for massive scalability? Even if you can provision the resources for the application, how do you build out a test network of millions of machines around the world? There are two ways to test scalability; use scale units and extrapolate the ability of the application to scale and/or use a third party testing organisation that has the capacity to perform the tests.

The scale test is the ultimate performance test for an application and, thanks to the cloud platform, can be performed a lot easier than with traditional applications. The scale tests intention is to simulate production load across workloads, features, time of day, durations and geographies. The scale test should be performed on the production platform, which should be relatively easy on the cloud, with production configurations, instances, instance sizes, data storage, health monitoring, and so on.

Building applications that need to scale massively, shows up any weaknesses because they are amplified at scale. The weaknesses extend beyond the application to the people and processes within the implementation teams due to their inability to cope with the stress, the lack of time to prep large applications for load, and the time taken to conduct root cause analysis when thousands of machines are running. Testers are not excluded from the pressure and are encouraged, if scale tests are necessary, to understand in detail how they are going to test at scale, develop their processes, test their approaches, and generally make sure that they know exactly what needs to be done when the time for scale tests starts.

While scale tests are important for systems that need to scale, it is necessary to understand how imperative they are and whether or not the implementation team has the skills and capacity to perform scale tests themselves. Applications that need to scale because the business founders think that their idea is cool and will go viral, differ greatly from an established brand that is going to be under massive load from launch. Scale tests need to be planned and conducted according to the realistic business need. In some cases, it may not be feasible to do too much scale testing (rather spend the money on features to attract users). In other cases, it may be preferable to outsource scale testing, at least for the front-end simulation, to a third party.

Additional considerations when testing at scale, specifically on a cloud platform, include:

- The data logging needs to be carefully considered. The amount of data that can be generated by millions of users can both clog up the logging systems (degrading performance), and be so vast that any meaningful analysis will be virtually impossible.
- The chosen datacentre may not have sufficient capacity for massive scale tests, and someone from Microsoft may call up to ask what on earth you are doing. It may be useful to engage with Microsoft before running massive scale tests.
- The scripting of provisioning and, importantly, deprovisioning needs to be properly figured out before scale tests begin. If deprovisioning is not done, you may find that thousands of instances are running and costing money, whilst waiting for a test to run that isn't ready yet.
- At scale things take time. Initialising a database with terabytes of data may take a long time to upload. Similarly with bringing test results and logs down for analysis. Even the spinning up of thousands of instances may take longer than expected.
- Scale tests will not happen often, and it is a good idea to have the application run by operations as a practice run for their processes; letting them try and respond to increased demand as they would in a live scenario.

Availability Test

The availability outcomes and influencers in the availability model infer that, from a testing perspective, most availability is tested by performing a good functional test, performance soak and other tests. It is the overall quality and responsiveness of the application under varying loads that ultimately determines its availability.

Tests for availability don't need to be as broad as one would think because other tests take care of it to a large degree. Remaining tests will target unplanned partial or complete failure, and the adherence to the 'design for failure' principles that are implemented by developers. This means that the availability tests are largely about shutting down services (breaking something) to see what else would break.

When developing availability tests:

- Go back to the requirements and design, to ensure that the failure of a service has been catered for. In some cases, architectural assumptions are made about the availability of a service, such as Windows Azure Storage, that is sufficiently high that there is little point taking on the cost of developing fault tolerance for the service. In other cases, there may be such a high dependency on a service, such as a credit card payment gateway, that there is simply no workaround other than a polite error message.
- Try and find ways to terminate services randomly. Terminating services is actually quite difficult on Windows Azure, as the Fabric Controller will do its best to try and keep things running.
- Try options of expired logins for services, as this can be a common fault that affects availability.
- Timeouts and latency can be the Achilles heel of distributed computing, so any tests that simulate timeouts and long delays will show up availability problems.
- Recoverability is part of availability and can be tested in conjunction with operational tests. What would happen, for example, if data storage was completely unavailable in a particular region? Is there a plan to get a basic site running, or stand up alternative storage? What would operations do in these cases?

Soak Test

A soak test is a long-running test that is used to establish if there are any defects that are only presented when an application has been running (preferably under load) for an extended period of time. Soak tests are frequently used to detect defects such as memory leaks and with cloud applications can also be useful to collect data about the underlying platform over an extended period of time (as it may vary due to multi-tenancy). The cloud makes it easy to run soak tests, since they can run on isolated and available capacity for long periods, even months.

Operational Test

There is a data centre adage that says something like "A backup is not a backup until it has been restored", illustrating the need to test basic operations. No test strategy or plan would be complete without ensuring that operational tests are performed. Again, there are some specific focus areas for cloud applications when performing operational tests:

- Health monitoring needs to be tested. The mechanisms that collect, aggregate, and view health data need to be included in test coverage. The accuracy, timing and usability of health metrics need to be given the same attention as any other feature as much of it will be new, unfamiliar, and hand-rolled.
- Operational processes need to be tested. The response of operations needs to be tested, particularly those operations that relate to availability. Can operations detect diminished health and respond accordingly in either a manual or automated manner?
- Storage, archiving, and restore of backups needs to be tested. Operations unfamiliar with the cloud will be used to accessing extensive and fast local storage for backups. Backups may be more difficult to manage on the cloud because they are not on the local network, or they may take too long to upload to the Azure datacentre.

Penetration and security tests

There is valid concern around cloud security, not just because of the increased attack surface, but because the security models may be unfamiliar to the implementation team. Testers have a responsibility to ensure that the security related tests are rigorous and beyond reproach. Specific aspects that need to be considered include:

- Security of storage keys, passwords, and other logins that are stored as part of the configuration.
- Penetration testing across the entire application extending beyond the obvious endpoints (such as web and service endpoints), and including the less obvious, Azure specific ones, such storage (which has a public endpoint), messaging subsystems, and logs.

- Testing of encryption and access to data, including cloud based backups.
- Testing of exposure of on-premise endpoints that have been opened up to integrate with cloud based services.

The testing team and the security team need to work closely together and establish who is responsible for what. The security team may be responsible for threat modelling, security practices and governance, while testers are responsible for making sure that it has been successfully implemented, by developing tests that specifically try to penetrate the defences.

Summary

Cloud applications offer opportunities for implementation teams to re-engage with testers and create a methodology that makes maximum use of testing skills, processes and disciplines. This is important to the entire team, not just because the cloud has risks that need to be managed through testing, but because the cloud offers the ability to test very early in the project on a production platform. This opportunity to test early, and with high coverage, should not be squandered.

Steps

1. Familiarise testers with cloud principles and how they apply to testing.
2. Include cloud specific aspects in the test plan
    1. Test schedule.
    2. Qualitative Performance Test.
    3. Quantitative Performance Test.
    4. Scale Test.
    5. Availability Test.
    6. Soak Test.
    7. Operational Test.
    8. Penetration and security tests.

License

CALM is published under an open source copy-left licence. The GNU Free Documentation licence requires that the license be included in all works and is therefore contained, in full, below.

GNU Free Documentation License

Version 1.3, 3 November 2008

Copyright © 2000, 2001, 2002, 2007, 2008 Free Software Foundation, Inc. <http://fsf.org/>

Everyone is permitted to copy and distribute verbatim copies of this license document, but changing it is not allowed.

0. Preamble

The purpose of this License is to make a manual, textbook, or other functional and useful document "free" in the sense of freedom: to assure everyone the effective freedom to copy and redistribute it, with or without modifying it, either commercially or noncommercially. Secondarily, this License preserves for the author and publisher a way to get credit for their work, while not being considered responsible for modifications made by others.

This License is a kind of "copyleft", which means that derivative works of the document must themselves be free in the same sense. It complements the GNU General Public License, which is a copyleft license designed for free software.

We have designed this License in order to use it for manuals for free software, because free software needs free documentation: a free program should come with manuals providing the same freedoms that the software does. But this License is not limited to software manuals; it can be used for any textual work, regardless of subject matter or whether it is published as a printed book. We recommend this License principally for works whose purpose is instruction or reference.

1. Applicability and definitions

This License applies to any manual or other work, in any medium, that contains a notice placed by the copyright holder saying it can be distributed under the terms of this License. Such a notice grants a world-wide, royalty-free license, unlimited in duration, to use that work under the conditions stated herein. The "Document", below, refers to any such manual or work. Any member of the public is a licensee, and is addressed as "you". You accept the license if you copy, modify or distribute the work in a way requiring permission under copyright law.

A "Modified Version" of the Document means any work containing the Document or a portion of it, either copied verbatim, or with modifications and/or translated into another language.

A "Secondary Section" is a named appendix or a front-matter section of the Document that deals exclusively with the relationship of the publishers or authors of the Document to the Document's overall subject (or to related matters) and contains nothing that could fall directly within that overall subject. (Thus, if the Document is in part a textbook of mathematics, a Secondary Section may not explain any mathematics.) The relationship could be a matter of historical connection with the subject or with related matters, or of legal, commercial, philosophical, ethical or political position regarding them.

The "Invariant Sections" are certain Secondary Sections whose titles are designated, as being those of Invariant Sections, in the notice that says that the Document is released under this License. If a section does not fit the above definition of Secondary then it is not allowed to be designated as Invariant. The Document may contain zero Invariant Sections. If the Document does not identify any Invariant Sections then there are none.

The "Cover Texts" are certain short passages of text that are listed, as Front-Cover Texts or Back-Cover Texts, in the notice that says that the Document is released under this License. A Front-Cover Text may be at most 5 words, and a Back-Cover Text may be at most 25 words.

A "Transparent" copy of the Document means a machine-readable copy, represented in a format whose specification is available to the general public, that is suitable for revising the document straightforwardly with generic text editors or (for images composed of pixels) generic paint programs or (for drawings) some widely available drawing editor, and that is suitable for input to text formatters or for automatic translation to a variety of formats suitable for input to text formatters. A copy made in an otherwise Transparent file format whose markup, or absence of markup, has been arranged to thwart or discourage subsequent modification by readers is not Transparent. An image format is not Transparent if used for any substantial amount of text. A copy that is not "Transparent" is called "Opaque".

Examples of suitable formats for Transparent copies include plain ASCII without markup, Texinfo input format, LaTeX input format, SGML or XML using a publicly available DTD, and standard-conforming simple HTML, PostScript or PDF designed for human modification. Examples of transparent image formats include PNG, XCF and JPG. Opaque formats include proprietary formats that can be read and edited only by proprietary word processors, SGML or XML for which the DTD and/or processing tools are not generally available, and the machine-generated HTML, PostScript or PDF produced by some word processors for output purposes only.

The "Title Page" means, for a printed book, the title page itself, plus such following pages as are needed to hold, legibly, the material this License requires to appear in the title page. For works in formats which do not have any title page as such, "Title Page" means the text near the most prominent appearance of the work's title, preceding the beginning of the body of the text.

The "publisher" means any person or entity that distributes copies of the Document to the public.

A section "Entitled XYZ" means a named subunit of the Document whose title either is precisely XYZ or contains XYZ in parentheses following text that translates XYZ in another language. (Here XYZ stands for a specific section name mentioned below, such as "Acknowledgements", "Dedications", "Endorsements", or "History".) To "Preserve the Title" of such a section when you modify the Document means that it remains a section "Entitled XYZ" according to this definition.

The Document may include Warranty Disclaimers next to the notice which states that this License applies to the Document. These Warranty Disclaimers are considered to be included by reference in this License, but only as regards disclaiming warranties: any other implication that these Warranty Disclaimers may have is void and has no effect on the meaning of this License.

2. Verbatim copying

You may copy and distribute the Document in any medium, either commercially or noncommercially, provided that this License, the copyright notices, and the license notice saying this License applies to the Document are reproduced in all copies, and that you add no other conditions whatsoever to those of this License. You may not use technical measures to obstruct or control the reading or further copying of the copies you make or distribute. However, you may accept compensation in exchange for copies. If you distribute a large enough number of copies you must also follow the conditions in section 3.

You may also lend copies, under the same conditions stated above, and you may publicly display copies.

3. Copying in quantity

If you publish printed copies (or copies in media that commonly have printed covers) of the Document, numbering more than 100, and the Document's license notice requires Cover Texts, you must enclose the copies in covers that carry, clearly and legibly, all these Cover Texts: Front-Cover Texts on the front cover, and Back-Cover Texts on the back cover. Both covers must also clearly and legibly identify you as the publisher of these copies. The front cover must present the full title with all words of the title equally prominent and visible. You may add other material on the covers in addition. Copying with changes limited to the covers, as long as they preserve the title of the Document and satisfy these conditions, can be treated as verbatim copying in other respects.

If the required texts for either cover are too voluminous to fit legibly, you should put the first ones listed (as many as fit reasonably) on the actual cover, and continue the rest onto adjacent pages.

If you publish or distribute Opaque copies of the Document numbering more than 100, you must either include a machine-readable Transparent copy along with each Opaque copy, or state in or with each Opaque copy a computer-network location from which the general network-using public has access to download using public-standard network protocols a complete Transparent copy of the Document, free of added material. If you use the latter option, you must take reasonably prudent steps, when you begin distribution of Opaque copies in quantity, to ensure that this Transparent copy will remain thus accessible at the stated location until at least one year after the last time you distribute an Opaque copy (directly or through your agents or retailers) of that edition to the public.

It is requested, but not required, that you contact the authors of the Document well before redistributing any large number of copies, to give them a chance to provide you with an updated version of the Document.

4. Modifications

You may copy and distribute a Modified Version of the Document under the conditions of sections 2 and 3 above, provided that you release the Modified Version under precisely this License, with the Modified Version filling the role of the Document, thus licensing distribution and modification of the Modified Version to whoever possesses a copy of it. In addition, you must do these things in the Modified Version:

A. Use in the Title Page (and on the covers, if any) a title distinct from that of the Document, and from those of previous versions (which should, if there were any, be listed in the History section of the Document). You may use the same title as a previous version if the original publisher of that version gives permission. B. List on the Title Page, as authors, one or more persons or entities responsible for authorship of the modifications in the Modified Version, together with at least five of the principal authors of the Document (all of its principal authors, if it has fewer than five), unless they release you from this requirement. C. State on the Title page the name of the publisher of the Modified Version, as the publisher. D. Preserve all the copyright notices of the Document. E. Add an appropriate copyright notice for your modifications adjacent to the other copyright notices. F. Include, immediately after the copyright notices, a license notice giving the public permission to use the Modified Version under the terms of this License, in the form shown in the Addendum below. G. Preserve in that license notice the full lists of Invariant Sections and required Cover Texts given in the Document's license notice. H. Include an unaltered copy of this License. I. Preserve the section Entitled "History", Preserve its Title, and add to it an item stating at least the title, year, new authors, and publisher of the Modified Version as given on the Title Page. If there is no section Entitled "History" in the Document, create one stating the title, year, authors, and publisher of the Document as given on its Title Page, then add an item describing the Modified Version as stated in the previous sentence. J. Preserve the network location, if any, given in the Document for public access to a Transparent copy of the Document, and likewise the network locations given in the Document for previous versions it was based on. These may be placed in the "History" section. You may omit a network location for a work that was published at least four years before the Document itself, or if the original publisher of the version it refers to gives permission. K. For any section Entitled "Acknowledgements" or "Dedications", Preserve the Title of the section, and preserve in the section all the substance and tone of each of the contributor acknowledgements and/or dedications given therein. L. Preserve all the Invariant Sections of the Document, unaltered in their text and in their titles. Section numbers or the equivalent are not considered part of the section titles. M. Delete any section Entitled "Endorsements". Such a section may not be included in the Modified Version. N. Do not retitle any existing section to be Entitled "Endorsements" or to conflict in title with any Invariant Section. O. Preserve any Warranty Disclaimers. If the Modified Version includes new front-matter sections or appendices that qualify as Secondary Sections and contain no material copied from the Document, you may at your option designate some or all of these sections as invariant. To do this, add their titles to the list of Invariant Sections in the Modified Version's license notice. These titles must be distinct from any other section titles.

You may add a section Entitled "Endorsements", provided it contains nothing but endorsements of your Modified Version by various parties—for example, statements of peer review or that the text has been approved by an organization as the authoritative definition of a standard.

You may add a passage of up to five words as a Front-Cover Text, and a passage of up to 25 words as a Back-Cover Text, to the end of the list of Cover Texts in the Modified Version. Only one passage of Front-Cover Text and one of Back-Cover Text may be added by (or through arrangements made by) any one entity. If the Document already includes a cover text for the same cover, previously added by you or by arrangement made by the same entity you are acting on behalf of, you may not add another; but you may replace the old one, on explicit permission from the previous publisher that added the old one.

The author(s) and publisher(s) of the Document do not by this License give permission to use their names for publicity for or to assert or imply endorsement of any Modified Version.

5. Combining documents

You may combine the Document with other documents released under this License, under the terms defined in section 4 above for modified versions, provided that you include in the combination all of the Invariant Sections of all of the original documents, unmodified, and list them all as Invariant Sections of your combined work in its license notice, and that you preserve all their Warranty Disclaimers.

The combined work need only contain one copy of this License, and multiple identical Invariant Sections may be replaced with a single copy. If there are multiple Invariant Sections with the same name but different contents, make the title of each such section unique by adding at the end of it, in parentheses, the name of the original author or publisher of that section if known, or else a unique number. Make the same adjustment to the section titles in the list of Invariant Sections in the license notice of the combined work.

In the combination, you must combine any sections Entitled "History" in the various original documents, forming one section Entitled "History"; likewise combine any sections Entitled "Acknowledgements", and any sections Entitled "Dedications". You must delete all sections Entitled "Endorsements".

6. Collections of documents

You may make a collection consisting of the Document and other documents released under this License, and replace the individual copies of this License in the various documents with a single copy that is included in the collection, provided that you follow the rules of this License for verbatim copying of each of the documents in all other respects.

You may extract a single document from such a collection, and distribute it individually under this License, provided you insert a copy of this License into the extracted document, and follow this License in all other respects regarding verbatim copying of that document.

7. Aggregation with independent works

A compilation of the Document or its derivatives with other separate and independent documents or works, in or on a volume of a storage or distribution medium, is called an "aggregate" if the copyright resulting from the compilation is not used to limit the legal rights of the compilation's users beyond what the individual works permit. When the Document is included in an aggregate, this License does not apply to the other works in the aggregate which are not themselves derivative works of the Document.

If the Cover Text requirement of section 3 is applicable to these copies of the Document, then if the Document is less than one half of the entire aggregate, the Document's Cover Texts may be placed on covers that bracket the Document within the aggregate, or the electronic equivalent of covers if the Document is in electronic form. Otherwise they must appear on printed covers that bracket the whole aggregate.

8. Translation

Translation is considered a kind of modification, so you may distribute translations of the Document under the terms of section 4. Replacing Invariant Sections with translations requires special permission from their copyright holders, but you may include translations of some or all Invariant Sections in addition to the original versions of these Invariant Sections. You may include a translation of this License, and all the license notices in the Document, and any Warranty Disclaimers, provided that you also include the original English version of this License and the original versions of those notices and disclaimers. In case of a disagreement between the translation and the original version of this License or a notice or disclaimer, the original version will prevail.

If a section in the Document is Entitled "Acknowledgements", "Dedications", or "History", the requirement (section 4) to Preserve its Title (section 1) will typically require changing the actual title.

9. Termination

You may not copy, modify, sublicense, or distribute the Document except as expressly provided under this License. Any attempt otherwise to copy, modify, sublicense, or distribute it is void, and will automatically terminate your rights under this License.

However, if you cease all violation of this License, then your license from a particular copyright holder is reinstated (a) provisionally, unless and until the copyright holder explicitly and finally terminates your license, and (b) permanently, if the copyright holder fails to notify you of the violation by some reasonable means prior to 60 days after the cessation.

Moreover, your license from a particular copyright holder is reinstated permanently if the copyright holder notifies you of the violation by some reasonable means, this is the first time you have received notice of violation of this License (for any work) from that copyright holder, and you cure the violation prior to 30 days after your receipt of the notice.

Termination of your rights under this section does not terminate the licenses of parties who have received copies or rights from you under this License. If your rights have been terminated and not permanently reinstated, receipt of a copy of some or all of the same material does not give you any rights to use it.

10. Future revisions of this license

The Free Software Foundation may publish new, revised versions of the GNU Free Documentation License from time to time. Such new versions will be similar in spirit to the present version, but may differ in detail to address new problems or concerns. See http://www.gnu.org/copyleft/.

Each version of the License is given a distinguishing version number. If the Document specifies that a particular numbered version of this License "or any later version" applies to it, you have the option of following the terms and conditions either of that specified version or of any later version that has been published (not as a draft) by the Free Software Foundation. If the Document does not specify a version number of this License, you may choose any version ever published (not as a draft) by the Free Software Foundation. If the Document specifies that a proxy can decide which future versions of this License can be used, that proxy's public statement of acceptance of a version permanently authorizes you to choose that version for the Document.

11. Relicensing

"Massive Multiauthor Collaboration Site" (or "MMC Site") means any World Wide Web server that publishes copyrightable works and also provides prominent facilities for anybody to edit those works. A public wiki that anybody can edit is an example of such a server. A "Massive Multiauthor Collaboration" (or "MMC") contained in the site means any set of copyrightable works thus published on the MMC site.

"CC-BY-SA" means the Creative Commons Attribution-Share Alike 3.0 license published by Creative Commons Corporation, a not-for-profit corporation with a principal place of business in San Francisco, California, as well as future copyleft versions of that license published by that same organization.

"Incorporate" means to publish or republish a Document, in whole or in part, as part of another Document.

An MMC is "eligible for relicensing" if it is licensed under this License, and if all works that were first published under this License somewhere other than this MMC, and subsequently incorporated in whole or in part into the MMC, (1) had no cover texts or invariant sections, and (2) were thus incorporated prior to November 1, 2008.

The operator of an MMC Site may republish an MMC contained in the site under CC-BY-SA on the same site at any time before August 1, 2009, provided the MMC is eligible for relicensing.

www.ingramcontent.com/pod-product-compliance
Lightning Source LLC
Chambersburg PA
CBHW080903170526
45158CB00008B/1969